COMMUNITY IN A BLACK PENTECOSTAL CHURCH

Melvin D. Williams

COMMUNITY IN A BLACK PENTECOSTAL CHURCH

✝

AN ANTHROPOLOGICAL STUDY

University of Pittsburgh Press

Library of Congress Cataloging in Publication Data

Williams, Melvin D., birth date
Community in a Black Pentecostal church.

Bibliography: p. 189
1. Negroes—Religion.   2.   Pentecostal churches—
Pennsylvania—Pittsburgh.   3.   Negroes—Pittsburgh.
I.   Title.
BR563.N4W523   301.5'8   74-5108
ISBN 0-8229-3290-3

to my wife
Faye
my children
Aaron
Steven
Craig

CONTENTS

FIGURES

ACKNOWLEDGMENTS

This study is the result of three years of anthropological observation of a Pittsburgh Pentecostal church, beginning in 1969. Much of this time was spent attending services, visiting in the homes of members, intensively interviewing a selective group from a range of members, recording sermons, testimonies, and prophecies, examining church documents, and attending state and international meetings.

The research was supported by funds from Community Action of Pittsburgh and a grant from the National Science Foundation. I am grateful.

Because of the sensitive nature of the information gathered, I have used pseudonyms rather than actual names. I have also used fictitious geographical locations for various international and state meetings. The name Zion Holiness Church itself is a pseudonym.

I am deeply indebted to the pastor, who permitted me to enter his fold, and to the members, who accepted me in my unique role. They realize far better than I can express here the great contribution they have made, and I would like to share with them the often repeated words of Bishop Jenkins, as he alternately clapped his hands and raised them to his shoulders, "Thank the Lord, bless the Lord."

Leonard Plotnicov and Arthur Tuden read the manuscript and its revisions and gave me valuable suggestions. They have been my academic paters for almost a decade now.

It is generally known that studies such as this require an entourage of attendants. I mention only a few of those who have been instrumental in the completion of this work. My wife and boys are my source of strength; I dedicate the book to them. My parents are unique, and what I am and what I can do, I owe to them. Margaret O. Brown, my student and research assistant, has labored beyond the call. L. Keith Brown, John P. Gillin, Ulf Hannerz, Donald Henderson, David Landy, Barbara S. Lane, Jacques J. P. Maquet, George Peter Murdock, Emrys L. Peters, Alexander Spoehr, Wayne Suttles, and Otto von Mering have been among my able mentors and supporters. Then there are those unique experiences that were brief but have had far-reaching ramifications—

a quiet talk with Thomas Weaver in the fall of 1969, the last day of a seminar with Jacques Maquet in 1968, and the effective touch of the great humanity of David Landy.

Finally, there is Carlow College, "far from the madding crowd," the pleasant academic setting that enables one with my temperament to work.

I have had ample assistance, but the failings here are my own. This has been a difficult task; perhaps I have not been equal to it. Zion is a group that has demonstrated its distinctive ability to recruit across traditional social boundaries—neighborhoods, subcultures, families, economic levels, and even ethnic groups (it has one Caucasian female member). It has cohered for fifty-four years. Zion has proved its solidarity and viability. But it has been my task to describe the nature, content, networks, and character of this group and its members. That description was written to illustrate how this group achieves its solidarity in spite of human conflict and why this group persists in the face of pressure from the larger society. This is a great aspiration. The insights I received very late in my participant observation convince me that much is yet to be learned about Zion. But this introduction to Zion is offered with the hope that further chapters may be contributed by a more seasoned student of human behavior.

COMMUNITY IN A BLACK PENTECOSTAL CHURCH

† 1 †

INTRODUCTION

Understanding Black people in the United States remains one of the critical tasks of the social scientist (see Ladner, 1973; Lyman, 1972). When such understanding comes, it will be a hallmark in its contribution to our knowledge of human behavior. As culture-bound observers of human phenomena, we have neglected to protect adequately our research on the poor urban Black from the distortions characteristic of man. With value-laden criteria of achievement, recognition, status, prestige, competition, material wealth, power, and yes, poverty, the social scientists analyzing the behavior of Black people have repeatedly failed to heed Lowie's (1922:160) warning:

> Important, however, as variety of information and interests doubtless are, one factor must take precedence in the scientist's equipment—the spirit in which he approaches his scientific work as a whole. In this respect the point that would probably strike most European or, at all events, Continental scientists is the rarity in America of philosophical inquiries into the foundations of one's scientific position.

As a result, our basic assumptions have consistently distorted our conclusions. That evasive truth has often escaped us, and the beauty and the good that reside in the adaptive life styles of poor Black people have been overlooked or misinterpreted.

I am convinced that one of the ways of approaching this problem is the writing of some good anthropological ethnography on the behavior of the poor Black man in the United States. This is what I attempt in this volume.

My observations of the Zion Holiness Church and its larger organization, the international group of the Church of Holy Christ, are not primarily designed to analyze and describe the religious characteristics of this Black sect. This has been done satisfactorily by others (Fauset, 1971; Frazier, 1971; Washington, 1970). My study focuses primarily on the distinctive quality of social relations, communal ideology, and

3

social behavior within the group (see Geertz, 1966). This congregation constitutes a closely knit group of individuals who intensively interact together in sacred and secular association. It is my conclusion that within the urban Black ghetto, where geographical mobility is high and neighborhood identification low, Zion, as an organized religious group, is most likely to constitute a community, for here the major portion of an individual member's social relations can be traced to church group functions (see Williams, 1973a). I have described and illustrated the ability of Zion to regulate and shape the life patterns of its members. I have also determined the critical social and cultural factors involved in rallying the commitment of these Black ghetto dwellers to this unique pattern of social relations.

The character of this group illustrates the complexity of even such a small component of ghetto life and aids us in defining the concept of Black ghetto life. Zion demonstrates the cultural range and variation in a complex society and patterns of cultural continuity between the rural South and the urban North. I have observed the mechanisms used to make life tolerable in this urban context. The Zion Holiness Church has been a manageable anthropological unit of research within which to investigate a system of behavioral content. This anthropological description of the nature of social relations within Zion is enlightening and heuristic for further research.

Pentecostalism has attracted considerable research attention. Calley (1965) investigated the assimilation quality of West Indian Pentecostalism in England. Cutten (1927) made a psychological analysis of glossolalia. Elinson (1965) tried to identify relations between Pentecostal beliefs and nonreligious attitudes and activities. Gerlach and Hine (1966) studied White Pentecostal groups in Minneapolis and emphasize conversion as "bride burning," a commitment to a new way of life. Holt (1940) studied Pentecostal groups along with others in the situational context of Holiness religious development. G. B. Johnson (1953) analyzed the values of Pentecostal ministers. Miller (1967) observed the distinct movement, growth, and spread of Pentecostalism in Argentina. Wood (1965) defined specific personality factors related to Pentecostal participation.

Others have treated Pentecostalism within studies of greater scope (E. T. Clark, 1949; Goldschmidt, 1947; Mintz, 1960; Morland, 1958; Pope, 1942). Poblete and Odea's (1960) study of Pentecostal sects is closest to mine in its objective. They hypothesize that these sectarian groups represent an escape from anomie and an attempt to reestablish "community" under conditions of alienation and absence of norms. My study attempts to examine the cohesive nature of the social relations and behavior of one Black Pentecostal group. The religious factor is a significant variable in the Black behavior I have observed and is exemplified by the nature of the community cohesion it creates among ghetto Black people considered to have loosely knit community ties. It is within a religious context that Zion has developed a shared definition of human experience. As Suttles (1968:41) observes:

> Religion is one of the most significant ways in which Addams area residents assure one another of their willingness to sacrifice personal designs in favor of joint concern. This does not mean that they are particularly religious or moral. Instead, religious affiliation must be taken for what it is—a public guarantee of one's amenability to group concerns, whether one happens to be "moral" or not.

The history of Black people in the United States has been one of constant geographical movement (see Franklin, 1947; Handlin, 1962; G. E. Haynes, 1969; Himes, 1965; Kennedy, 1969; Meier, 1966; Park, 1919; Reid, 1939; Ross, 1934; Scott, 1969; U.S., 1935). They were uprooted from Africa and shuttled about in Plantation America, and their mobility continued after legal slavery ended. Immediately after Emancipation, Blacks migrated into the cities of the South in numbers larger, proportionately, than those of Whites. For the next ten years Blacks gradually moved into many southern cities. Prior to 1916, about 90 percent of the Blacks were in the South, and of this number, 80 percent lived in rural areas (Frazier, 1971:47).

World War I stimulated mass migrations of Blacks to northern cities. The war created a great demand for unskilled workers in northern industries and simultaneously prevented the normal immigration of unskilled workers from Europe. Migration from the South was encouraged by a multitude of factors—economic deprivation, unscrupulous landlords, exploitative merchants, and boll weevil despoliation. After an initial wave this migration decreased, but Blacks still moved to northern cities until the Second World War, when they were again attracted by war industries. As a result of this constant geographical movement, among other factors, Blacks have seldom discovered in the New World the combination of ethnic, economic, social, and political

factors that create and maintain community. Theirs has been a history
of impermanence and inability to control their own destiny.

The statistics on internal migrations in America are not comprehen-
sive. Much of the information has to be derived from census data on
population variations from region to region and from decade to decade.
In any case, we know that in 1915 the Great Migration of Blacks began
in the United States, and it has continued ever since. As Myrdal (1962:
183) points out:

> The proportion of all Negroes living in the North and West rose
> to 23.8 percent in 1940, which signifies a total net migration
> between 1910 and 1940 of about 1,750,000 from the South.
> Negroes constituted, in 1940, 3.7 percent of the total Northern
> population. Practically all of the migrants had gone to the cities.
> In 1940, 90.1 percent of all Negroes in Northern and Western
> states outside of Missouri lived in urban areas. New York City
> alone claimed 16.9 percent of all Negroes living in the North and
> West. If the Negroes of Chicago, Philadelphia, Detroit, Cleveland,
> and Pittsburgh are added to those of New York, the proportion
> rises to 47.2 percent.

Black migration to the North decreased during the industrial depres-
sion of 1920 but resumed again in 1922, when industrial activity in the
North began an upturn. In 1910, 78.8 percent of Blacks in the South
lived in rural areas (Frazier, 1968:199), most often in the cotton belt:

> The Cotton Belt, one of the most highly specialized agricultural
> regions in the world, consists of many sub-regions, but is bound by
> temperature and rainfall. On the north it follows the summer aver-
> age temperature of 77 degrees; on the south the belt has its bounds
> set along the Gulf and Atlantic Coast by an average rainfall limit
> of over 10 inches during the autumn. Beyond the northern tem-
> perature boundary the growing season is likely to be ruined by
> rains. Cotton production is found throughout the southern states
> extending from eastern North Carolina to Western Texas. The
> Belt is 1,600 miles long and varies from 125 to 500 miles in width,
> the average width being 300 miles. In an area of 295,000,000
> acres, less than 3 percent of the world's land area, is grown about
> 55 percent of the world's cotton.

I have made no attempt here to offer all the reasons and motivations for the rural southern Black migrations to the North. It would be impossible to consider the many individual motivations involved—death of a relative, romance, and personal fortune. Relatives and friends living in the North wrote "back home." These letters, or their contents, were frequently distributed within the community. The Black press was active nationally and printed employment ads as well as editorials and news comments that praised the better conditions the North offered the Black man. Northern industries sent representatives to the South with promises of jobs and traveling expenses. Even when these agents did not appear in person, rumors of their coming had the same impact. And there were jobs during the war, as well as the growing myth of northern prosperity. These attractions created a movement of southern Blacks to the North between 1910 and 1920 that was fundamentally different from earlier Black migrations, during which most Blacks had come from states bordering upon the North. As J. A. Hill of the United States Census Bureau points out (Frazier, 1968:192):

> Even as recently as 1910, 48 percent, or nearly one-half, of the southern-born Negroes living in northern states came from two states—Virginia and Kentucky. The migration between 1910 and 1920 reduced the proportion born in these two states to 31.6 percent. On the other hand, the proportion of northern Negroes coming from the states farther south, or from what we may term the cotton-belt states, including in this class South Carolina, Georgia, Florida, Alabama, Mississippi, Arkansas, Louisiana, and Texas, increased from 18.2 percent of the total number of southern-born Negroes living in the North in 1910 to 40.5 percent of the total in 1920. The absolute number of Negroes in the North who were natives of these States increased from 75,517 in 1910 to 298,739 in 1920, so that there were nearly four times as many in 1920 as there were in 1910.

The southern rural Black (peasant) has never been encouraged to display economic initiative. For him to act on ambition has required courage and often personal risks (see Powdermaker, 1939). He has never had the advantage of legal privilege necessary for successful economic endeavors. His security has been rooted in associations with powerful and protective whites in his community (see Dollard, 1962). His low income has prevented the accumulation of investment capital.

He has been denied credit because of his race, and his educational opportunities have been meager (see C. S. Johnson, 1934, 1967). Blacks traditionally lived on plantations where small landholdings were rare and those for sale rarer still. Even when such landholdings were available and Blacks were able to buy, it was rare for potentially valuable holdings to be offered to them. (See Myrdal, 1962, for a fuller discussion of plantation conditions for the rural Black southerner.)

At the turn of the century, the social and structural conditions of the Black were no better than his economic condition. The caste system, Jim Crow legislation, inferior schools, legal injustice, and lynchings were ever-present conditions of Black life in the rural South. During the 1890s the Negro's "place" in society became a matter of law in every southern state (Lincoln, 1967). The approved doctrine of "separate but equal" completely isolated the races in every facet of public life. The use of schools, trains, buses, public buildings, parks, playgrounds, beaches, waiting rooms, and water fountains was racially qualified. Facilities for Blacks were always inferior to those provided for Whites. Booker T. Washington had established the "separate fingers" doctrine in which he encouraged Blacks to concentrate on meager material advantages to the neglect of social equality through agitation or militancy.

Blacks in the rural South were thus not in competition with Whites socially or economically. Paternalistic Whites treated them as inferiors and encouraged them to live simple, uncomplicated lives. Their social contacts consisted of neighborhood and extended family groups that relied on their own members for companionship and support in economic crisis and human uncertainty. Their intimate association created an atmosphere of free expression and unlimited toleration for human inadequacies. Temporary social leadership in these small intimate groups usually derived from charisma, and standards of social status were very fluid. Thus a member of any small Black community in the rural South found his social, economic, and psychological security bound up in the qualities of these relationships, which gave acceptance to his personal identity from birth to death. There was little stress on achievement, competitiveness, status, prestige, wealth, or material aggrandizement in these small communities. The emphasis was upon family relationships, rites of passage, and word-of-mouth news that was of interest to the membership. The critical components of this community were intimacy, freedom of expression, face-to-face contact, and familiar social and physical surroundings. As we shall see later, it was these familiar characteristics that the members of Zion Holiness Church who migrated to Pittsburgh prior to 1919 sought to preserve in their religious order.

According to Frazier (1968), the church was the most important association next to the family in the Black rural South (see also Billings, 1934; Brunner, 1923). The church and its membership often determined the limits of the rural community, which frequently bore its name. The church was the most important means of community expression, and rural southern Blacks made financial and material sacrifices to maintain it. The church was frequently a center for recreational activities, and its building often served as a schoolhouse. These rural communities had organizations for mutual aid, especially during death and sickness. Many of these organizations (see Helping Hand Club, 1948) grew out of the church and then further developed into lodges like the Good Samaritans, Prince Hall Masons, the Odd Fellows, and the Knights of Pythias. Recreation in the rural South was primarily limited to visiting friends and relatives and attending church services.

Religion also had its restraints. In the small, intimate rural communities, social conduct usually proceeded under the watchful eye of "elders" who were very observant of "sinful behavior." One of the pleasures of going to town on Saturday afternoons was to escape from the boredom of the rural setting and let loose behavioral impulses that had to be repressed at home because of religious influence. In town, from Pullman porters and dining-car waiters who worked the rails throughout the South, one could hear fabulous stories about the northern cities, where freedom and exciting adventure awaited the migrant. One could also meet migrants who had worked in lumber and turpentine camps where they had a first taste of personal and sexual freedom and a certain amount of anonymity. Often a Black wanderer of this sect seduced a simple rural girl on her Saturday afternoon visit to town with romantic tales and strange words of love that he had acquired in his urban wanderings. (See Frazier, 1968, for a full discussion of Blacks outside their traditional rural setting.)

The migration to cities created a social crisis, for it separated masses of Blacks from their rural life style and destroyed the social organization which gave meaning to their segregated rural southern society. The northern city was less than the "promised land" Blacks sought, but it was an improvement over the impoverished southern condition that they fled (see Drake and Cayton, 1962). These rural Black southerners were mostly unskilled, and their employment had generally been limited to jobs in common labor, domestic service, and sharecropping. And even these economic means were threatened in 1915 and 1916, when cotton plantations were devastated by swarms of boll weevils.

After World War I the movement of Blacks to northern cities slowed, but it continued and regained some of its momentum again during World War II. Frazier (1971) has compared the movement of Blacks to cities during this period to the crisis created by Emancipation. The crisis, he explains, was the separation of Blacks from their customary way of life and social organization. This social organization, Frazier (1971:48) continues,

> represented both an accommodation to conditions in the rural South and an accommodation to their segregated and inferior status in southern society. In the city environment the family of the masses of Negroes from rural areas, which lacked an institutional basis and was held together only by cooperation in making a living or by sympathies and sentiments generated by living together in the same household, was unable to stand the shock of the disintegrating forces in urban life. . . .
>
> In the cold impersonal environment of the city, the institutions and associations which had provided security and support for the Negro in the rural environment could not be resurrected. The mutual aid or "sickness and burial" societies could no longer provide security during the major crisis which the Negroes feared most. In fact, in the crowded slums of northern cities, neighborliness and friendship no longer had any meaning. The Negro could not find even the warmth and sympathy of the secret fraternal organizations which had added colour and ornament to a drab existence in the South.

Another significant crisis in the life of the Black migrant was the loss of his church. His church had been the focal point of his social life and to some extent had given meaning to his life, which was otherwise largely isolated from mainstream America. Frazier (1971:49) describes the impact of this condition:

> In the strange environment the Negro endeavored to explain his new experiences in terms of his traditional outlook on life which was saturated with his religion and the image of the world provided by his knowledge of the Bible. This is shown vividly in the letter a migrant to Pittsburgh undertook to describe the marvel of

the gigantic blazing steel furnaces by writing that they were just like what would happen on Judgement Day.

The northern Black churches had memberships larger than those in the South, but in spite of their opulence and power, they failed to attract the Black masses who were seeking religious association more intimate and conducive to creating status. These conditions created what Linton (1943) has described as a rational, revivalistic, nativistic movement typified by Zion Holiness Church, where I gathered my data. Zion revived the images of the rural South as well as the intimate religious association conducive to creating status.

Social systems perpetuate themselves. Children of the membership at Zion have always been reared among the members and in their ideology. In second and third generations other categories of Blacks, because of other cultural factors, have felt the need for the intimacy of Zion. The Black urban ghettos offered many attractions that helped those oriented toward sex, gang life, alcoholism, athletics, and drugs to find their niche and flower as members of the Black ghetto subculture (see an Italian example in Whyte, 1961; Keiser, 1969). But for people whose temperaments and propensities were incompatible with those orientations, the human isolation was dreadful. Zion, like religions in mainstream society, has operated as a residual institution to legitimate and fulfill the needs of Blacks whose human and social characteristics have not otherwise been satisfied in any dignified manner (Yinger, 1970). In addition, many Blacks have been forced to earn their living as unskilled laborers and domestics. In many instances, the structure of their life in the urban milieu has not included a rewarding and abiding associational pattern, and churches of many varieties have come to represent for them a critical form of organized social life.

The Church of Holy Christ (the international organization of churches to which Zion belongs) allows urban ghetto Blacks to reorganize and revitalize their ideas about God, the world, and the self (see Battle, 1961; Bloch-Hoell, 1964; Braden, 1963; Catton, 1957; W. A. Clark, 1937; Conn, 1956; Discipline of the Pentecostal Holiness Church, 1937; Hawley, 1948; LaBarre, 1966; Lindsay, 1949; Mays, 1968; Paulk, 1958; Spain, 1967). The members seek to establish a church that intimately belongs to them, a church where they are the performers rather than the audience. As Frazier (1971:56) says, their religious activity is distinctive:

The chief religious activity of the members of the Holiness cults is that form of ecstatic worship which is known as "getting happy" or "shouting." This frenzied behavior is often accompanied by drums, guitars, or tambourines. The worship in these Holiness churches is the type of behavior which Daniel studies in the nine ecstatic cults. They insist that Christians shall live free of sin and in a state of holiness. They refuse to compromise with the sinful ways of the world. By sin they mean the use of tobacco, the drinking of alcoholic beverages, cursing and swearing, dancing, playing cards, and adultery. All of such activities are regarded as "carnal mindedness." In recounting their achievement of a state of holiness, some members tell of having visions of heaven. They claim, as a pastor of a Holiness church said, that they "are the common ordinary people that Jesus dwelt among."

Of the five classes of Black religious cults enumerated by Raymond Julius Jones (in Fauset, 1971:9)—Faith Healing, Holiness, Islamic (a broader classification would be "nationalistic"), Pentecostal, and Spiritualistic—the Church of Holy Christ might fall into all except the Islamic and the Spiritualistic. The members of Zion conceptualize themselves as healing by faith, as a Holiness church, and as a Pentecostal religion. They were originally motivated to organize by a desire for the intimate, spontaneous, imaginative worship they had known in the rural South.

Historically the economic resources of most Blacks in America have been meager. Yet all human groups attempt to structure life so that they can perceive and experience pleasure, meaning, and reward. Blacks have traditionally achieved this by intensive interaction. They have entertained one another and exploited one another for the sake of entertainment, pleasure, and reward. During slavery they sang together, danced for one another, told stories, and joked among themselves about their mutual plight. Rapping and shucking, jiving, running it down, griping, copping a plea, signifying, and sounding (Kochman, 1970) are all variations of the peculiar mode of Black intensive interaction. A distinct characteristic of this intensive interaction is uninhibited laughter. This laughter is a catalyst, reward, cue, and stimulus for further intensive interaction. Ghetto Black children are socialized into this behavior early, as many of their teachers know, having lost control of their classroom of students after a snicker suddenly grew into a tumultuous roar of uninhibited laughter and spontaneous interaction among the students. This socialization creates identifiable cues in conversation and lyrics—which I suggest are expressed in the term "soul." Blacks have developed social interaction into an art, whether gambling, arguing (usually a prelude to a fight), conversing, or seducing. Thus, Blacks skillful at manipulating the verbal cues can create entertainment and reward out of almost any situation.

The key to Zion's social interaction lies in its extension of these behavioral characteristics. The original members of Zion were accustomed to intimate, familial interaction in the rural South; thus the role playing characteristic of the urban establishment was new to them. Zion has been a successful attempt to perpetuate the intimate interactions of the rural South in a new geographical and social context—the urban North.

Pentecostal churches like Zion have taken the idealized intimate model of the American nuclear family and the biblical code of ethics for their mode of behavior and nature of social interaction. They have chosen to isolate themselves from urban society by means of a different life style. Zion boasts, "We are in the world but not of the world." They have patterned this approach to living upon a primary group within which one can expose one's personal inadequacies, vicissitudes, and emotions. Being a member means being "closer than a sister or a brother." One has a kissing relationship with every member, a paternal relationship with the pastor—"the protector of his flock"—and a maternal relationship with the church mother. These paternal and maternal relationships have been generalized to include, to some extent, all the older members of the church, and they have been solidified and reinforced three times a week by testimonial services in which members stand and express their problems and anxieties and ask for the prayers of other members. Financial emergencies are openly admitted to the membership, who then come to one's aid with a "freewill offering." Zion, as an intimate group, demands that "love" determine all relationships.

The primary group intimacy in Zion also fills this community with anxieties, stresses, fears, jealousies, and competition that are expressed in member-to-member relationships. At the same time, it provides a meaningful, attractive, time-consuming, energy-absorbing way of life. The intense ambivalence makes these relationships of great interest to the members. They express that interest and react to the group dynamics through gossip, division, and threats of division. They release emotions generated by the stresses and anxieties of these intimate relationships through purging church services. Thus these potentially disruptive dynamics are kept at a level the community can tolerate.

It is my contention that the intense dynamics of these relationships in Zion create a vital community that so absorbs members' interest that they can spend a lifetime in Zion, in a subculture of their own relatively isolated from the larger society. Most of the members and all of the core members (see chapter 3) spend most of every day discussing, thinking about, or working for Zion. Spouses and children who themselves are members often express jealousy over the time, money, and energy that their mates and parents give to the church.

Thus a quality of interaction common among "poor" Blacks is intensified in Zion to create a viable community in a strange urban context by means of a combination of the intimacy of the rural South, the love doctrine of the Bible, and the idealized conception of the roles within the American family. This is the basis for their subculture; this has determined their social structure; this has created community.

The critical features of the character of interaction in Zion are intimacy, conflict, competition, and cooperation. The members have preserved the intimacy, freedom of expression, face-to-face contact, and symbols of familiar social and physical surroundings that were once a part of the rural southern style. But in a growing international organization, these qualities have been structured into a system of competitive enterprise for the sake of the growth of the group. Indeed the influence of American commercial organization—growth, expansion, power, and wealth—is much apparent.

Tremendous efforts toward the development of intimacy and solidarity in Zion create a social environment conducive to tolerance for a wide range of individuals who find acceptance difficult in the general population outside the church. In its efforts toward resolving its high level of conflict, Zion emphasizes the expression of love among its members, a love that extends to all members in spite of their physical handicaps, mental disturbances, or marginal behavior. Thus in Zion one sees tolerance for a number of people who would be considered deviants in the society at large.

This book is organized into nine chapters, beginning with this introduction and a brief description of Zion's historical development as one of the churches in the Church of Holy Christ. My purpose in describing the history of Zion is not only to provide a background but also to give the reader some appreciation of how the behavioral dynamics of Zion have played a crucial role in its development. In the chapters that follow, then, not only do we examine categories of membership; instrumental and expressive church activities; distinctive style, ideology, and design for living; and cohesive social interactions, sanctions, conflict, division, and status hierarchy; but we discover, as well, how these phenomena have resulted in the Zion that exists today.

The members of Zion are both the components of a religious social system and the embodiment of a distinctive subculture. In the discussion of membership, I attempt to give some idea of the character of those who participate in, manipulate, and use the symbol subsystem of Zion. Within Zion are distinct categories which give us insight into how the members of Zion perceive one another in a structural framework. My discussion of core members, marginal members, and membership hierarchies will give the reader information about Zion as a community of interaction and may allow us to identify the human phenomenon in Zion as one that could well be found in various other Black subcultures.

Intrinsic to Zion are the many structural contexts in which the members operate. If we are to understand Zion we must observe some of the expressive and instrumental activities that Zion provides (chapter 5). By observing members at picnics, funerals, moving expeditions, and travel, as well as in services, we may learn something about the cohesiveness that keeps this group together. When the members relate that the Church of Holy Christ has a junior college, a theological seminary, a printing press, and an impressive international headquarters, one can appreciate the pride and status that come to this group by means of their own self-conception, and one can gain a little more insight into what it is we call Zion.

The distinctive style of life, design for interaction, ideology, or subculture of Zion is expressed in verbal symbols. The ways the members of Zion arrange their verbal symbols to create a distinctive outlook on urban life are the focal points of chapter 6. That a group can take the simple resources of a rural southern experience and a "poor" Black ghetto environment and mold them into a distinctively different design for living and meaning for life is a fitting anthropological point of departure. My discussion of the Zion system of verbal symbols is designed to show how this community has developed and utilized its own communication procedures to support its group identity.

Zion does not have the geographically demarcated patterns of interaction of traditionally conceived communities. But as a gathering place where familiar faces take refuge from an inhospitable world, as a source of identity, and as a matrix of interaction for the members, it may be considered as a community. It is the storage place for the system of symbols that creates, transmits, and enforces rules and standards of belief and behavior. It allocates social status, provides for social mobility, resolves conflicts, and gives meaning, order, and style to its members' lives. If I can define community as patterned interactions among a delineated group of individuals who seek security, support, identity, and significance from their group, then Zion is a community as well as a church (the subject of chapter 8).

† 2 †

HISTORY

Zion is located in the lower Hill District of Pittsburgh. The Hill District contains approximately forty thousand Blacks and is one of three major concentrations of Blacks in the city, whose total Black population is approximately one hundred five thousand persons (city limits, 1970 census). Many of the residents of other areas used to live in the Hill District but have been forced to move by redevelopment or encouraged to move by upward mobility into better neighborhoods. Zion has been in the Hill District since the church's inception and seems destined to remain there into the distant future.

The lower Hill is a maze of narrow streets and alleys saturated with churches, bars, tenements, burned-out stores, and abandoned houses. It is a typical Black ghetto, lacking major or effective city services, the pride of ownership, and neighborhood cohesion. It is a panorama of street-corner life, where men congregate daily to discuss the vicissitudes of their lives. It is primarily a residential area, but its inhabitants are the transient poor and the captive Blacks whose movement around the city is restricted. The lower Hill, like most Black ghettos, has numerous drug users and pushers whose activities are widespread and obvious. It has a police station, a fire station, a movie house, and several brothels. Evenings in the lower Hill still find the prostitutes soliciting their white customers boldly, even in this era of Black militancy. There is even a concentrated network of male homosexual prostitutes who congregate in a specific neighborhood of the lower Hill. All of this makes night life in the district exciting, to say the least (see Epstein, 1969, and Buni, 1974, for an expanded discussion and Reid, 1930, for an earlier description).

The enforcement of environmental health codes and building inspection codes recently extended to the lower Hill has exposed hundreds of dwellings as unfit for human habitation. Most absentee landlords have dumped these dwellings on unsuspecting Black renters, while others have abandoned them to demolition at public expense. A few buildings

---

Some of the information in this chapter was taken from church documents.

in this area have been purchased for rehabilitation by corporations which invest large sums of federal loan money in refurbishing these long-neglected shells.

The lower Hill contains two Catholic churches, two Methodist churches, two Baptist churches, five Pentecostal churches, and several storefront missions of various denominations.

The Zion Holiness Church lists ninety-one official adult members on its roles, drawn from throughout the Pittsburgh area: East Liberty, Homewood, Penn Township, St. Clair Village, Horning, Arlington Heights, Manchester, North View Heights, West End, Beltzhoover, Central North Side, Garfield, Wilkinsburg, Lawrenceville, Lawrence, Glen Hazel, Hendersonville, Freedom, and the Hill District. Eleven members originally came from Georgia, eight from Florida, three from Mississippi, thirteen from Tennessee, seven from Kentucky, sixteen from Virginia, nine from Alabama, eight from South Carolina, three from North Carolina, and ten from Pennsylvania (three members have not been active for nine months and were not interviewed). Thirty members are over fifty years of age, thirty-nine are between thirty and fifty years of age, and twenty-two are between twenty and thirty. Thirty-six of the households represented earn under five thousand dollars a year, two earn between eight and nine thousand dollars a year, and two earn over fifteen thousand dollars a year. Forty-seven members have been in this church for more than twenty years.

Zion Holiness Church is one of thousands of small Pentecostal churches located in Black urban ghettos throughout the United States. There are about twenty such churches in metropolitan Pittsburgh and approximately one hundred in Pennsylvania, organized under two state organizations and under the leadership of two different bishops. The Zion Holiness Church is neither a storefront church nor part of the large and prosperous mainstream. Its members worship in a mortgage-free, four-story, brick building, the second floor of which has been remodeled for religious services. The congregation moved to this building in 1937 from a horse stable which they had converted into a church. The church services had been held in tents and members' homes before they purchased the horse stable.

The history of the Pentecostal sect to which Zion belongs began in the South. In 1895, a group of Black ministers was ousted from the Black Baptist church organization in Jackson, Mississippi, when they insisted upon preaching that one could not be "saved" without "holiness." These ministers established a new denomination, the Christ

Church. After two years, the leading founder, I. H. Jenkins, broke from this new group and established his own denomination, the Church of Holy Christ. (The former organization, the Christ Church, has grown and prospered.) Nine years later Jenkins introduced a new doctrine of the baptism of the Holy Ghost accompanied by speaking with tongues. He was purged from his latest group when his fellow ministers refused to sanction this doctrine. So in that same year, 1906, Jenkins gathered together a new group of elders who would follow this doctrine and organized them under the same name, Church of Holy Christ. This organization has persisted to the present as the Church of Holy Christ, and its chief apostle is its founder, Bishop I. H. Jenkins.

The Zion Holiness Church had its beginnings in Pittsburgh's Hill District around 1918 when a woman known as Mother Beck started a "mission" in her home with a group of women. (Black women have frequently founded Black churches.) When Mother Beck's mission achieved success, she wrote Bishop Jenkins to send her a pastor for her people, and he sent Elder Baxter in 1919. Elder Baxter had separated from his wife but he had to rejoin her to be accepted as a pastor there. She came to live with him shortly after he arrived, and he then assumed his role. Baxter was a dynamic man who "spoke his mind and ruled with an iron fist." These personality traits repelled some sophisticated people who were attracted to the faith, but Baxter drew many others, and the church grew and prospered. Elder Baxter was the first pastor appointed to the state, and he became the overseer of Pennsylvania and Delaware. His wife was appointed by Bishop Jenkins to be the state mother, an office she held in addition to that of church mother.

Elder Baxter died in 1925, and Bishop Jenkins himself assumed the pastorship of the church. He appointed a series of ministers as his assistants to function as pastor, since he himself lived in Tennessee and had to travel extensively throughout his church organization. Bishop Jenkins notified the officers of the church, "I am going to stay here to keep fellows from running in here. I am going to put my name here." By this he meant that he was going to eliminate the competition among several ministers who were vying for his position. He also meant that as pastor of the church he would receive all the tithes (10 percent of all the members' earnings), plus a monthly offering, for the remainder of his life.

After the death of her husband, Mother Baxter became the center of church power in Pennsylvania. She was instrumental in removing several ministers from the position of assistant pastor of Zion. Whenever one of the assistant pastors displeased her she requested that Bishop Jenkins remove him. She was strongly supported by Jenkins, who respected her obvious power and influence in his church.

In the fall of 1925, Bishop Jenkins appointed Elder Simpson to replace Elder Baxter as overseer of the state of Pennsylvania and as pastor of a mission in Philadelphia. This mission had been "brought out by Mother Williams," a pioneer in the church's development in eastern Pennsylvania. Mother Baxter remained the state mother of Pennsylvania and worked in that capacity with Elder Simpson until her death in 1941. After her death, Mother Williams, who had worked as her assistant, became the state mother, and for the first time the church's power in Pennsylvania shifted entirely to the eastern part of the state.

Another church member, Elder Judd, became pastor of the mission in Beaver Falls about 1920. That mission had shared close ties with the church in Pittsburgh, and the members often came to Pittsburgh to worship. Elder Judd was ambitious, and his church increased in size and stature. When Simpson gained control of the Pennsylvania structure, Judd aided in the development of the church throughout the state. As a result, he was rewarded with the position of chairman of the council of ministers in the state organization, which allowed him to review problems concerning the ministers. Elder Judd, who had worked closely with Mother Baxter, later married her and consequently was elevated to superintendent of a state district.

In 1938, Bishop Jenkins appointed Elder Judd assistant pastor of Zion in addition to his pastorship in Beaver Falls. This appointment was the result of the influence and encouragement of Judd's wife. It was also evidence of the growing influence of Elder Judd and his wife upon Bishop Jenkins and in the state of Pennsylvania. The Judds in western Pennsylvania were becoming a growing threat to the seat of church power in eastern Pennsylvania. As a consequence of this threat, a conspiracy developed to undermine the growing power of the Judd team. A previous wife of Elder Judd was brought before the officers of Zion as evidence that Elder Judd had two wives. This woman was divorced from Elder Judd and had remarried, but according to the Zion doctrine she remained his wife nevertheless. The decree of Bishop Jenkins was that "you would not marry if you have a living wife," and this precept was invoked against Elder Judd and his wife. They were notified that they would not be supported as leaders if they "lived together in sin." Judd was removed as assistant pastor in Pittsburgh and his wife's position as state mother was threatened. They separated under this pressure, and "Mother Baxter didn't live long after. It broke her." Elder Judd continued to pastor in Beaver Falls, and he had the legal title of his church arranged so that Bishop Jenkins could not remove him as pastor there (a precedent that has flourished among pastors in the international organization).

In 1949, Bishop Jenkins "split the state" of Pennsylvania. The state had grown and prospered under the leadership of Elder Simpson and Mother Williams. But the power and influence of Elder Simpson (appointed bishop by now) had soared to the point that he was competing with Bishop Jenkins. Elder Simpson had built up an international youth organization so large that it began to create jealousies among other international officials. These officials made the growing power of Elder Simpson appear a threat to Bishop Jenkins, and they also convinced Bishop Jenkins that the revenues from the state of Pennsylvania could be increased substantially by having two state organizations there. Pennsylvania was thus divided into an eastern and a western organization. The organization in the east remained under the direction of Simpson and Williams; that in the west was headed by Bishop Jackson (who had proved his loyalty to Jenkins, financially and politically, as an assistant pastor in Pittsburgh) and Mother West (who had worked as Mother Williams's assistant). All these officials became wealthy and powerful in their positions.

As was pointed out earlier, this organization is a vehicle for achievement for economically and politically deprived Blacks, and this is a structural basis for its continual schisms. The church has judged this world irredeemably wicked and the worldly fate of the economically dispossessed, hopeless. The members have created their own alternative—a new society in which the criteria are all in their favor. They have adopted a new set of values which transforms the meaningless struggle for subsistence into "self-denial for Christ." A potential leader need only be redeemed to become a voice for God. If he is intelligent and eloquent in speech, he can influence large congregations and, in turn, accumulate wealth and power for himself and some of his subordinates. Thus by a different route a few acquire most of mainstream society's badges of achievement, and the remainder secure a viable pattern of living.

Leadership is represented in this church by the power of the pastor and the "obedience of the flock." It is actualized by many reciprocal relationships, such as pastoral recognition of financial "captains" who receive public acknowledgment during church services and a voice in church administration. The officers, captains, and auxiliary heads, who assert themselves in financial support and directives, run the church. The pastor bears the final responsibility for success or failure and reaps the major financial harvest.

To understand better how church leaders obtain and exercise their power, let us look at an actual instance of schism in the church, the interplay between Pastor Jackson and Leader Jodie of the newly emerging congregation. Jackson met Jodie in 1929 when he became a layman in the church, where Jodie was already a member. They became the "best of friends." Both were members of the "prayer band" who went from house to house praying for the sick. This activity gave them opportunities to develop many friendships among the members as well as to gain intimate knowledge of each other's habits and relationships. This intimate relationship was the foundation for the two men's stable friendship and parallel careers in the church. Jodie became the chairman of the trustee board and Jackson a member of the deacon board.

Both men had come from the South with backgrounds in farming and would later use farm-animal illustrations in their sermons to explain life to their congregations. Both were ambitious, though uneducated and unskilled laborers. They were handsome men and, by their own admissions, attractive to the ladies. Both were extremely frugal. Jodie raised ten children. Jackson had no children but raised his siblings who came to Pittsburgh with him and his wife after his mother died in Kentucky. Jodie came from Georgia with his young bride and their children and started afresh in Pittsburgh, where he worked as a city street cleaner and a truck driver for a film company until retirement. Jackson had worked as a coal miner in Kentucky but became a building superintendent in an office complex in downtown Pittsburgh. Both men were slow to speak, to change, to be persuaded, and to trust. Both dominated their households with authority.

In 1942, when the church officers took steps to oust the assistant pastor, Jodie, by dint of politicking with the local hierarchy, was one of those responsible for the ordination and consequent naming of Jackson to the post. Bishop Jenkins remained official pastor until his death even though Jackson assumed considerable authority as a leader.

Jodie did not foresee that Jackson, in his powerful position, would run his program as he perceived it to be most beneficial to himself, largely oblivious to the ambitions of his supporters. Jackson's utmost concern was to keep Bishop Jenkins's financial support at an impressive level, and this he did, even to the extent of loaning the church money to "bring up" his offering when the members failed to contribute a sufficient amount. Jackson's stratagem worked, as he knew it would, for he was aware that Bishop Jenkins defined loyalty in terms of financial support and deference to him, and Jackson was astute in both. But this approach required that Jackson emphasize heavy financial support, so that he could "come up with his report" for Bishop Jenkins and the church could "take a front seat" in the international meetings.

Soon after Jackson became assistant pastor, Jodie, as chairman of the trustee board ("he ran the church because he knew business"), felt the effects of Jackson's growing confidence. Jackson began to usurp more and more authority, with the help of officers who sensed his growing power and were anxious to stay in his good graces. Jodie became more isolated in his business policies, most of which he felt were sound and for the benefit of the church. But Jackson was more concerned about the flow of money to himself that would enable him to carry out his program. This resulted in numerous encounters in the "back room" between the two men. Jodie constantly tried to persuade the other officers that Jackson was not interested in the church, but only in "his own power and money for himself." He had known Jackson as an intimate friend and was not awed by him as many of the officers were, so he often spoke his mind in Jackson's presence.

By 1949 Jackson's strategy had paid off so well that when Jenkins decided to split the state, he appointed Jackson to preside over the western part and promoted him to bishop. This maneuver not only upset Simpson and his supporters in the east but also gravely disturbed many in the west who felt that they were more educated (Jackson never went to high school), more experienced, more capable, and more popular than Jackson. Meanwhile Jodie seemed to be developing bitter envy of Jackson's growing power as well as deep resentment because he was being "pushed aside and overlooked" in church policy decisions. He began to refer to the officers who supported Jackson as "pantywaist men" and "petticoat men." In short, his influence in the back room was at a low ebb. But Jodie was the superintendent of the Sunday school, and he began to use this position as his platform to fight Jackson.

Throughout this time, Jackson never attempted to remove Jodie from his official capacities either formally or subtly. He never chose to antagonize Jodie any more than his program forced him to, and he never attempted to "set him down" (take away his offices). He explained this by saying, "I don't fight dirty."

As superintendent of the Sunday school, Jodie had the task of offi-
cially closing school each Sunday. This gave him approximately an
hour just before regular services began, when most of the Sunday worshipers were present, to speak "as the Lord led him." The Lord led him
consistently to speak against Jackson's program. He talked about cars,
preachers' offering, and money raising, comparing them with the poor
financial state of the church. He complained about preachers' families
running the church, the poor morality of preachers in general, and the
"money-hungry pastors who never get enough." But he never mentioned Jackson by name. Each Sunday on his Sunday school black-
board he wrote mottoes that seemed to be directed at Jackson. Jackson
confronted him about one such motto, asking that it be taken down
because he believed Jodie was referring to him. Jodie denied the reference but removed the motto.

Jodie began to use these opportunities to preach what amounted to
a Sunday message before the official one. His success and his following
at these Sunday sessions sparked an obsessive ambition which was to
drive him to his subsequent position of power. Jodie discovered that
he could indeed preach! His critical remarks about "hypocriting saints"
and "preachers going to hell" encouraged his supporters to call him
"young Baxter," whom the "old-timers" remembered earlier railing
against the "so-called saints of God."

In the spring of 1956 Jodie announced to his friends that the Lord
wanted to use him, but not until he had cleared up some matters,
because when he started to preach he wanted to be free of all burdens.
In 1957 Jodie and his followers organized to have Jackson removed by
Jenkins as so many other assistant pastors of the church had been
removed. But Jenkins was satisfied with Jackson. Consequently, instead
of meeting with the officers, Jenkins called for a full church meeting
to decide the matter and asked everybody to speak his piece. Many
were intimidated by the large audience, and those who spoke were discreet in this public situation. Moreover, for some reason which is not
clear, Jodie had asked his supporters to stay home. In the end, Jackson
remained, and the next year, Jodie took his flock (forty-one members,
or about half the church) out of Jackson's church and established
his own.

This success was sweet to Jodie, and he was encouraged. He waged
a relentless attack against the existing leadership (Bishop Jackson and
his lieutenants) in the western part of the state, and he preached constantly on themes that were critical of Jackson's program. Jodie was

prodded by his own sense of inferiority and his obsession to equal and surpass the achievements of his former buddy. He immediately began plans to build a new church. This was done by soliciting pledges to establish a building fund, negotiating for the purchase of selected land, and requesting that members with equity in their homes pledge it for collateral for the new church. During this period it was discovered that he sought to purchase a church building that he had advised the officers of Zion *not* to buy because the foundation was undermined by water. He later abandoned that plan, but Jackson supporters interpreted it as a device Jodie had used to prevent Jackson from buying a modern church at a time when Jodie was already anticipating the launching of his own career.

The people with whom Jodie started his church were all firm financial supporters. He went to the savings and loan association where he had dealt for a considerable time for his own personal needs and secured a loan to build a new church. He enlisted his members and his family to help him in the construction of the building, hiring contractors only for jobs he could not have done by amateurs. He completed his church in 1966. A year later, Jodie started to broadcast on the radio twice a week, thus extending his contacts and resources. He purchased three buses and a station wagon to bring his growing membership to church services and built himself a new home in a prestigious part of the city. Thus in 1968, when the organization of western Pennsylvania began to argue about whom they would support in an international dispute, Jodie was being called a "wonder" who had built a church after he was sixty.

Elder Bostem was at that time the president of the state youth organization. He insisted on supporting a rebellious faction in the international organization, even after being warned against it by the state bishop (Jackson), who consequently removed him from his state office. This gave Bostem and a group of rebellious ministers in the state organization the excuse they needed to attempt to split the state. They wanted to set up their own state organization in the hope that leadership, titles, and financial rewards would then be theirs. Thus, according to the members, even after the international dispute was settled in court, they continued to plot for their own state organization. Each minister in the plot had hopes of being the bishop of the new organization, and this hope attracted even more dissenters. Eventually nine pastors organized the "New State." There were several meetings to select officers, with the result that Jodie was finally selected as the

leader of the organization, and Bostem, disappointed because he was
not made leader, was given the same job he had had before—president
of the youth department. When it was decided that age, experience,
seniority in the church, respect, and prestige would be the crucial factors in determining the leader, all the pastors reluctantly agreed that
Jodie was the best candidate because he had the largest church, the
largest membership, and the largest financial resources. Two disen-
chanted pastors quit the organization after this decision and returned
to Jackson's organization, and Jodie continuously validated his leadership by having his church participate in all the subsequent meetings
en masse. He insisted at these meetings that his members stand separately, bring their offerings separately, and that each offering be publicly announced separately.

Jodie now had a radio broadcast, a new home, other real and personal property, two churches (he had purchased another in a suburb
of Pittsburgh), three buses, a station wagon, and leadership of the New
State with which to challenge Jackson. He waged a bitter and unceas-
ing attack against Jackson at every opportunity, but Jackson still
seemed to want to retain his dignity and not "fight dirty." He possessed
little to qualify as a leader to his members and his state organization.
But the social network to which he belonged played by different rules.
Although he did not need the badges of mainstream society, he had to
use some device to control this heated contest. He employed supernaturalism, building up in the minds of his members and subordinates
his image as God's prophet who was being persecuted by the devil.
Over and over he stressed that God, not man, had put him where he
was, and "he who would undo God's work would be damned." He
became so obsessed with the idea that he preached a variant of it every
Sunday and at every possible opportunity in his state meetings. He
asked his members and subordinates to pray for him. His wife con-
fessed that she needed a "whole lot of prayer," apparently to live with
him during these turbulent times. Thus, when any misfortune came to
members of the New State, it was easy for Jackson and his supporters
to conclude that "God was working" or "death was ruling" or "death is
still riding" to those present and still opposing him.

But Jodie persuaded the other pastors one by one. He worked to
make their offerings attractive. He announced the New State meetings
on the radio broadcast and allowed one of the other pastors to speak
occasionally. He bought another church, in Uniontown, and put it in
the New State organization. But impressive as he was, he knew that

his organization had to be recognized by the international organization. ("Recognition" means that the leader of the new organization is made a bishop in the international organization.) The international organization was reluctant to encourage these schisms, but at the same time it was reluctant to refuse the financial reports sent to the international office from these organizations. So the international organization took the financial reports but announced a freeze on the appointment of any more bishops. This ruling appeased the existing state organizations, which wanted these new organizations crushed, and also the international organization, which feared that the new groups would change their affiliation if not recognized in some way.

Jodie died on March 3, 1970. His grueling ordeal was too much for an old man. Elder Mousey, Jodie's assistant, felt that he should succeed him as leader, but he had none of Jodie's qualifications. The New State attempted to garner the support of Jodie's wife for their organization (she was a respected mother in Jodie's church), but she was having disputes and threats of a congregational schism in her own church and needed all her energies to keep the church intact. The pastors could not decide upon a successor to Jodie, and in consequence, the New State failed. They gradually returned to the old organization.

The history of Zion to a large extent is a history of its characteristics—an intimate primary group in which anxieties, stresses, fears, and competition proliferated. As the history shows, these characteristics are a basis for dynamics that operate in Zion. Thus when I describe below the quest for solidarity, the emphasis on fellowship, and the many idioms of identity utilized, one can appreciate why these are required to mitigate against the conflicts in Zion—fission, threats of schism, conspiracy against leadership, and membership competition. Zion is a community straining to keep the levels of church tension and controversy tolerable; at the same time such tensions and controversies make Zion an interesting and energy-absorbing community for its members.

† 3 †

ORGANIZATION IN ZION

Zion is one of many Pentecostal churches located throughout the world within the organization of the Church of Holy Christ, which prescribes the same formal organization for each of its affiliated churches. But Zion is also a closely knit community with a mission to validate the lives of the poor and the socially immobile by means of "love and fellowship." It is also a group settled in the urban context where the competitive ethos prevails in social organization. These social dynamics of fellowship and competition are translated into Zion's informal organization, where the conflict of thwarted ambition exists side by side with the solidarity of love and fellowship.

The formal organization of Zion groups the members into formal categories (see figure 1). It also serves as a means for identification within the larger church superstructure, the Church of Holy Christ. A member can travel to affiliated churches throughout the world and feel comfortable in their services because the formal structure and the format for religious service are similar to those in Zion.

The pastor presides over Zion. He is the highest official and is appointed by the international bishop for as long as he performs satisfactorily in the latter's judgment. Zion has a "pastor's helper" who presides over church services when the pastor is absent. The pastor's helper is not an assistant pastor, for that would validate him as being capable of pastoring. On the contrary, he has no official title; he is merely a minister who helps the pastor. Zion's deacon board consists of nine deacons who are responsible for the general operations of Zion. A nine-member trustee board is responsible for the business transactions of the church. There are a choir (where, for twenty-five years, two of the most influential women in Zion have sung), a chorus, a young people's choir, an usher board, a church secretary, a church treasurer, a church announcer, church nurses, a pianist, and an organist. Zion has a Sunshine Band, a group in which children learn the Bible and memorize speeches for holiday pageants. The members of a pastor's aide group provide personal assistance to the pastor and his wife. There is also a group of financial captains who organize and lead financial drives.

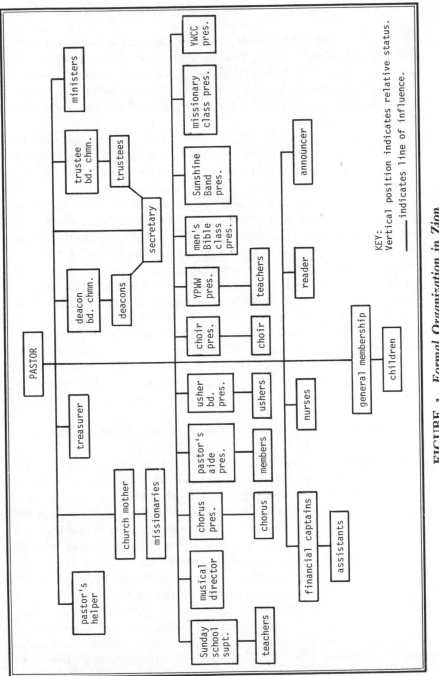

FIGURE 1. *Formal Organization in Zion*

An official church reader reads the Bible during the pastor's sermon. The Sunday school, Young Women's Christian Council, missionary class, Young People's Willing Workers, and a men's Bible class are all Bible-teaching groups. Zion has a prayer band which holds weekly prayer sessions, ministers who preach occasional sermons, and other miscellaneous officers.

Any male in the Church of Holy Christ who believes that God has called him to preach can become a pastor by attracting some followers to support his calling. The church can be housed in a storeroom, a member's home, or almost any kind of shelter available to the congregation. After the pastor has established his church he may then ask the state bishop for membership within the Church of Holy Christ. This request is almost never refused, because it means increased financial support for the state and international organizations. Ministers in Zion or in other churches in the international organization can be appointed pastor when a former pastor dies, retires, or "backslides," that is, relinquishes the faith. These appointments are usually reserved for those who have been loyal to the particular bishop in whose state the vacancy occurs. But often the congregation where the appointment is to take place is adamant about whom they want for pastor, and since they must financially support the pastor, the state, and the international organization, their feelings are usually considered. This means the bishop will often try to "feel out the people" before he makes such an appointment.

The pastor's helper is peculiar to Zion. This position is usually occupied by a minister who would be considered the assistant pastor in other affiliated churches. The title "assistant pastor" means that this minister has all the authority of the pastor when the pastor is absent and when he acts for the pastor in official capacities. Such a minister is expected to become pastor when a successor is needed. Because the pastor at Zion does not want an assistant with such status and prestige, he has refused to appoint an assistant pastor. Instead he has selected one of his loyal ministers to assist him when called upon without having the duties, responsibilities, and powers of an assistant pastor.

The deacons in Zion are appointed by the pastor on the basis of their loyalty and financial commitment to the pastor's program. They are members who have demonstrated by their service to the church, loyalty to the pastor, and financial contributions that they are committed to the mission of Zion. The deacons are responsible for the functioning of the physical plant, the welfare of the members, and the obligations of the pastor. They exert the necessary energy and effort to assure that Zion is operated so that it will grow and prosper. When the deacons become dissatisfied with any of the workings of Zion, it is their responsibility to initiate the proper changes in consultation with the pastor. The deacons can even take action to remove the pastor if they can determine and demonstrate that he has been derelict in his duties. Such action is begun by an appeal to the pastor's senior officer (the state or international bishop) in the Church of Holy Christ. The chairman of the deacon board is usually selected from that board. He is most often the deacon who has served on the board the longest and has demonstrated the qualities of deaconship to the greatest satisfaction of the pastor. The church treasurer is usually appointed from the deacon board and has the responsibility of accounting for and disbursing funds in Zion.

The trustee board consists of church members with characteristics similar to those on the deacon board, but trustees are usually not held in as high esteem as deacons. They are selected to supervise the business transactions of the church. The members of the trustee board oversee dealings with tenants living in church rental property and negotiate the sale and purchase of real estate and church equipment. They see that church debts are paid, and, at present, they are negotiating the preparation of church land and plans for the building of the new church. The chairman of the trustee board is usually the oldest and most capable trustee. In actual practice the deacons and the trustees work together closely, and the power of any individual board member depends largely upon his personal characteristics. The superintendent of the Sunday school is usually appointed from either the deacon or the trustee board.

Women as well as men can be called by God to deliver sermons, but there is a distinction between the "teaching" of the female missionaries and the "preaching" of the male ministers. Women are inferior to men in Zion. Only a man can be "the head," and only a man can stand in the pulpit in Zion and preach. Women missionaries must stand below the pulpit platform to "teach." But women missionaries can travel about delivering sermons in various churches, and they can become well known and prosperous as long as they recognize that they are subservient to a man who is "the head." The church mother in Zion is appointed from among the missionaries and is usually the woman who has demonstrated the most ability for keeping the women members "in line." She has sufficient longevity, Bible knowledge, and commitment to the faith to command the respect of the other women in Zion. Loyal and capable missionaries are also appointed by the pastor to be president of the missionary class, president of the Sunshine Band, and president of the Young Women's Christian Council. This group of missionaries has reached a status among women in Zion similar to that of the minister among men. Thus, when the superintendent of the Sunday school appoints Sunday school teachers, he seeks women who are missionaries and men who are ministers.

Financial captains are men and women in Zion who have demonstrated a high level of loyalty to the pastor's program and an ability for securing funds inside and outside the church. These captains are highly competitive about fund raising, and a successful captain who has secured financial resources inside and outside Zion sufficient to be "the biggest money raiser" is most influential in Zion policy. Captains can be recruited from among any of the members, but they are usually dedicated members who are totally committed to Zion and the full-time efforts required of captains. Captains can be seen day after day and week after week soliciting money in the church, on the job, and in the street. Consistent efforts are required to accumulate the funds and to make the required substantial financial reports. It is these efforts that make pastoring at Zion a financially rewarding enterprise and enable Zion to meet its state and international financial commitments.

The secretary of the church is a confidante of the pastor, appointed by him from among loyal female members. She must be articulate and poised because she is "always before the people." She must be a "seasoned member, able to digest strong meat," because she will be exposed to all the problems of church affairs. She must be loyal to the pastor, because she is always in a position to influence the officers of the church concerning church policy. The secretary keeps the church records, writes the church communications, and participates in all church meetings. If she is an able secretary, she is charged with much of the authority and responsibility that reside in the deacons and trustees.

All other officers in Zion are appointed by the pastor. Such appointments are rewards for demonstrated commitment in Zion, and the pastor attempts, to the extent that the pressures for appointments allow him, to appoint members to duties that they will be most qualified to perform.

My analysis of the informal organization of Zion is based on my observations and may not apply to other affiliated churches in the Church of Holy Christ. Zion's informal organization is a distinctive synthesis of the achievement orientation of the wider society and the mission of Zion as a group. The informal organization of Zion (see figure 2) provides members with the mechanism of mobility and culminates in the system of ranking found within Zion. Access to financial resources within or outside the church (by solicitations) which flow into Zion is the prime basis for mobility and status. Favor with the pastor based upon loyalty to him and allegiance to his program is the second basis; charm, "a way with the people," is a third; and exposure, "being put before the people," is a fourth. Combinations of these enhance one's potential for moving up and for maintaining one's position there. Formal positions in Zion are often the means of conferring title upon and validating those who have achieved informal status on one or another of the bases noted above.

In describing the informal organization of Zion, I have found it useful to distinguish among marginal, supportive, core, and elite members. The elite is the top category in the system of ranking within Zion. It is this category of members whose policies, attitudes, and decisions directly influence the pastor's behavior. The elite can determine who will be promoted and demoted. They can directly influence church policies concerning spending, fund raising, sermons, and allotment of space for ministers to preach and missionaries to teach. They have a critical influence on the interactional dynamics of Zion as well as on its structural changes. The elite members are usually seated within or around the "sacred inner space" (after Erikson, 1968; see figure 3, p. 144), and many of their formal functions take place within in. The elite consists of the church secretary, who has achieved her position by means of loyalty and exposure; the president of the pastor's aide group, who has financial mobility; the chairman of the deacon board, who has loyalty mobility; and the church treasurer (also a deacon) who has loyalty mobility. The elite also includes certain members of the pastor's immediate family who have demonstrated their loyalty to him. They are a sister who is the only female trustee, the usher board treasurer, and president of the Young People's Willing Workers; a sister who is state field worker for the state Sunday school organization (not a Zion office); a sister who is president of the usher board; a brother who is a deacon; and a brother who is a trustee. These phenomena are derogatorily referred to by jealous members as "kinfolk's religion."

The core members are ranked immediately below the elite. The core and elite members are critically concerned about the operations of the church, for their future ambitions and day-to-day life perspectives depend upon these operations. But the core members do not have the power or the influence of the elite. They pay their tithes and all other financial commitments asked of them by the pastor and participate in all the activities of the church. They attend on Tuesdays, Fridays, and Sunday nights, and accompany the church on its travel itineraries. They are the members who respond when people are needed to cook, clean, and perform other functions related to annual state meetings and festivities in which the church building is used. They plan and attend special functions such as teas, banquets, pageants, and dinners. Thus, the core members are vital to the church operations, and herein lies their power, especially when they have strong alliances among themselves and with certain elite members. The core members consist of:

1. the deacons
2. the trustees
3. the pastor's aide group
4. the financial captains
5. the choir
6. the adult members of the chorus (there are also seven teen-agers)
7. the missionaries
8. the ministers
9. other miscellaneous officers mentioned above who are not members of the elite category

The core and elite members are those most concerned about recruiting and retaining members and about the threat of the church's demise.

The supportive members are ranked immediately below the core members. They normally come exclusively to Sunday morning services, annual meetings, and special occasions like musical programs, pageants, church dinners, church banquets, and funerals. They seldom participate in the planning or policy decisions for these events. They are valued for their weekly offerings, recruitment to ad hoc committees, presence in Sunday morning services, their names that expand the membership list, noninterference in power maneuvers, and contributions to major financial rallies. They are the members whom the core and elite members are constantly encouraging to participate more; they give meaning to the comparative categories of core and elite. They are often referred to as "Sunday-morning Christians" and "fair-weather saints."

Marginal members are ranked below the supportive members, in the lowest level of membership in Zion. Often the only distinction between

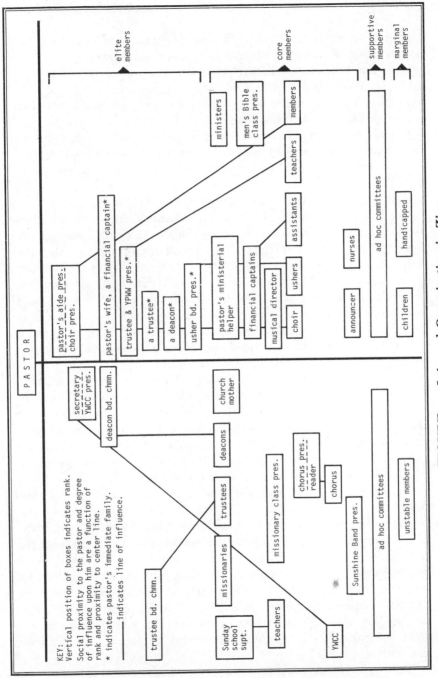

KEY:
Vertical position of boxes indicates rank.
Social proximity to the pastor and degree
of influence upon him are a function of
rank and proximity to center line.
* indicates pastor's immediate family.
————— indicates line of influence.

PASTOR

pastor's aide pres.:
choir pres.

pastor's wife, a financial captain*

trustee & YPWW pres.*

a trustee*

a deacon*

usher bd. pres.*

pastor's ministerial
helper

financial captains

musical director

choir

ushers

assistants

teachers

members

men's Bible
class pres.

ministers

announcer

nurses

ad hoc committees

children

handicapped

elite
members

core
members

supportive
members

marginal
members

secretary-
YWCC pres.

deacon bd. chmn.

church
mother

deacons

trustees

missionary class pres.

chorus pres.-
reader

chorus

Sunshine Band pres.

missionaries

teachers

Sunday
school
supt.

YWCC

trustee bd. chmn.

ad hoc committees

unstable members

FIGURE 2. *Informal Organization in Zion*

marginal members and visitors is that marginal members have their names on the church rolls. Marginal members consist of:

1. teen-agers, whose financial contributions and physical energies play a minimal role in Zion
2. chronic backsliders, who come in and out of Zion and never attain a specific role or status there
3. a residual group of members whose physical, mental, and financial inadequacies are such that their participation in Zion is limited, but whose presence serves to demonstrate the range of acceptance that is Zion's
4. the children, who are conceptualized as the future church

The formal organization in Zion is a variant of that in the Southern Baptist Church and has little direct relationship to the themes that have developed and operate in Zion. The informal organization, on the other hand, is distinctive, for it is peculiarly adaptive to the conflict and solidarity that are Zion. Each member of the elite derives his position from the influence he commands, which can be translated into financial resources, loyalty, alliances, exposure, or a combination of them. Charm and exposure are particularly important factors in gaining the support and alliance of the church members; financial resources and loyalty usually gain the powerful support of the pastor.

Thus, the elite position depends upon alliances or potential alliances in Zion, and any conflict among the elite filters down among the respective core members who support them and becomes very disruptive to the operation of the church. Such conflicts must be kept to a minimum or be quickly resolved by reconciliation lest they lead to schism. The membership recognizes the potential for such conflict, and this recognition reinforces one of their major concerns—fellowship. The elite are especially aware of potential conflict; thus they make a concerted effort not to antagonize one another. Elite members will often confront core members or other elite members concerning the undesirable behavior of another elite member rather than confront him directly and risk potential antagonism. This procedure allows them to dissipate their antagonistic energy in directions other than toward the offending elite member. Often an antagonism is of such proportions that an elite member will continue to communicate his displeasure to others until word reaches his antagonist that they must come to some understanding soon. This procedure is not always successful, as the case of Elder Jodie demonstrates.

Elder Jodie, an elite member, was outspokenly critical of the pastor's program. His alliances among the core and supportive members were strong and numerous. He argued that the elite category in Zion was closed and that the financial resources of the church were directed overwhelmingly to the pastor's private coffers. He proposed that mobility in Zion be increased and that the money be used more for the benefit of all members. Both the pastor and Jodie avoided open and direct confrontation with each other, but Jodie "put it where the pastor could get it" by relating his displeasure to members who were allied and loyal to the pastor. The pastor directed his displeasure against the core members who supported Jodie strongly, usually by means of "not recognizing them," which meant they were denied the exposure in church services to which they were accustomed. The pastor acted thus to signal to core members and others that their support of Jodie was "blocking the pastor's program." This was also a warning to Jodie that the pastor would take stronger measures against him if he did not cease his opposition. (The pastor was in a position to demote Jodie from his positions as Sunday school superintendent and chairman of the trustee board.)

These admonitions might have succeeded in most circumstances, but Jodie's alliances were too powerful. He had the membership support to challenge the pastor and the awareness that if he were defeated, he could establish his own church with his Zion members. The pastor's measures encouraged undecided core members to avoid supporting Jodie, and they persuaded other core members to attempt reconciliation between the core supporters of Jodie and the pastor. The elite members were very anxious. Some of them secretly agreed with Jodie's suggestions, but they were afraid of the potential disruption his methods might bring to the church and their positions. Any evidence that they supported Jodie brought an immediate indictment from the pastor and the risk of his sanctions. The elite were loyal to the pastor and opposed to Jodie's maneuvers, but often their attempts to reconcile this opposition aroused the pastor's suspicion. Nevertheless, they worked feverishly to mend the breach between Jodie and the pastor, but Jodie's alliances were too strong; he could not be intimidated or persuaded. He used the pastor's sanctions against his supporters as a means of solidifying his alliances and his opposition. He promised his supporters that if he failed to change things in Zion he would move Zion elsewhere, and he assured them that he had the resources with which to do it. The members failed to resolve these differences, and Jodie subsequently asked the international bishop to remove the pastor for incompetence. When the bishop refused because of lack of evidence, Jodie took his supporters out of Zion and started a sister church in the Church of Holy Christ.

The formal organization of Zion is recognized by all its members. The behavioral content and the structure of the informal organization are recognized by some, participated in by most, and manipulated by a few who are cognizant of the Zion power structure and in some cases capable of moving through the channels of mobility in Zion. As I pointed out above, the formal positions in Zion are often the means of validating informal power, and the informal organization is thus translated into the formal structure of Zion. With that idea in mind, I have selected crucial members of the formal structure as a means of explaining their roles in Zion in terms of the informal categories.

The chairman of the deacon board is a member of the elite. He has been a member of Zion for forty-six years and a member of the deacon board for forty-five of those years. He served on the deacon board when the pastor was a deacon also and claims that he was instrumental in the ordination of the pastor as minister and his initial appointment as assistant pastor to Zion. He has been very supportive of the pastor throughout his period of leadership at Zion. On several occasions when the international bishop was called to Pittsburgh to review charges against the pastor as a prelude to moving him, Deacon Paint fought courageously at the latter's side. When Elder Jodie took forty-one members out of Zion to establish his own church, Deacon Paint remained at Zion and attempted to heal the wounds created by that split.

Deacon Paint works incessantly to motivate the membership to support the pastor financially. He is admired by most of the members despite the fact that he is limited by a lack of formal education, a speech impediment, and a meager retirement income. (He has spent most of his life in Pittsburgh as a maintenance employee for a food chain, during which time he has never earned more than seventy dollars a week.) The members perceive this deacon as one who has given of himself as well as his income "above and beyond the call of duty." Not only has he contributed to the support of the pastor and the church, but he has also given "from his pocket" to help individual members in need. He is described by the members as one who has "a lot of influence in this church." Every church service is ordered in such a way that Deacon Paint has "words." These "words" are usually designed to rally financial support for the pastor, the church, or a member in need. It is to Deacon Paint that core members take their offering when they cannot be present at a church service, for he will always announce that a member "left his offering with me." Deacon Paint knows the state of church affairs at all times, and he receives many phone calls each week from core and supportive members who want to know the implications of actions and decisions at Zion.

Deacon Paint has very close relationships with other members of the elite. They call each other to discuss church business as well as personal fears, anxieties, and emotional traumas that result from interactions at Zion and in the wider world. Deacon Paint gained much of his renown at Zion as the deacon with whom the international bishop stayed when he came to town. In fact, Deacon Paint's wife has recalled to me the many hours at night when she "rubbed Dad down from head to toe for his arthritis" ("Dad" is the intimate term used for the international bishop and founder, Bishop Jenkins).

Sister Ulrich, president of the pastor's aide, is another member of the elite. She has been a member of Zion for twenty-five years, a member of the choir for twenty-three years, and the president of the pastor's aide for fifteen years. Since the death of Sister Backler, who was the former president of the choir, Sister Ulrich has had more influence in Zion than any other member. She is the "top money raiser" in Zion. In her position, which is competitive financially, she is intensely envied by the other members and especially the other elite members. Her only indisputable emotional ally is the pastor, who frequently finds it necessary to encourage and praise Sister Ulrich from the pulpit, providing exposure, as well as to "put down" her adversaries. Sister Ulrich is not only Zion's most prolific fund raiser, but as president of the pastor's aide, she administers to the pastor's many personal and private needs. Her seat in the choir places her directly behind the pastor's seat, and it is well known in Zion that any attack upon Sister Ulrich is an attack upon the pastor or his program.

The pastor is required to be very discreet when praising female members, for this praise and encouragement must always be gauged upon a female ranking system in which Sister Ulrich remains in the top category (see Figure 2). Recently one of the core members "asked for her letter" (changed her membership to another church) when her ambitions were thwarted by the awareness that Sister Ulrich's social position could not be encroached upon at Zion. The pastor made an earnest effort to keep this sister in the fold, but he could not pacify her without antagonizing Sister Ulrich.

One time Sister Ulrich angered the pastor's entire family by planning and organizing a golden anniversary banquet for the pastor and his wife against the repeated wishes of the family that they be allowed to plan and organize this affair. To add fuel to the fire, the pastor was required by loyalty to Sister Ulrich to praise the event and Sister Ulrich for an entire month. The pastor's family has taken concerted action to wrest some of this power from Sister Ulrich. They have managed to put one of the pastor's sisters on the trustee board (the first female ever), and they have manipulated his wife into the position of a financial captain even though most of the members feel that it is an "unseemingly" (inappropriate) position for a pastor's wife. Moreover, the pastor's wife has, on two occasions, untactfully raised more money than Sister Ulrich, thus forcing the pastor to explain on both occasions that his wife "only beat her out" because the "whole family helped my wife." As a result of such actions, Sister Ulrich receives the deference of most members but the love of very few.

Sister Mainway, the secretary of the church, is a member of the elite. She has been a member of the church for forty-five years and the church secretary for twenty-four of those years. In addition, she has been the president of the Young Women's Christian Council for twenty-three years. The pastor employs her services for his church affairs and frequently his state affairs. She is a confidante of the pastor, and he relies upon her not only to administer church and personal affairs, but also to be loyal enough to practice extreme discretion in her communications with others.

Sister Mainway's husband has been on the trustee board for twenty-five years, and for a number of years this husband-and-wife team were, respectively, the secretary and treasurer of the church. Until recently Sister Mainway was the only woman who had the privilege of "going in the back room" (the officers' room). She has a seat in the sacred inner space, between the pulpit and the seating of the general audience, where she is highly visible. To accentuate this seating arrangement, she normally sits in the audience and then at strategic times during the service proceeds back and forth to the officers' room and the secretarial chair. In her role as secretary she is visited at the secretarial chair during the financial part of the service by officers of the church and members making financial reports. At the point in every church service when the church "doors are opened," if someone applies for membership the secretary has to proceed to the front of the church, where the pastor is receiving the potential member, and record the name. The pastor frequently calls upon the secretary to leave her seat in the audience and come to the front and center of the auditorium to read various reports. Since she sits in the second row, but on the far side from the center of the auditorium, this requires that she walk approximately thirty feet to where she reads her report. Thus, the secretary's constant movement about the church auditorium, in and out of the officers' room, and in and out of the pastor's study (for private conferences) is legitimated in Zion by the status and role which Sister Mainway manipulates for exposure mobility, and there is little doubt that she exploits this exposure. She is one of the best-dressed women in Zion, and the variety of her hats and outfits is impressive. She moves about with her head high and an air of dignity about her which the members describe as "acting her part."

The pastor's immediate family consists of his wife, two brothers, and four sisters, all members of the elite. The pastor's wife's recent appointment to the position of a financial captain is the only official position she has in Zion. Mother Jackson is lethargic and seldom expresses her emotions overtly, but she is frequently seething with anger because of the enactment of policies which she has openly opposed. In conversations with her I have noticed these emotions as well as her firm conviction that "the bishop's wife has to go through something; I need a lot of prayer." The members give her "love tokens," take her out to dinner, and purchase gifts for her, but none of this seems to give her much pleasure. She is a "homebody" by her own admission and would be quite satisfied living a simple homemaker's life. Her health is failing, and this aggravates the anxiety created by the constant pressure to attend "so many services." Because she recognizes her political impotence and has always been close to her husband's family, she has cast what influence she has with the lot of the pastor's brothers and sisters and acts with them on most crucial decisions. She has had a stormy emotional life, for the rumors and realities of the pastor's church problems have sometimes been disconcerting, but she believes that a wife should do all she can to help her husband, no matter what sacrifices this entails.

The pastor's two brothers are officers and members of the elite. The older brother is a deacon; the younger, a trustee; and both exert their influence on official decisions. The older brother married a member of the church after his first wife died and has only been a member for approximately five years. The younger brother has never been married, but he has been in the church most of his life. He has enjoyed the prestige of being the pastor's brother, and one of the rewards has been the attractiveness he has held for the female members, by several of whom he has fathered children.

Of the four sisters, all of whom are members, one is a trustee, president of the Young People's Willing Workers, and treasurer of the usher board. She is frequently appointed to collect money from the members for international meetings. Another sister is president of the usher board and a financial captain. The third is the state Sunday school field worker (not a Zion position), responsible for raising funds and making the financial report to the international Sunday school organization. She is also responsible for a financial report for the state Sunday school superintendent and the state bishop. For her services she receives a financial "day" and expenses to travel to the international Sunday school meeting. The oldest sister is the matriarch of the family; their mother died at an early age and she reared the younger children. She has no official capacity in Zion and does not appear actively to seek any power, but she has the respect and deference of all members of the family. It is this group—the immediate family of the pastor—that I refer to as a unit among the elite. This family unit competes with the other members of the elite, especially recently, since the signs of the pastor's age and suspicions of his growing susceptibility to influence are threatening to them.

The core members are the foundation of the Zion enterprise. Deacons, who are core members, see to it that the church doors are opened in time for service and secure when the service is over. They execute the responsibility for cleanliness and maintenance of the church building. They are concerned about the welfare of the members, reporting to the church and administering to the needs of the widows, the sick, and the desperate. The deacons are perceived as protectors of Zion. When someone becomes unruly (for example, Elder Harmin, see p. 77), they are expected to perform the necessary actions. When intoxicated visitors, the homeless, and the mentally disturbed come in off the streets and appear to be a threat, the deacons respond like the dominant males in a baboon troop until they are satisfied that there is no imminent danger. The deacons perceive of the church building, the church organization, and the church morale as their intimate personal property and responsibility. They are rewarded with the prestige, propriety, and magnetism that come with their positions. The core members, supportive members, and marginal members court the deacons' favor, and the latter are frequently in the limelight among the congregation. They take the offerings, adjust the windows during the service, check the radiators, adjust the fans and lights, conduct business among the members, welcome visitors, chat with the pastor, and move in and out of the officers' room and the pastor's study all during the services. The deacons are frequently expressly recognized during the pastor's sermons. They play a crucial role in organizing all church events and are perceived as significant components of any such organization in Zion.

Trustees in Zion, who are core members, "look after the business of the church." Most of what was stated above about the deacons also applies to the trustees. It is the trustees' responsibility to take control of all business transactions between the church and outside agencies. They are responsible for paying the taxes on property other than the church building and bills for water, sewage, electricity, gas, and building maintenance. The trustees collect rents, negotiate leases, and make the necessary contacts for initiating building plans and repairs. In reality much of this responsibility is shifted to the secretary, but the trustees have the authority. The reciprocal rewards of this authority are couched in the status, prestige, and deference the trustees enjoy among the congregation. In this respect their position is similar to that of the deacons.

The pastor's aide, who are core members (except for the president, who is an elite member), consists of five women, including Sister Ulrich, who is the president. It is their duty to provide for the comfort and convenience of the pastor and his wife. When the pastor is out of town they assure the church members that his wife will not be alone for long periods of time. They provide transportation for her, take her out to dinner, assist her with her cleaning, accompany her shopping, and encourage her to spend most of her time in their company. When the pastor is at home, they initiate plans for periodic banquets, dinners, and other special affairs in his honor. They give him and his wife "love tokens" on the days that he preaches his annual convocation message, on Mother's Day, Father's Day, and on their wedding anniversary. They organize special flower-pinning ceremonies on Mother's and Father's Days. The pastor's aide is the group in Zion which assures the pastor that his "name will stay before the people."

Financial captains, also core members, are a special group whose responsibility is to organize the collection of funds for the church's expenses and the pastor's offering. It is a competitive group because one's rank and influence with the pastor depend upon one's ability to raise money. These members must be keenly motivated to build their influence and thus anxious to demonstrate their prowess at raising money, and they are selected for their positions accordingly. The financial captains are periodically exposed to the church. On his "day" each month when he takes complete charge of the financial part of the service, a financial captain stands at the head of a line which includes all the members who are cooperating with the quota the captain has set. (This quota ranges from five to twenty-five dollars.) After the line is complete, with all members who are going to give the requested amount, the line marches down the center aisle, away from the pulpit, around the rear end of the left section of pews, and back up the left aisle toward the front of the church, again proceeding to the secretary, to whom they relinquish pledged funds. Captains also gain exposure during special financial rallies (for the pastor's annual "appreciation," to raise property-tax money, or for large projects, such as painting the entire interior of the church building). During these special rallies each captain is permitted to read the names of all who contributed to his individual totals. The individual totals are announced, and each captain is given the sound of approval, "Amen," the loudness of which depends upon how successful his efforts have been. Most of the financial captains also hold other official jobs in Zion. They are held in esteem by most of the members and are usually described as "our good workers."

The missionaries of Zion, who are core members, are all women over fifty years of age. All of them have been in the church more than twenty years and are recognized as having been called by God to bring the message to God's people. The missionaries' sermons are characterized as teaching in contrast to preaching, which only a male minister can accomplish. The missionaries are not allowed to go into the pulpit but must teach from a position in front of the pulpit at the audience level. The missionaries are the revered women of the core membership. They are considered to be in close touch with God, and they demonstrate this by their prophecies, dreams, and knowledge of the Bible. There is a "missionary corner" in Zion which is in the same general location as the male officers' seating but at the opposite side of the church (see figure 3, p. 144). The pastor depends upon his missionaries to respond to his sermons, in which he frequently mentions them. Missionaries are the female spiritual leaders in Zion and exercise considerable influence.

The pastor's ministerial helper, a core member, has been a member of the Church of Holy Christ for approximately thirty years. He left Zion fifteen years ago and returned in 1969. Soon thereafter he was appointed the pastor's helper, a position designed to be unofficial and ambiguous. Because he has no official capacity, he also has no official power and no right to church resources. He is at the mercy of the pastor, who frequently allows his helper to preach for him in the state itinerary as well as at Zion, where he gets a financial offering in each case. The established duties of the helper are to carry on the church services as minister in charge whenever the pastor is not there. These duties have created an unofficial position for him which some members describe as "assistant pastor." Although he is not exposed to the official church business and is not given an official title or position, he enjoys some of the esteem that usually accrues to an assistant pastor.

Members of the choir and the chorus have maximum exposure to the congregation. Each group sings two songs during every Sunday morning service; they sit facing the congregation and at the highest point in the auditorium; the choir wear robes and the chorus, special uniforms. There must be close cooperation for rehearsals and special events organized by the two groups. The activities of the choir and chorus put their members in frequent contact with the officers of the church and other core members. They rehearse during the week, follow the pastor on many of his itineraries, and organize special programs as a group (serving in the kitchen, sponsoring a musical program, or presenting the pastor with a token of love). The presidents of the choir and chorus have historically wielded great influence in Zion. These groups appear to be fertile ground from which to "grow," or achieve upward mobility, in Zion.

Zion has six ministers (core members) other than the pastor and his helper. They sit in the pulpit and encourage the pastor or whoever is preaching by responding enthusiastically. The ministers recognize themselves as a group; they have their own financial captain and periodically sponsor programs. They are permitted to go to other churches if they have a preaching assignment there but are expected to stay at Zion if not. The ministers are recognized by the congregation as healers, prophesiers, and prophets of God. They are addressed as elders and are frequently given the opportunity to preach at Zion.

The members of Zion believe that one's influence is increased by exposure to the other members. As indicated earlier, the pastor, who feels he must tip the balance of influence in his favor if he is to lead, frequently reminds his lieutenants to "keep my name before the people." Sister Ulrich, who is the most influential woman in Zion, insists that the pastor constantly praise her activities, a demand that often causes other women of Zion to say that "Sister Ulrich gets all the credit" for their efforts. Based upon this ethos of exposure, every member of the elite has systematic means for frequent exposure to the membership, and those core members who aspire to elite positions seek every opportunity for such exposure.

The interest of the female members in hats (at a time when this interest is declining among women in the larger society) seems a typical fashion interest to the casual observer. But upon gaining further insight into Zion's informal social organization one discovers that hats are instruments of attention for those who systematically design means of being exposed to other members. They are a means of being distinguishable in the membership, of becoming well known to the members, and of attracting the interest of other members, all of which are mechanisms to achieve social alliances and thus power in the Zion community.

The Zion membership also believes one's influence is increased by demonstrations of love and fellowship. This approach is especially important for those core, supportive, and marginal members whose potential for exposure is very limited. Some of these members have developed this demonstration of love to a fine art, and their ability is often seen as a threat to the elite who sometimes refer warily to these "artists" as being "so sweet that the honey flows out of their mouths," or "they have butter-mouthed tongues." Not only has intimacy in Zion been a survival of custom from the rural South, an attraction to potential members, and a reward for present members; it has also been an instrument of political alignment. A "sweet sister" (charming woman) may find herself surrounded by the status, prestige, and power that come to a woman in Zion whose personal influence extends to other members. But this position may be competitive and thus fraught with emotional stress, such as fear and anxiety. This stress is alleviated through testimony, emotional outbursts, dance, speaking in tongues, prophesying, singing, retorting to the sermon, the practice of "love," and financial generosity. All these factors have the potential for creating member support and for enhancing political alignment, thus creating personal power in Zion.

Members believe that Zion's greatest attraction is its demonstration of love and fellowship. The aging pastor, whose deacons, trustees, and elite often beleaguer him with complaints about falling church attendance, constantly stresses that it is not his responsibility to attract newcomers but rather the responsibility of the members to do so by love, kindnesses, and fellowship. This basic belief in the powers of love and fellowship is the rationale for the alliances operating among Zion's membership. Marginal, supportive, and core members explain their allegiance to certain elite members as a response to his or her being a "wonderful person," "a fine saint," "a person so full of love." But such allegiances have reciprocal advantages such as a prestigious contact, an occasional free meal, transportation, or exposure to the membership. Such allegiances and demonstrations of love and fellowship are the one basis for the Zion theme of solidarity—a solidarity that mitigates against disruptive conflict. That is an integral part of mobility and status in Zion.

In short, Zion is an aggregation of southern rural migrants who settled in Pittsburgh and attempted, by means of a religious community, to reestablish the nature of the life they had known in the rural South. They perceived this effort as one of exclusion, isolation, and boundary-building. They would live *in* the city but they would not be *of* the city. Or, as they would explain it, "in the world but not of the world." This mode required intensive solidarity among the members. But in the urban context, members were more exposed to the nature of power, position, prestige, recognition, wealth, and social mobility in the larger society. They recognized Zion as their own available means for achieving these values. This quest for upward mobility in Zion is the major basis for conflict in this church and is perceived as the greatest threat to solidarity. Zion's response to the distinctive nature of coexistent solidarity and conflict is:

1. to couch both solidarity and conflict within Zion's own system of symbols
2. to provide a variety of opportunities for intensive secular and sacred interaction
3. to provide a wide range of membership tolerance which includes acceptance of those who are upwardly mobile and those who are helplessly immobile
4. to provide mechanisms of mobility and a system of ranking within Zion

† 4 †

BEHAVIORAL DYNAMICS
OF THE MEMBERSHIP

The ideology that supports the interaction of members in Zion is in the nature of virtues (love, fellowship, humility, self-deprivation, "purity of heart," generosity, charity, and "satisfaction in Christ") to which the members subscribe but, as in all human groups, fail to achieve fully.

The members say that the love of money is the root of all evil, and that greed destroys "many a man." Most of them are poor; their incomes do not exceed five thousand dollars a year. But poverty is no obstacle to full participation in the functions of Zion. The members conceptualize themselves as "poor folks" and believe that the only significant achievement is to be "a good soldier in the army of the Lord." Worldly achievements are acknowledged but are not decisive for mobility within Zion. In fact, superior educational, financial, social, and political status in the wider society frequently generates suspicion among the leaders of Zion and the Church of Holy Christ and thus may hinder one's mobility there. Ambition of all kinds (especially among the leaders) is frowned upon, in theory, among the members of Zion. They say, "What God has in store for you, you will get. You don't have to plot, plan, and undermine to get to the top." One of the characteristics of the upwardly mobile members in the Church of Holy Christ organization is the constant demonstration of humility and love among the members. Thus humility and love are cogent instruments for rising within Zion, as these ambitious members seek to convince the membership that mobility in the wider society is not a part of their way of life. Social and political achievements are not part of "Christ's plan." The Zion charter is inconsistent with the attempt to achieve social and political power in "the outside world."

The ideology and the charter for Zion are distinct from the actual behavior one can observe in member-to-member relationships, however. Chapter 3 demonstrates the primary importance that money and the ability to secure it for Zion play in this religious community. Achievement, although structured in the idiom of the Zion community, is a driving force among the members. Ambition is a key component of the keen competition that pervades the elite members in Zion; and social and political power is noticeable in the organization of Zion in spite of the ideological disdain the members attach to those who seek upward mobility within and outside the church.

Zion, like possibly any human community, finds little discrepancy between its ideology and its members' actual behavior; those discrepancies discerned are given only superficial significance unless they contribute to the personal advantage of those who are making the observation. Thus we have in Zion a community whose ideals hold worldly values in contempt but whose operations and driving forces are pervaded with those same values—money, achievement, ambition, mobility, and social and political power.

This church may be said to be designed for the poor, Black, peasant immigrant from the rural South, and the group ideology supports its membership. But in the northern American city, social organization is prescribed by the norms of the larger society, such as ranking, social distance, and instruments of mobility. When they attempted to organize their church, these rural southerners discovered that they had little alternative. They created a system of ranking, but they provided an ethos which accepted within this church both the upwardly mobile and the hopelessly immobile in their design for association. This chapter shows the nature and range of the members of this closely knit group.

Observing actual behavior among the upwardly mobile in Zion, one finds there are conflicts to be resolved, sanctions to be administered, social controls to be inculcated, decisions to be made, leaders to be selected, rank to be determined, authority to be conferred, status and role to be validated and legitimated, domains of power to be gained and manipulated—all in the Zion idiom.

Zion consists of a variety of social themes. To understand Zion is to understand this variety. How does Zion manage to integrate these and its social order? How has it survived or integrated successfully the dynamics of human interaction? Has it attempted to direct most of its hostility upon the "world" and the "devil"? How has it validated the distribution of rank and wealth? How do the authorities in Zion coerce and punish? How do they abuse this privilege to punish? The answers to some of these questions may be sought in the analysis of networks of interaction, shared norms, and socialized tendencies toward order discussed in other chapters. But a fuller understanding requires considerations of political behavior such as we shall now explore.

There are factions in Zion that must be recognized. These and expressions of power or feelings of impotence create conflict which requires mechanisms to confine it to tolerable limits. Someone must rule in Zion, but that authority must be constantly validated and legitimated by other levels of power. Sanctions exist as a basis for compliance with established authority, but personal influence can manipulate that authority, making it more flexible. Personal success is couched in terms of rebellion and special alliances, but each is modified by the Zion idiom. Thus rebellion has its ritual, and support its ceremony. There are political aspects to all of Zion's major symbolic themes—theology, food, animals, death, human anatomy, the physical world, and the supernatural (see chapter 6). The interactional features of Zion—intimacy, conflict, fission, status, prestige, group competition, and alignment—also have political aspects. It is beyond the scope of this discussion to analyze all of these, but an attempt is made below to describe some features of membership that underlie the behavioral dynamics of this church.

THE CHARACTER OF LEADERSHIP

This sect is characterized by poor and uneducated Blacks who, upon discovering some charisma in themselves, launch an uncertain and competitive career for status, prestige, and material possessions via religion. It is commonly assumed that in order to lead people, one must be "a leader," with all the images of ability which that symbol projects. Yet historically the leaders in this sect have had none of the symbolic baggage that mainstream society accepts as leadership insignia. They claim no significant bloodline, no land or wealth aristocracy, no education, and no exceptional practical experience. "God can call anybody to preach" and thus lead. The ability to organize and rally people to one's support is the crucial factor, and this recruitment implies a precarious and demanding life style. (Bishop Jackson, the leader of Zion, lives in constant fear that he is being undermined, and indeed he is.) Leadership in Zion is neither well constructed in mainstream symbols nor clothed in sufficient mainstream ritual. (Jackson constantly reminds his officers and intimate supporters to keep his "name before the people.") As a result, the new, educated breed of Pentecostal preacher represents a threat to traditional leadership and is being constantly reminded of the impotence of his seminary training and his Ph.D. He is distrusted and required to pay constant homage to his uneducated superiors, who rigidly control upward mobility in this church organization.

The ministers (always male) are the acknowledged leaders in Zion, the symbolic representation of the group (see Kelley, 1970). They must be able to satisfy the yearning of members who wish to identify with something larger, wealthier, more powerful, more articulate, and more flamboyant than themselves in order to obscure the poverty, insignificance, and powerlessness that dominate their lives. Leaders must be able to use the idiom of Zion. They must be willing to communicate the anxiety and traumas inherent in leading this "troublesome" group. Thus we see throughout these pages the statements of a leader who constantly confronts his followers with the issues of today, the anxieties of the moment, within the idiom of the Zion code.

But leadership in Zion also has its instrumental obligations. The church has its expenses and must maintain an organization capable of amassing the income necessary to defray these expenses. The point has been made that leaders in churches like Zion have traditionally come from among the poor, the uneducated, and the socially immobile (see Gelman, 1965; Mitchell, 1970; Pipes, 1951; Pope, 1942). But it is evident that these humble beginnings present no significant obstacles to the development of the leadership qualities one finds in churches such as Zion. It is a fitting refutation of the long-standing myth that the lower classes lack all the qualities necessary to achieve success in any domain.

These ministers must be able:

1. to create emotional excitement in the congregation by integrating experiential empathy with religious aspirations and biblical accuracy in a sermon that begins with a text and ends in emotional frenzy (see J. W. Johnson, 1927)
2. to interact with the members so that they demonstrate their love for "everybody" yet maintain the appropriate social distance concomitant with their position.
3. to create an air of distinctiveness around their individuality by appearances, wealth, education, political astuteness (support of powerful church members among the elite and core or support of national leaders or strategic members of the wider secular community), glibness, intellectual prowess in recognition of the Zion idiom, ease of interaction and identification among various subcultures (in the "world" and in Zion)
4. to jest and entertain the congregation within the limits of propriety determined by Zion

  5. to motivate the congregation to work to maintain the physical
     plant and to raise money; to organize
  6. to appreciate the symbols and values in Zion so as to be upwardly
     mobile without undue threat to the vested interests of superiors
  7. to conduct their personal lives so that they do not create church
     or public scandal
  8. to withstand gossip, the threat of schism, feminine guile, and the
     pressure groups within Zion and in the international organization
  9. to support the international and state organization in membership
     and finances
  10. to attract new members, whether with programs or personal
     appeal

No leader has all these characteristics, but these are the strategic
qualities employed to gain and maintain power.

To amplify the above list: a potential leader in Zion is a man "who
knows the Bible from cover to cover." He can translate this knowledge
into vivid "parables" utilizing themes of food, animals, human anatomy,
death, Black folk beliefs, and items of traditional Black folk behavior.
He is well groomed, has a sense of humor, and is emotionally expressive. He has organizational ability and is adept not only at attracting
"womenfolks" but also at organizing them into an effective fund-raising
machine. The potential leader is sensitive to the local, state, and international political overtones of his actions. He realizes that often one
must find favor within the local power structure to succeed in the
Church of Holy Christ, but there are times when validation from the
state and international level is more strategic for local success in spite
of the competitive fears and jealousies it generates. The successful
preacher, who is usually the potential leader, entertains his congregation. The expected fun he injects in his Sunday morning sermons is well
received. The lively gestures he uses as he manipulates his body at the
height of his arousing sermons are a phenomenon to which every member of the congregation can relate. The members value the minister
who can "rare back" and preach a "knock-down" sermon. He is
described as making the folks "cut up" or "cut a step." The members
say he can really bring the message, and if he has "a way about him"
too (that is, a knack for communicating and encouraging the members),
then he is a ripe candidate for potential leadership in Zion.

Bishop Jackson

The example of Bishop Jackson and his particular combination of
talents clarifies the qualities of leadership required. There are other

leadership determinants than those I have described. International and state leaders have several times awarded positions of leadership to their relatives. Bishop Jackson has no children, but I mentioned in chapter 3 the power that accrues to his siblings by virtue of his leadership. Both Elder Jodie and Bishop Jackson surrounded themselves with loyal, committed, and seemingly indefatigable elite members. Both were physically attractive to their female constituency, and both expressed vivid memories of membership interaction in "days gone by." Both provided for intimate contacts with important members. Bishop Jackson, through his prayer line, gave various core members the opportunity to "rub him down" (a firm massaging which reinforces prayer) and pray for him. His nurses were selected to put his cape on after each sermon, and core and elite members had free access to his private study. Jackson finds it difficult and often annoying to communicate with his members, although they are anxious to have the privilege of talking with him and being seen in his company. He prefers to be alone or with a few trusted members or his immediate family. He is able to maintain his distinctiveness by means of his meticulous grooming, his display of wealth, and his political astuteness.

Jackson's concern about his personal appearance is extreme. He often leaves the pulpit, especially after any emotional display, to check his appearance in the mirror in his study. He has his hair cut each week, and he has a habit of smoothing his hair with his hands to assure that it is lying down neatly. He has his fingernails manicured. He seldom preaches in his street clothes but removes them whenever possible and replaces them with a robe. Then after the sermon, he takes the robe off and dresses again. He uses a facial powder to prevent an oily appearance. He is concerned about talking directly to someone at close range for fear that his breath may be unpleasant, so he covers his mouth with his hand.

Bishop Jackson is aware that he "doesn't take to people." He knows that his success has been based upon the major financial contributions he made to the international bishop, Bishop Jenkins, during his lifetime, as well as the humility he displayed vis-à-vis Bishop Jenkins's leadership. He never finished elementary school and is not a glib speaker. His ability to organize is not impressive. He has had problems with his personal life and its public discussion. And his recruitment capabilities are not great. But then he has shown a stalwart ability to withstand gossip, fission, feminine guile, and pressure groups. He has demonstrated an acute facility to avoid unduly threatening vested church interests at the same time that he has been upwardly mobile. He

has been a strong proponent of the values in Zion, because they are the
only values to which he can legitimately subscribe (that is, one is called
by God to be a preacher, the Lord gives the message, the church program is the program of God. God gives one all the worldly goods one
possesses as a reward for doing his bidding).

Bishop Jackson has assiduously avoided any conflict with the international officials. When there was an international upheaval in leadership in 1968, he was accurately accused of "straddling the fence" until
it was evident where the power lay. Even after he had committed his
allegiance to the dominant group, he continued to reassure the congregation that he "loved" the leader of the losing faction. He has consistently met his financial quotas in the international organization, even
when the membership and financial support he got from his state
organization required that he contribute "out-of-pocket monies" to
supplement the report.

He is a stoic person, lethargic most of the time, but he makes the
necessary effort periodically to jest with his congregation. Because of
his temperament the congregation is especially appreciative of these
jocular moods. He is "down-to-earth" in his analogies and frequently
amuses his congregation inadvertently. He has considerable experience
in creating the excitement that culminates in emotional frenzy during
the final moments of every sermon. Despite many shortcomings, these
positive characteristics make Bishop Jackson an acknowledged leader
of the Church of Holy Christ.

Elder Jodie

Elder Jodie was another example of the leadership qualities that
have been recognized and rewarded in the Church of Holy Christ. He
began to demonstrate early, as a superintendent of the Zion Sunday
school, his ability to influence the members. He also exhibited his ability to organize by obtaining the commitment of forty-one members in
Zion before he "pulled out" to form his own church. He convinced his
cohorts that Bishop Jackson had strayed away from the traditional
Church of Holy Christ ideology and behavior. He supported the belief
within this disgruntled faction that Bishop Jackson was "out for himself" and no longer concerned about the community of fellowship of all
the members. Elder Jodie began to preach in a style that imitated Elder
Baxter, the first pastor of Zion; he even used those "rough words" for
which Elder Baxter was remembered. Elder Jodie's followers began to
refer to him as the "young Elder Baxter," even though he was seventy

years old. He further demonstrated his organizational abilities when he led his members to pledge their homes for security to build a new church and induced many of them to contribute their own physical labor to the structure. His success in his venture reached the point of rivaling that of Zion, whereupon Elder Jodie made a bid for Bishop Jackson's job as leader of the state organization. It is evident that Elder Jodie could organize.

He also created a distinctive air about himself by his conspicuous wealth. He had worked two jobs most of his life and had always been frugal. He owned property in the Hill District and in Homewood. He induced his members to buy two Cadillacs and four school buses, and he built himself a new home in the suburbs. It seemed to the majority of his members that he "had money." He also had a canny ability to relate to leaders in the wider business community. He persuaded the city to rezone the property upon which his church was built as well as to sell him the property at a price far below its value. He persuaded a lending institution to give him a sizable mortgage (there is doubt about the exact amount) on a property in the Hill District which ordinarily would not have qualified. These favorable maneuvers caused his members to describe him as a "good businessman" and contributed to the distinctiveness which characterized Elder Jodie.

He was an able entertainer. His comments about "miniskirts, naked thighs, these wigs, sissies, and Bishop Hightowers" kept his members enthralled. His political maneuvers and tirades against "Bishop Hightower" (Bishop Jackson) generated excitement among the members in the Church of Holy Christ throughout western Pennsylvania and other parts of the nation. This was compounded by his use of a radio broadcast to continue the attack.

Elder Jodie also subscribed intensely to the values of the Church of Holy Christ, for as with Bishop Jackson, they underlay his claim to social status. He was not only able to withstand gossip, fission, feminine guile, and pressure groups; he even seemed to thrive on these pressures. He was not an impressive preacher in the traditional style, but his tirades against sex and the hypocrites in the church were an ample compensation for this inadequacy. Elder Jodie's life was a "clean and open book." He had been able to live down the early gossip about his conduct before he "was called to preach." He had a record of not only asking his members to invest in the church but of also being willing himself to invest in his members' private ventures. Some of his members expended more time maintaining the physical plant and the church buses than they spent in gainful employment. His career was too short to make possible a final judgment of his ability to manipulate in the international organization, but upon his death he had achieved the strategic support of several international figures.

Elite and Core Members—A Role in Leadership

Leaders must have followers, and the nature of those followers is a determinant of the character of leadership. One of the major problems in Zion is accumulating sufficient funds to pay church expenses and to support the life style of the pastor. This is understandable when one considers that most of the members are poor. This means that members who are able to secure substantial sums from outside sources for the coffers of Zion command respect from the pastor and the other administrative officers. Such status inevitably leads to influence and control in decision-making. But others achieve such status by means of strategic alliances with other members, as a result of their charm, exposure, and loyalty. Then there are members whose status comes from consistent and faithful service necessary to a group like Zion. Some members have nothing to offer except loyalty to their pastor, but where divisions and factions accrue this is a valuable offering. So leadership has its reciprocal dependencies, and these dependencies constitute the part these members play in leadership.

As I indicated in chapter 3, the elite members play a critical role in the decision-making process in Zion. Each member of the elite has a power base predicated upon his ability to raise money or his widespread influence and support within the general congregation and/or among the international or state leaders. Sister T. K. Ramsey achieved great power and influence in Zion because of her relationship with Bishop Jenkins. She attended all the international and state meetings, and she worshiped Bishop Jenkins as if he were God. This relationship resulted in her appointment to both international and state secretarial positions, from which she continued to obtain strategic advantages in social relationships as well as monetary rewards. Her fame in Zion resulted from the fact that her influence with Bishop Jenkins ("Dad") grew to the point that she could "move" pastors at Zion at will. The members describe her methods thus:

Dad liked her. When he came in town he would often stay at her house. She would cry and cry like a baby telling Dad all the wrong the pastor was doing. Then Dad would tell the pastor,

"Son, we're gonna have to send you away." Some of the pastors would cry. There was nothing they could say once Sister Ramsey got to him. She had a forked tongue. She could talk out of both sides of her mouth. Sometimes I wished God would cut her tongue out. She moved a lot of good pastors. She moved one because he wouldn't preach her brother's funeral even though he wasn't even a member of the church. She moved the others when she couldn't boss them around.

Elite or core members who had considerable influence with international or state leaders were often in a favorable position to increase their influence among the international, state, and local memberships. The rest of the members are anxious to be "good friends" with elite or core members who have such "pull." Ofttimes some of these same members, including Sister Ramsey, built reputations in the wider neighborhood as prominent churchwomen and thus increased their power base even more. Bishop Jenkins stayed at the home of Sister Ramsey on many occasions, and as a consequence her husband eventually was appointed chairman of the deacon board and received considerable support from Bishop Jenkins and the membership. Deacon Paint (at whose house Bishop Jenkins stayed before using Sister Ramsey's house) told me that it was his own decision that resulted in the ordination, pastoral appointment, and state position of Bishop Jackson, who was once on the deacon board with Deacon Paint. After Bishop Jackson obtained the state position and became the object of considerable envy of pastors who had more education and experience than he, he became obsessed with the maneuvers of these pastors to unseat him. He arranged that Bishop Jenkins would stay in no one's house (especially not Sister Ramsey's) but his own when he came to Pittsburgh. Bishop Jackson was aware that his political rise in Zion was due to his influence with Bishop Jenkins, and after the death of Bishop Jenkins he experienced continuous anxiety over threats to his state position. Members like Sister Ramsey were one of his major concerns.

Another of the groups on which the leader is dependent is the missionaries, many of whom have been in the church forty years or more. They are well known throughout the state and international organizations and have considerable influence among the members of Zion. They can always exert this leverage, through elite members or the pastor himself. Many of the core and marginal members have close friendships with elite members, as well as intimate peer group associations in Zion. This complexity of relationships often makes the decision-making process in Zion tedious.

Bishop Jackson frequently makes decisions and tells the church officers, "Don't let this get to the people." This requires extreme loyalty from the officers, who participate in a complex network of telephone gossip among members. This particular procedure recently resulted in pressure from the bishop's immediate family to put his sister on the trustee board so that they (members of the elite) would "know what's going on in the back room." This indicates how much the support of the church officers is required for decisions, but the pastor has considerable influence of his own and is often able to make decisions to which many of the church officers do not agree. The extent of such freedom is determined by the nature of the decision and its effects on Zion as the church officers perceive them.

Since all members have access to international leadership, any major controversy over decisions with far-reaching ramifications has potential for involving international leaders. Bishop Jackson's state job as overseer of western Pennsylvania is subject to the approval of Bishop Mormon (the present international leader) and his staff. There is constant grouping and regrouping of members over church issues such as building a new church, pressures to raise money, buying an existing structure, using building-fund money for current expenses, excessive praise for some suspected favorite of the pastor, opportunities for various ministers to preach, neglect in handling church affairs, availability of the church bus, offerings for the leaders of the church auxiliaries, the influence of the pastor's family, the importance of any individual member, and appointments of church officials. The cohesiveness and impeditive potential of these groupings are determined by how quickly and satisfactorily the motivating issues are solved. If allowed to flourish because of unresolved issues, these factions may lead to church fission. The pastor must maintain a constant awareness of the strength of support for any controversial actions.

MEMBERSHIP AND CONFLICT

The pastor is the chief official of Zion, with the elite members next in rank. Some church officers are subordinate to the elite members, although a strategic alliance can at any time tip the scale of rank. The pastor's international prestige is always at stake, depending upon how adept he is at controlling his local church and his state organizations. Thus he can determine the personal success of all members in these organizations. But as I have tried to indicate, such authority is couched in a matrix of political ramifications and thus, what would seem to be clear-cut political power is actually a part of a complex of social relationships that must be reckoned with in any political decisions. The church issues form a continuous basis for conflict, which results in constant grouping and regrouping of church factions as well as lively gossip. These conflicts are an integral part of the character and dynamics of Zion, and the ability to keep them within acceptable range determines the quality and longevity of a pastor (see Gluckman, 1954, 1959; Simmel, 1908).

Conflict reaches a peak of intensity when the position of the pastor is being contested. When Elder Jodie had realigned forty-one members of Zion to his political support and called the international leader to Zion to request that he be made pastor, the levels of disorganization, instability, and anxiety reached a point that strained the very fabric of Zion's social system. The charges and countercharges (see chapter 2) that were designed to undermine Bishop Jackson mitigated against whatever prestige and status he had with which the members identified. When the international leaders confirmed Bishop Jackson as pastor, and Elder Jodie rebelled by removing himself and his followers from Zion, the remaining members and the pastor were forced to endure a period of traumatic realignment. The political contest between Bishop Jackson and Elder Jodie did not end here but continued until the latter's demise.

The micropolitics within the various auxiliaries and peer groups form another dimension of Zion's political nature. The president of an auxiliary frequently has members within that group who are competing for his position. There is a constant concern that such competing members not gain influence with the pastor, church officers, and important members to undermine the auxiliary president's position. A member competing for the president's job may be not only eager to originate new ideas and programs (usually designed to raise money) but also anxious to communicate to the pastor and appropriate members her part in the success of any such enterprise. A member of a certain auxiliary may also be a member of the church elite and thus create a strained relationship with the president of the auxiliary. Auxiliaries compete with one another in raising money and gaining the resultant influence and praise from the pastor. Such praise may create conflict between presidents of auxiliaries and members of the elite, church officers, core members, and factions within the auxiliaries themselves. Such conflict may support the ambitions of a member to achieve an auxiliary presidency. The dynamics of such micropolitics occur similarly within all the official groups in Zion.

The severe nature of conflict is also significant as a basis for political compliance. The pastor and the members are fully aware that failure to comply with the dynamics of the political structure will have definite social and political consequences.

Other bases for political compliance form a significant part of the Zion symbol subsystem (see chapter 6). The threat of death "hangs over the heads" of all members who interfere or disrupt the political structure or "program" at Zion. Even sickness is sometimes thought to be a punishment for one's political behavior. The pastor and the members constantly threaten sanctions for misbehavior, which may include noncompliance with political authority, lack of "respect for leadership," and not "going along with the program." Any member who disrupts the political dynamics in Zion can expect to be the subject of malicious gossip. Depending upon the nature and the intensity of political disruption, witchcraft can be a sanction. This usually means, for the members involved, that unusual circumstances can be explained by their adversaries' "working stuff." Depending upon the nature of the political disruption, the member may be threatened with "the loss of his soul," which means that if he dies he will go to Hell. The pastor and the ministers who violate the political code of Zion can be the victims of withheld financial support, lack of attendance when they are scheduled to preach, and denial of congregational response during their sermons and the songs they lead. All groups in the church periodically sponsor programs and rallies to raise money, and it is always a potential sanction for a member to refuse to attend or to withhold financial support from such programs.

It may be clear from the earlier discussion of statuses and roles as determined by sex that even though men hold the highest positions in Zion, the dynamics of political relationships are such that the influence of the female members may tip the balance of power at a given moment. For example, Sister Ulrich is the president of the pastor's aide, a financial captain, and a member of the choir. None of these positions outranks the office of chairman of the deacon board, but her alliance with the pastor is such that she can effectively challenge the authority of that chairman. The same could be said for other female members of the elite as well as female core members, especially missionaries. Thus the political nature of mobility in Zion is determined not only by certain stable structures, but also by a flexible system of political alliance which at any given moment may shift the locus of political power.

MEMBERSHIP CASE HISTORIES

One approach to examining the nature of membership is by means of case histories. The descriptions given below are unequal in detail, but in each case the description is designed to give enough information to indicate some distinctive characteristics of elite, core, supportive, and marginal members. I also attempt to give some descriptive features of the life styles of these members. However, I have omitted case histories of elite members, which were given in chapters 2 and 3.

Elite Members

Elite members in Zion are those who are most aware of the instruments of mobility in their church and who are ambitious, articulate, and capable enough to manipulate those instruments. The elite members are the most keenly competitive. They raise the most money, demand the most exposure to other church members, plan the church activities, and determine church procedure. And the pastor must deal with them in making any decision. The elite are the members the pastor frequently telephones to determine their attitudes on church policy and to persuade them, if necessary, before announcing his decisions about such policy. Elite members are very conscious of the status hierarchy and frequently precipitate serious rumblings in Zion when that hierarchy appears to have been violated. Some elite members have local, statewide, and international influence in the organization of the Church of Holy Christ. For all these reasons the elite members of Zion are those whom the pastor must reckon with.

Core Members

The core members have not yet reached elite status. They may not have been in the church long enough for elite validation, especially in Zion, where length of membership is an often expressed value. Core members seldom command the impressive financial resources that flow into Zion via the elite. They do not make the plans, but they do the work. They do not participate in decision-making, but once the decisions are made they put them into effect. Core members are the ushers, the nurses, the kitchen help, the cleaning people after special occasions, the cook helpers, the officers, the janitor, the choir members, the chorus members, the missionaries, the ministers, the church announcer, the pianist, the organist, and the presidents of various church auxiliaries. The core is the largest group in Zion, from which a selected few periodically move into the elite category. Core members recognize themselves as the providers of the service that keeps their Zion functioning. They enjoy their role in sustaining the church, and most of them ask no more reward than periodic praise from the pastor. The power of the core members resides in alliances among themselves and with certain elite members. The older core members gain special recognition for their seniority and especially for persistent and unwavering loyalty to the pastor.

Trustee Anderson and his wife are representative of the older core members with a wide range of alliances. They are recognized by the pastor not only as two who have given long and faithful service to Zion but also as members who have been loyal to him during many attempts by others to replace him. The Andersons are representative of the "poor" Blacks in this church whose status is in no way connected to their economic level.

Trustee Anderson and his wife have been members of this church about as long as anyone there (since 1930). Sister Anderson had attended a small, rural, Black Baptist church in Tennessee, and she joined Zion soon after her arrival in Pittsburgh in 1928. The church was the only source of her social life in a strange city. Joseph Anderson's family were not churchgoers in suburban Atlanta, and he met Sister Anderson in 1929 while on a curiosity visit to the church. He "knew Sister Anderson was his wife as soon as he saw her." Joseph Anderson found it very difficult to court his future wife because she was not allowed to court "unsaved boys" and because her older sister thought he was a "ne'er-do-well." But he joined the church and deceived his wife into believing that he was "a big shot" by his dress and manners. So in spite of the protests of the older sister, the Andersons were married. It was then that Sister Anderson found that her husband had neither a steady job nor a "nest egg" to get them started. Their life in the Hill District became a series of crises—short-term jobs, sickness, evictions, children, and money problems. During this time they received aid from the church and their families. They lived on church property for a year in 1931, paying rent when they were able. After "mother's assistance" was established by the state of Pennsylvania and Sister Anderson began to receive a check for her family, they set up a more permanent residence in the Hill District in 1935. They subsequently reared six children in a five-room house in the same district. Brother Anderson has worked in painting, gas station service, construction, steel mill labor, and as a hospital porter.

The Andersons are not and have never been concerned with nutrition, tasteful home furnishings, college education for their children, community participation, their children's ambitions, a savings account, or a home of their own. They are concerned about their religious symbols and their social network within the church. This is their "saving grace," the means by which they achieve in this life, the group of people who are relevant to their self-conception, and the solution they perceive to most of life's problems. They are aware of mainstream society and culture but do not participate directly, and they are not comfortable when directly confronted by it. Education, money, middle-class styles of life with all the material gadgets are fine, "but they won't get you in [heaven]," and this group does not require them. In fact they are skeptical of them because they are a threat to their symbol subsystem.

Mrs. Anderson does not visit her neighbors. ("They are all worldly people.") She is cooperative in neighborhood crises, but otherwise she is a good churchwoman whom neighbors expect to be distant. To most of her neighbors, Mrs. Anderson is a "sanctified" freak. She is a "Holy Roller." She is "nobody really." But at Zion, Mrs. Anderson is a missionary and a "big shot" to the extent that she tactfully ignores me (whose status and position she admires) when she is involved with the church officialdom of which she is a part. This is a consistent pattern among church officials.

Hardly a week passes that Mrs. Anderson does not have a funeral, wedding, missionary meeting, speaking engagement, or special service to attend at Zion or one of its affiliates in western Pennsylvania. There are few evenings when she could not attend some function, and her husband, who is not active, often chides her about how busy she is "worrying about those church folks." He says she cannot eat, read the paper, talk to visitors, or rest for the telephone and "Child, have you heard the latest." Mrs. Anderson admits that if she did not have her telephone she "would go crazy" worrying about her health, age, etc. "The telephone makes me forget my own problems." She is upwardly mobile in Zion. She would like to be a member of the elite, and her activities and alliances may help her to achieve this soon. Mr. Anderson is satisfied as a core member, but he enjoys his wife's growing influence among his fellow members.

Sister Boyd, another core member, is a member of the usher board and a faithful churchgoer. She attends services at least twice and frequently three times a week. She is a faithful financial supporter of the church in all special drives (the building fund, pastor's anniversary fund, state and international meeting quota funds, district officer offerings, etc.) as well as offerings to support Zion and its pastor. Sister Boyd is a prolific dancer in the church who exerts tremendous energies when she "shouts." During her dances, she generates great interest on the part of the members, who often anticipate her hat falling off (she is a committed and fanciful hat wearer, as are most women in Zion). Sister Boyd is considered too young (thirty-two) and unambitious to be a threat to the elite members, and as a consequence she appears to be well liked by almost everyone in Zion.

Sister Boyd is separated from her husband and on public assistance. She has four children and lives in a four-room rear apartment in a Black ghetto. In spite of her apparent economic plight, Sister Boyd is a well-integrated core member of Zion. Besides being a member of the usher board, she is a Sunday school teacher. She spends most of her time raising money to assist the usher board in making its financial reports, and she is astute in that capacity. She is well liked by the pastor, his immediate family, and most members.

Sister Boyd's life is filled with church affairs. Her money-raising duties require that she frequently serve in the kitchen and participate in organizing other programs. Sister Boyd's parents are dead, and she expressly admits that Zion is her family. Her round of life is crucially influenced by the Zion community, and it is this community rather than her economic and social plight that colors her outlook on life. Sister Boyd is a vivid example of Zion's core members who spend most of their time supporting the Zion community and receive much in return.

Mother Chips has been in Zion longer than any other living member, so she is well known throughout the state and international organizations. She is not a candidate for elite membership because she is not ambitious. She is devout, committed, and God-fearing. She epitomizes the Zion member with a "butter-mouthed tongue" or "honey flowing from her mouth." She is reluctant to offend anyone and probably comes closer to the practice of loving everybody than anyone I have ever

known. She is a true Christian woman who makes every effort to practice her creed. She has poise and an air of dignity, yet she periodically
dances while possessed of the spirit, a characteristic not typical of elite
members. She is even committed to helping those who are not members
of Zion. As she explains, "I am always fearful of mistreating strangers
because I know no matter who the man or woman might be, that he is
some mother's son and she is some mother's daughter, and I really
believe God wants us to truly love everybody." Mother Chips has been
loyal to the pastor as long as she has known him, and she has never
"sided with confusion." But her lack of ambition among the competitive
and her lack of financial resources have denied her membership in the
elite. The pastor is growing old, however, and he is more and more concerned that loyal members surround him. It appears that on the eve of
this writing Mother Chips may be scheduled for an appointment that
her service deserves and her longevity demands. This appointment will
automatically carry elite status in Zion as well as state and international
recognition in the Church of Holy Christ. There is tremendous pressure
from the members of Zion to make Mother Chips the living example of
"if you wait on God, you'll get what's coming to you."

Mother Chips is the mother of the church. She was born in 1900 in
Tennessee. She joined the Methodist Church at the age of fifteen, and
her husband was a Methodist trustee. They came to Pittsburgh in 1919,
a married couple. Some of the women she met began to take her to the
tent services. She enjoyed them, but her mother and father had also
been Methodists, and as she explains, "I thought you were trying to be
too good if you were sanctified." She considered herself a good woman
already: "I stayed at home and didn't bother anybody, I just got angry
sometime." A visiting minister had a great impact on her conversion to
sanctification. A women's group was taking him from house to house to
teach, and they brought him to Mother Chips's house. "He was clean,
intelligent, and a nice-looking man, and I was particular. He convinced
me." She was saved on June 8, 1921, and she joined the church three
days later. She has attended here ever since. Her husband joined two
months later: "We were very close, never had any big fusses." Two
years after that, her mother joined. She reared two children "in the
church," both of whom finished high school and went to college.

Mother Chips leads prayer service each Monday at noon. It is
attended by the women and men who are free during that time of day;
six or seven members are considered good attendance. As official
church mother, Mother Chips concerns herself with the sick and the

undutiful. She is constantly encouraging the members to "come out" to all the services (Monday for prayer, Tuesday, Friday, Sunday, district meetings, and special programs). Mother Chips is a district fieldworker for the central district (one of five), which includes her church. This job consists of organizing the member churches to raise money for state and international financial quotas. For this she "gets a night" on which an offering is raised for her (usually to aid her in traveling to a national meeting). Mother Chips is a captain for raising money for the pastor each year for his anniversary and twice a month for his compensation. Mother Chips plays an important financial role. Even in her role as church mother she uses her announcement periods each Sunday to remind the members of the pastor's service and to make their financial reports. Yet she is a pensioner, and her personal income is very limited; thus she must depend upon soliciting family and friends for her quotas.

She has been the official church mother for thirty years and attempts to exert a strong maternal influence on the church members. Her serious concern, she says, is that "young people carry on the standards that we have set. . . . We are willing to step back and enjoy youth taking over." Most of the deacons and trustees expressed similar desires for the youth to continue their work and were disappointed that their pastor was so reluctant to allow young people to use their ideas in services. They felt this was largely responsible for the limited interest of young people. When Mother Chips was confronted with the idea that those in power were reluctant to allow others to manifest their ideas about the direction of the church, she felt these were the exceptions. But she is adamant in her consistent exposure before the members. She insists upon using five to ten minutes each Sunday morning to talk about the events that have transpired during the week—the sicknesses, deaths, her personal travels, meetings she has attended, and past, present, and future church programs—in spite of the fact that the pastor constantly complains about conserving the time on Sunday morning and requests each Sunday morning that all announcements be submitted to the announcer.

As we drove to Aliquippa to a service held to assist a financially troubled pastor there, Mother Chips recalled some of her cherished memories of traveling by car in groups to Philadelphia once a year to the annual state meeting (when the state was one unit and not split three ways). "We had the best times eating and joking and stopping on the road to rest." It was a time of social solidarity for all the members of the state organization. They saved all year for this occasion, and when it was upon them they bought new clothes, arranged their rides, "got their quotas together," and left with great expectations of "good messages," "good singing," "good food," and great social reunions. Mother Chips has spent her life raising money for this church, but to her it has been a full, rewarding, meaningful, and good life.

On one occasion when I was in Mother Chips's home, Elder Jodie "took low" in the hospital. Her phone rang continually with people calling about this and other events. She said that Elder Jodie was "low," hospitalized and not improving: "Some had him dead"; "Do wrong and you just have to wait on the Lord"; "You can't get no place with God like that"; "I have always tried to live a clean life and my neighbors always said that about me"; "It is the little foxes that destroy the vine"; "Each little thing makes your strength less and less." She was expressing her feeling that Elder Jodie was wrong and had mistreated her pastor, Bishop Jackson. She continued, "But all wrongdoers is some mother's son and it's just that the devil's got him." "He [Jodie] had a whole lot of zeal and no understanding." This time, as always, before I left we had a ten-minute prayer in which she exhorted God to bless me in my endeavors and keep me interested in God's work. On several occasions this prayer was interrupted by the phone, which she answered and returned to pray as if there had been no interruption.

Mother Chips acknowledges that "my church is my life." She "wouldn't know what to do if I didn't have my work in the church." Besides her Monday prayer meeting, as mother of the church she is the official head of all the women in Zion, and in that capacity attempts to keep the duties of these women executed, organized, and satisfying. She has the major responsibility for assuring that the money-raising activities of her women are carried out efficiently. As a church financial captain she has that same responsibility as an individual. Mother Chips has functioned long and effectively in Zion, and because of this and her loyalty to the pastor she today holds a state organizational job as district missionary. Her manner is extremely pleasant and enables her to reconcile the many conflicts that arise within the membership; she fills her role as "mother" vividly. She is another example of these core members in Zion whose efforts and dedication stand as the foundation of this community.

Sister Dankins, age twenty-nine, is an example of the younger women in the core-member category at Zion. She is also an example of the matrifocal family life style in the "poor" Black ghetto. Sister Dankins's age as well as her limited access to financial resources mitigate against her being an elite member. She is a dutiful core member, and she manipulates well those instruments of mobility at her disposal. She offers her service at any and all church functions. She never misses a chance to be exposed before the membership by means of dancing and spiritual possession. She is a member of the usher board and ushers at every opportunity. Because of such constant exposure she is a well-known member in Zion in spite of her youth and limited financial contributions. Added to her ability for exposure is her loyalty to a large network of other core members and especially to the pastor. Sister Dankins is ambitious, and on the basis of her past record of exposure and loyalty her bid for elite status cannot be denied for long.

Sister Dankins lives in the Hill District. She has four children and no husband, and she lives in a four-room apartment. Sister Dankins receives financial support for herself and her children from the Department of Public Assistance. A large portion of money is spent for her own clothes and cosmetics. She is a faithful churchgoer and requires her children to attend church regularly. She is noted in the church as a vigorous "shouter" (dancer), especially since she has acquired an uncanny skill for retaining her wigs and hats in spite of vigorous movement.

Sister Dankins does not think her children are unruly, although her oldest son is a juvenile delinquent and the others are discipline problems. In spite of this obvious contradiction, she takes pride in their churchgoing and is convinced that this activity will make them into men and women of character. She demands that her children go to the altar for prayer every Sunday morning when "the church doors are open." Her oldest boy sings in the adult choir, and the rest of her children sing in the young people's choir named after the pastor. Her children, like the children of most members, use their church attendance time to communicate with one another and to engage in games, pranks, and other mischief. This means that Sister Dankins frequently has to threaten them by gestures, eye contact, and sometimes physical punishment in the corridors outside the church auditorium.

In spite of this, Sister Dankins's children, as well as the children of all members, find the church an appropriate place to enjoy childhood communication. Children are allowed to talk (as long as it is not loud enough to disturb the services), play, sleep, shout, sing, and laugh at members who engage in religious gestures.

Sister Holiday illustrates the core member in Zion who is keenly aware of the instruments of mobility within and outside Zion. She identifies very closely with the symbols of prestige characteristic of both Zion and "the world," and she insists upon practicing the behavior considered prestigious in the outside world, disregarding the fact that such behavior creates doubt in the minds of some members about her full allegiance to the Zion commitment. Sister Holiday is an example of the range of tolerance for members' behavior in Zion, because she makes every attempt in her life style to disavow poverty, ignorance, and the lack of social poise. But then she has other assets that make her acceptable. Like her sister, Mother Chips, she has a very pleasant personality, a friendly disposition, and a cordial manner of speaking. She makes it difficult for those who are disgruntled about her life style to make a case against her. Her treatment of her fellow members is above reproach. Sister Holiday would like to be an elite member, but she expends too much of her income upon her life style to satisfy the criterion of extreme financial support for Zion. She is too dignified to practice the constant exposure of dancing and spiritual possession, although she does practice these enough to validate her membership in Zion. Her approach is to gain mobility through charm and loyalty, but in spite of her abilities in both it appears that her thrust is inadequate and she is destined to be a core member until age and longevity (she is now sixty-one) add another asset.

Sister Holiday is president of "hospitality" and a financial captain. Her husband is a Baptist minister who heads his own church. They are childless. Sister Holiday is a tall, elegant woman (6' and 150 lbs.) who dresses in the latest fashions and is noted for her wardrobe and for the elegant affairs she hosts for the women leaders in the church organization who visit the Pittsburgh area. Her home in the Schenley Heights section is expensively furnished, and she likes to entertain in her official capacity as president of "hospitality." She makes an effort to use tact and correct grammar in all her communications. She is a very pleasant person to talk with.

Her church position requires that she often address the church to give reports and to make special announcements, and she is noted for her unusual poise. Her ability was recently recognized when she was appointed special secretary for the pastor's appreciation (an annual fund raised for the pastor). But her ability to raise money for the pastor and the church is exceeded by that of Sister Ulrich, and this requires that she be given less recognition than Sister Ulrich. Yet she is within the age group of women in the church who feel very competitive for the pastor's attention and recognition, and she uses her resources to maximum effect.

She gave several teas at her home during the year to raise money and to give visiting guests an opportunity to meet the leaders of the state organization in Pittsburgh. She plans and participates in the planning of large banquets by leading churchwomen in the Pittsburgh area. She takes the pastor's wife out to dinner when he is out of town on church business and sees that his wife is not left without assistance around the house.

The church is her life, as she tells it, and she is reluctant to discuss the day work she does in "private family" to supplement the income from her husband's small church. She has been working thus since she has been an adult and thanks God that she has always been able to "get nice people."

Mother Brice illustrates the core member in Zion who is a constant thorn in the pastor's side. She is financially secure and thus feels superior to most of the members in Zion. She is convinced that her relative success in worldly matters qualifies her as an important decision maker in the church. She is not impressed with the pastor's program and is convinced that she could devise a far superior one. Mother Brice has the advantage of longevity (she is seventy-one), but her advantages will probably never move her into the elite. Her loyalty to the pastor is questioned, she makes no attempt to charm, and her first financial commitment is to her family. But Mother Brice has the advantage of prestigious status in her neighborhood as a property owner and landlord. She seems to have forsaken mobility in Zion and is resigned to the pleasure she gains from participation and fellowship with the membership. She is another example of the range of behavior that Zion tolerates as well as the varied life styles one finds in the "poor" Black ghetto.

Mother Brice lives on the North Side of Pittsburgh with her husband and only daughter. In 1919, as a young woman, Mother Brice attended the Zion Holiness Church even though she was not a member. Her mother forbade her to go because the ministers "in those days were too rough." Their language was crude, and they rebuked the sinners in unsophisticated words such as referring to someone's "backside." But she would sneak to the tent service in the summer and to service in the old horse stable in the winter. A building had to be purchased after the tent was struck by lightning and the members were afraid to worship there any longer. She remembers the march to the building on March

17, 1937: "There was a great snow on the ground and the sun was shining."

Mother Brice was married in 1919 and became her "own woman." She continued to attend the church meetings, although she lived in Buffalo, New York, for a period. She was attending (although not "saved") in 1924 when a faction "came out of the church" because of "some money trouble and if you spoke about it Elder Baxter would put you out." His famous expression was "scratch their name off the books." That faction had a "fight among themselves over a name because Elder Baxter said there would never be a Church of Holy Christ in Pittsburgh" except his own. This meant that they had to belong to another denomination. The faction split up over the disagreement, and the "women stuck together" and led the group. They met at the home of Mother Brice and her mother, who had been "saved" under her daughter's influence in 1923. They again appealed to Elder Baxter for a pastor and he again refused. So they remained another denomination by necessity. Mother Brice was "saved" in this group at her mother's home.

Mother Brice rejoined Zion in 1934. She subsequently left again and joined another church in the same organization (they had begun to multiply). She returned to Zion, the mother church, in 1940 and has been there ever since.

Mother Brice has some interesting ideas about the operation of the church and its affairs. Bishop Simpson was on his way to Philadelphia to preside when Bishop Jenkins's first wife died. "Bishop Simpson and Elder Judd built up Pennsylvania; at that time there were no district elders and others organized." Elder Judd was dedicated, and the church in Beaver Falls was the first in western Pennsylvania. It was there before 1919. When he obtained control of the state he started financial quotas "of begging." In Elder Baxter's time, the church "used to be packed, you had to stand up to hear the service" in a horse stable and a tent. "But in 1934 when I came back it seemed as if Jesus was behind a screen and the church began to decline and the preachers did everything they wanted, but later they moved the screen and let Jesus out for service." "The old-timers [preachers] were interested in souls, not money." She continues:

> Bishop Jackson is a double-minded man, and a double-minded man is unstable in all his ways. He changes too much. If Jackson could only shake off his folly, he preaches well.
>
> These preachers bewitch the folks with the devil. If Jackson

would come down off the pulpit with a basket and say I am collecting all the pocketbooks a lot of those women would put theirs
in it.

I left the church again and went with . . . because of dissatisfaction with the policy, but when he told us that we were going to
mortgage our homes to build that new church, I got up in the
church and told them if my husband wanted me to put my money
into a house in which I could only use the kitchen [no women
preachers], I wouldn't give him a dime. Brother Tate mortgaged
his home and later found he could not get any credit on it until
the church was paid off and it destroyed him.

. . . has a photostatic copy of the old agreement with [Jodie's
church] and he waved it one night and said, "I got something that
will straighten out this church." Mother Jodie got up after and
said, "The devil is here, he is just being quiet."

Jodie first gave coupon books and each member knew what
interest he had in the new church but when the church was almost
paid for he called them all in.

They asked me if Jodie made it in [to heaven], I say can a rob-
ber make it in? Jodie's churchmen were bewitched, put their
business in a bucket and trust someone else to dump the bucket
instead of being men and seeing to it that their business was
disposed of properly!

Mother Samuels is another example of the core member in Zion who
interprets the operation of the church as being largely dependent upon
herself. For her, the development of this church consists of the events
in which she has played key roles. She makes these interpretations in
spite of the fact that most of the other members would disagree. But
she represents the nature of belonging that is characteristic of Zion,
and she exemplifies the extent to which that nature determines the
members' interpretation of the operation and development of the
church.

Mother Samuels has been affiliated with the church since 1923. Some
of the "pioneers" (women) asked her to "help out," and she began with
"both feet in," even though she belonged to another affiliation, the
Christian Missionary Alliance—"Pentecostal too." "They needed me,
but Elder Baxter was too frank and my husband told me he didn't want
me in that mess." So she "helped out" in the services without joining the
church. She explained that Elder Baxter's frankness consisted of his

crude terms for female anatomy. He talked about one's "belly," called sinful women "hussies" and "whores," and told women "your dress was too high," all from the pulpit. In 1929 Elder Baxter was dead, and "I liked their method and preaching." Also, she was being reprimanded for teaching Sunday school without membership, so she joined. Mother Samuels emphasizes that the women started these churches with the little missions in their homes, but they could not preach, so the men were sent in to pastor.

She explains that in 1956 the church had revivalistic proclivities and that Jodie sensed this and began to suggest it. So when he began to preach he patterned his preaching after Elder Baxter ("you old woman lover, you sissy, get your hat if you don't like it, you old whoremonger, you"). When he "split the church he got all the old members."

She perceives her role as historically very strategic. In 1942 Elders Booker, Saxton, and Jackson were all assisting Pastor Jenkins, who would say, "You boys take care until I come back." She felt that this had to be stopped because "it was too much on the church" financially and politically. She said, "The brothers called me in to decide and I chose Jackson as the assistant pastor." Several members have told me they made the decision so I think they all contributed to it. She says that Elder Saxton was a studious, well-read, self-made man who used big words but had no understanding of people. She says Bishop Jenkins appointed her church mother after Mother Baxter died, but she turned it down because two powerful women in the church, Mother Beck and T. K. Ramsey, wanted to be her assistants. She states that after she turned it down Bishop Jackson did not want either of them, so she recommended Mother Chips, and "she got it." Prior to this she says she had refused the same position so that Assistant Mother Bloom could succeed to the position.

Supportive Members

The supportive member provides limited service to Zion (ad hoc committees, etc.) and receives support from Zion in the form of security. These members' lives are not integrated into Zion as are those of the core members, and they have no hope of participating in its power structure as elite members. But in most cases these members are not active heads of nuclear families and seem somewhat adrift from social attachments in an urban context. Zion fulfills a special need for them in spite of their limited capacity to provide the services Zion requires from its core and elite membership.

Sister Saber is a supportive member. She has been a member since childhood, when her parents (elite members) insisted that she attend. Sister Saber, now fifty-one, has been hospitalized several times during her life for emotional illness. She attends church regularly on Friday and Sunday nights and Sunday morning. She takes the same seat (or very close to it) at every service, and if she were not present she would be missed. But she has no official duty in Zion, and she does not seem to be seeking any.

Sister Saber participates enthusiastically in every emotional singing and dancing part of worship as an active dancer, clapper, and singer. If someone starts a song and that song reaches an emotional pitch that precipitates a dance, Sister Saber will move over to the singer and give her visual support by standing near and clapping, singing, smiling, and otherwise demonstrating her response to the singer, even by touching her during moments of spiritual possession. Sister Saber has a distinctive holler when she is possessed, the shrill sound of which seems to stimulate the congregation. She is a friendly member, and she enjoys the fellowship during and after worship.

Brother Henry Tucker is a supportive member in Zion. He has been sexually attracted to other men as long as he can remember. At the age of eighteen Henry joined the Zion Holiness Church because "the members welcomed me with open arms." He began to sing in the choir and soon thereafter he joined with a group of five men and seven women to form a gospel singing group that traveled around and gave singing programs for the various churches in the Church of Holy Christ. Henry has belonged to four different churches in Pittsburgh (all in the Church of Holy Christ), as from time to time he has been enticed to closer associations by his series of intimate friends. But in 1967, "I'm getting old so I thought I would come back home" to the Zion Holiness Church.

In 1968 the members and friends gave Henry furniture for a four-room apartment in Homewood. He and a male friend decided to set up housekeeping together and only needed to purchase a few small things from some used furniture stores. Up until this time he had been living "off and on" with his mother and in furnished rooms. Three months after they began living together, the friend left Henry, and he began to have difficulty keeping up the expenses ($70.00 a month rent plus utilities) with his spasmodic employment as a dishwasher, unemployment compensation, public assistance, and job training corps checks. Henry got further and further behind in his rent and utilities as his lenient landlord accepted partial payments. Seeing no other "way out," he packed a suitcase with a few clothes, thirteen months after having moved in, and walked away leaving clothes, dishes, furniture, and all. He stayed with his mother for a month and then rented two furnished rooms in the Hill District.

Henry's gestures, intonation, diction, dress, and voice are feminine. He speaks very good English and is a high-school graduate. He stands 5' 2" tall and weighs 107 pounds. He states that he was a "misfit" until he found this church, and these members are just like his family, "even closer."

Brother Henry Tucker attends church every Sunday but seldom during the week unless there are special programs being offered. The amount of money he gives to Zion is limited, and he is seldom given major responsibilities for church programs. But the members of Zion welcome his presence on Sundays and his consistent financial contributions, meager though they may be. He is always willing to provide physical labor for cleaning the church, serving food for dinners, helping to move a member, or acting as a pallbearer. Thus Brother Tucker supports the Zion community in his limited capacity, but, like other supportive members, he is not crucial to the propagation of the Zion community.

In certain respects, Henry's case is similar to those of several other supportive members. Sister Boodie is crippled, she has a speech impediment, and her face is severely disfigured. She weighs about one hundred and ninety pounds and walks very slowly and haltingly with the aid of a stick. When she is in public, passers-by stop and stare if they are not familiar with her, and children laugh. But in Zion she is an accepted member who sings (as best she can) and testifies. The church bus picks her up near her home, and she never misses a service night. As she puts it, "I don't know what I would do without the church."

Brother Evans, another supportive member, is forty-six years old. He was born in Pittsburgh and has spent his entire life there. He lives alone and works at two jobs—in the day as a gasoline station attendant, and at night driving a cab. He has been separated from his wife for eight years, and a member of the church seven years. He lives in a five-room apartment which he keeps immaculate. He prepares his own meals and does his own housework. His gestures and mannerisms suggest feminine proclivities; he divorced his wife because "she was too dominant and aggressive." As he puts it, "she would beat me." He says he was very lonely after the divorce. He joined the church because the members seemed to be a warm and friendly group of people who really cared about one another. Brother Evans contributes very liberally to the church and has been asked to be an officer several times, but he refuses because of his work schedule.

Brother Barker is a supportive member. He is a quiet man of fifty-five who refuses to sit more than halfway toward the front of the church auditorium. The members are constantly trying to persuade him to move farther toward the front, and the pastor sometimes asks him from the pulpit, but he returns the next Sunday and keeps his distance. Brother Barker meets his financial obligations at Zion, but he has no desire to become more involved than to give and attend. He would be a valuable new asset to the membership, and the pastor has frequently stated from the pulpit that he would be a "nice deacon or trustee," but none of the enticement has succeeded. He seems very relaxed, and the pastor remarked once during his sermon, "You know I envy Brother Barker. He seems to have so much peace of mind. He sits back there and doesn't seem to have a trouble in the world." Such members are a target of recruitment for the other members, especially if they seem to have Brother Barker's potential to be an officer who can afford the financial responsibility. But Brother Barker, a rural southerner from Tennessee, enjoys the service but refuses to get further involved.

Marginal Members

Marginal members in Zion are those with physical, mental, or behavioral characteristics that render them ineffectual for significant contributions to the church. Yet they impressively swell the church rolls. They contribute to sought-after church attendance, and they provide a resource for the constant recruitment of "new souls," for in this category there are frequent "backsliders." The marginal members are also the objects of the core and elite members' efforts to bring them "closer to God." In these ways marginal members play a vital role in Zion.

Sister and Brother Atwell are marginal members. They have been attending Sunday worship for six months, since they first moved to the city. Their attendance is unpredictable and they always come late and together. In spite of entering the church late they invariably walk up the center aisle to take a seat in the first row of seats. They remain unemotional throughout the worship. They may clap, but this too is casual. They observe but do little participating. They are strangers to the city, and Zion is a receptive community. But they do not seem motivated to learn the cues, behavior, and idiom of Zion to participate fully, and thus the members are suspicious of their presence.

Sister Float is a marginal member. She was introduced into Zion by one of its core members, Sister Washington, and she has been attending for over three years now, always in the company of Sister Washington. She comes in with Sister Washington, and she sits with Sister Washington. The level of her participation in the worship services seems to be determined by the involvement of Sister Washington. When Sister Washington gets "happy," Sister Float invariably gets "happy" also. When Sister Washington dances, Sister Float also dances. Sister Float never seems to enjoy the service more than when Sister Washington is intensively participating in some emotional climax and thus she also has sufficient rationale to become most involved. Sister Float enjoys the worship at Zion, but she seems to be unsure of her abilities to interpret the cues and respond with the correct behavior. She has a childlike dependence upon Sister Washington, and Sister Washington enjoys that dependence as well as the acknowledgment she gets for being instrumental in recruiting another member. Sister Float holds no offices, has no ambitions, and will probably never be able to perform in an official capacity in Zion. But she is a welcome member and another example of the tolerance one finds in this church.

Brother Bouie is another marginal member. He is severely crippled from birth defects. He was introduced into Zion by his adoptive mother, and he has attended ever since his adoption twelve years ago. Brother Bouie, age forty-three, is not able to participate fully in Zion because of his physical handicaps. He has a severe speech impediment as well as his other physical distortions. But Zion is a friendly community for Brother Bouie. He is welcome whenever he chooses to come, and there are not many places in this Pittsburgh urban sprawl where Brother Bouie would be welcome. He participates in the worship to the extent that his handicaps allow him, and he always comes forth "when the church doors are opened" to new members and converts. Thus, Brother Bouie plays a vital role in Zion. It is frustrating for the pastor to preach a dynamic sermon and not to convert any souls upon opening the doors of the church. So, when Brother Bouie and the children in Zion (some coerced by their parents) flock to the altar after a sermon, it is a visual reassurance to the pastor and the church that the message has been successful.

Elder Harmin is a marginal member of Zion and is rumored to be mentally "touched." He has been in the church forty-one of his fifty-five years and has been preaching and playing the piano for the past twenty-five years. Today he is difficult to communicate with and does not speak coherently for long periods of time. He does not appear to be in good physical health: he weighs only ninety pounds though he stands about 5'4". The Church of Holy Christ in the Pittsburgh region has been his means of support for many years—allowing him to preach on weekdays and taking up an offering for him as is customary for any preacher in this organization. But for seven years now he has not been allowed many opportunities, because he is not "up to it any more." So periodically the various churches he visits take up an after-offering for him even though he does not preach, or he is allowed to stand at the entrance after service with a pan and beg. He often confronts individual members of the various churches on a personal basis and requests specific amounts, and he usually gets something.

At Zion he is allowed to indulge in all these practices as well as to demand money from the church "poor treasury." The Zion officers recently attempted to "get him on relief," but Elder Harmin refused to cooperate, stating that he did not want charity. The officers insisted that they would no longer help him if he did not cooperate, and he finally submitted. Thus today he gets a subsistence check as well as his church itinerary donations.

Recently Zion gave Elder Harmin a special fund-raising night, and approximately seventy dollars was raised for him. All money received in the church is counted by at least two church officers and taken into the officers' room where it is packaged for the recipient. Elder Harmin did not wait for the officers to count his money; instead, he disrupted the service, walked up to the offering table, and took the money. The members overlooked this for "he doesn't know any better." The next day Elder Harmin bought a car with the money even though he does not drive, and the same day he was requesting some of the members to push his car with theirs as it was not running. The following church service night he told the church officers they had to give him fifty dollars to buy a battery for his car. Needless to say, this episode angered some of the members. It will not be long, however, before all is forgotten and he gets another special night.

Harmin is a good example of the tolerance of the church for strange behavior, as long as it does not interfere with the church. He lives in the dirty basement of one of the regional churches, in the midst of discarded debris. He does not seem able to care for his toilet or cleaning needs adequately and is assisted only sporadically by devout members. He has few clothes and always appears at church services unkempt but in a coat and tie. The children are frightened of him because of his bedraggled appearance and the rumors that he carries dead rodents in his pockets. At the church services he moves about without purpose but manages to refrain from disturbing the service for those who are familiar with him. What does he give the church? He attends services regularly and helps to bolster poor attendance on unpopular weekday nights. His presence provides assurance to other members that after they have given a lifetime of service, "God will take care of you."

Among the marginal members are the children (under eighteen), some of whose names are not on the membership roll, who attend regularly with or without their parents, sing in the chorus, act in the holiday programs and participate in the youth services (Sunday school, young people's religious service, Sunshine Band, etc.). Also in the group are regular visitors who do not want to be identified with the church but find solace in attending, being publicly recognized by the pastor, and constantly sought by the members.

There are also members who refuse to give such a large part of their income and labor to the church or who are not articulate, aggressive, or ambitious enough to engage in the church politics of mobility. Sister Bond is in the latter category. She lives one block from the church and is usually present at all services. She does not dress, give in offerings, or behave competitively. She has a severe speech impediment and is angered very easily. She shows no desire to lead any of the auxiliaries, but she enjoys belonging, and members enjoy being able to count her head in those weekday services which attract few. Sister Cody is also a marginal member. She has a history of confinement for emotional disturbances and has had several altercations in the church. She is welcomed as a member but no effort is made to recruit her for auxiliary leadership or functional duties, and she seems content to belong and participate very actively in the service.

Elite, core, supportive, and marginal categories of membership give us some clues to the extent and range of membership integration in Zion. The elite members constitute a well-defined power structure. They provide meaningful input to decision-making processes and help to decide and implement direction for this church. The roles of the elite are the attractions for the core, supportive, and marginal members who would conceptualize the rewards for mobility in Zion.

Elite members are "old-timers." They have been in Zion for many years and have proven their ability to organize, utilize, and manipulate the symbols in their church. They have learned well the values of Zion—loyalty, financial resources, exposure—which culminate in strategic alliances in Zion and thus create power. The elite are the pastor's "right arm," and both the pastor and the elite must constantly recognize this reciprocal dependence.

The core members are the "workhorses of the church." They give to Zion in service what the elite give in planning and leadership. They manifest the spirit they express when they say, "If you don't work for Zion, there won't be no Zion." Zion belongs to them, and they make every effort to assure that it survives. Elite members are recruited from the ranks of the core, and it is here that members learn their commitment to Zion, so that upon becoming elite members they can bear the ambiguities and disillusionment that come with leadership. Core members have no direct voice in decision-making, but through their membership alliances they can influence those decisions. Even officers of the church take their orders from the pastor and carry out the policies that he establishes. Thus, officers in Zion do not necessarily make decisions, whereas elite members without important offices may have a direct influence on policy. The core is the largest group of members, and it contributes most to Zion in terms of service to the church and participation in its idiom.

Supportive members in Zion are those recently recruited to the fold or those who choose not to become totally involved in this community. Supportive members fulfill their financial obligations to Zion but refrain from participation in most of the activities of the church. They come on Sunday morning, sometimes Sunday night, and occasionally Friday night. But they restrict their involvement to these worship contexts and seldom experience the total community that is Zion. They do not hold or compete for offices in the church, but they enjoy their sense of belonging and the participation in the worship, especially the emotion-packed parts of the religious service. Zion does not discriminate against its supportive members, but even makes a greater effort to make them feel welcome. They are a constant target of recruitment efforts for ad hoc committees and for greater involvement.

The marginal members of Zion are the residual category into which fall, in large part, members who are not able to participate fully in Zion because of some personal inadequacy such as age, physical handicaps, emotional instability, or lack of time and energy.

I have attempted to present here some selective insight into the nature of membership at Zion. Such insights help to explain the quality of interaction of members and leadership at Zion as well as in the various informal categories I have enumerated. The descriptions I have given are not full but are designed to give the reader some of the critical characteristics of individual members which exemplify the nature of Zion as a huddling place for a wide range of "poor" ghetto Blacks.

† 5 †

CHURCH ACTIVITIES

This chapter illustrates the nature of sacred and secular association among the members of Zion. This interaction tends to level the social hierarchy in the church. It provides the members with situational contexts to demonstrate an important component of their ideology, "fellowship," and validates the group tolerance for the poor, "outcasts," and "despised few."

The quest for higher status in Zion creates competition among its mobile members. Successes and failures in mobility generate animosities and jealousies within the membership, and the display of ambition causes anxieties. Such potential conflict, left unchecked, would disrupt Zion. But actual conflict is kept at tolerable levels by Zion's quest for solidarity. A significant component of that solidarity (love and fellowship) is Zion's provision of a variety of opportunities for both secular and sacred interaction, some of which can be described in terms of church activities.

Zion is not only a membership of individuals; it is also a continuous round of expressive and instrumental activities. It is difficult in the context of this discussion to describe all of these activities, but some indication can be given of the nature of the activities that have traditionally attracted and continue to attract the membership into social interaction. Some of the programs—teas, concerts, revivals, pastor's anniversary, men's day—are peculiarly structured to raise money and thus lack some of the rich informal action that one finds in trips, picnics, funerals, and household moving. For this reason I will describe the latter events in detail. But it is the church services themselves which form the consistent nucleus of activities in Zion, and they must be understood to appreciate the critical role that Zion plays in defining and maintaining a small community.

Membership gives license (see Plotnicov, 1962). Members can walk, talk, and sleep during sermons or prayer. Members can commit any sin and be forgiven. The cohesiveness of the group takes precedence over the ideals of the creed. One's financial support and loyalty are far more important than one's "life." Of course, behavior is always commented on within the membership network. It can be the rationale for denying upward mobility, but it is not critical for belonging.

Competition is keen, and among the members who seek mobility the manipulation of the appropriate symbols is crucial. Financial support, which is made public, is highly competitive, for the largest contributors have the greatest influence with the bishop.

The members think of themselves as "the same kind of people." If there is a community picnic, two or three of them will inquire of the others if they are going. If so, they will arrange to ride together or inform one another as to where they will sit or eat. Even if some of the members are not aware of who in the membership is attending, they will invariably meet at the park grounds and spend much of the time in one another's company. During such meetings, the crowd, the behavior, and the activities will be discussed from the perspective of their church—"These young girls are almost naked." "Now you know there is no sense in acting like that." "You'd think they wouldn't let them drink out here." "I don't know what this world is coming to." "Child! you couldn't pay me to ride on those things." Eventually the conversation will turn to church matters, and the latest church news will be analyzed. At the end of the day most of the membership, those who attended and those who did not, know who attended and what occurred by means of the telephone network.

The members form work parties to do certain jobs around the church —move furniture, clean the fourth floor for residence during the annual state meetings, clean the kitchen for serving, remove accumulated debris from the basement, replace broken window ropes, and seal the windows for the winter.

Two or three members are continuously attending district meetings and other churches' services, and wherever a member goes, he is an informal representative of Zion. He will invariably share his experience by telephone, testimony, casual conversation, or all three, so that the services and controversies in sister churches are reported through this network.

While the church prides itself on the warmth, love, fellowship, and "sweet communion of the holy ghost" that are manifest among all its members, fellowship does not extend to the members' homes. Most meetings take place at the church or are church-sponsored activities, for one's home is not perceived as a place for entertainment. Only two members of the total ninety-one have occasional teas at their homes to raise money for the church. The only other entertaining by the members in their homes is wakes, in which most of the visitors bring cooked food to enable them to eat without requiring the host to stir.

Most members were embarrassed to discuss why they do not invite their fellow members to their homes or do not visit one another. Some explanations were: "We all work and we spend all our time in church, we don't have time to traipse to the saints' houses." "We see each other enough in church." "I don't have time to run from house to house unless they're sick and need prayer." The pastor, too, was embarrassed by the question. He spoke of his many friends across the country and in the city, but "I am too tired of folks when I come home to have them coming to my house too." They all recognize the custom of entertaining at home, but their social network does not require it of them, and their economic means do not allow it. Entertaining in the home is part of the middle-class mainstream syndrome where the home is a symbol of one's status, mobility, and decorative sophistication. Most of the members of Zion have chosen a different route.

How does this fellowship manifest itself? Several feasts are prepared each year for special events, and food is served for sale to members and neighborhood residents about one hundred days of each year. There are choir rehearsals, chorus rehearsals, drama rehearsals, and rehearsals for children's ceremonies. Several bus trips to metropolitan areas occur each year. There are work group meetings, auxiliary group meetings, officer meetings, prayer meetings, conventions, bishop's meetings, international meetings, and state meetings of all kinds.

Church Dinners and Kitchen Activities

An example of a feast is the "anniversary dinner." After a week of raising money for the pastor's anniversary, the church provides a free dinner for the members in the large fourth-floor dining room. Ten or fifteen women who are noted for their cooking skills organize themselves to prepare the meal. Several members volunteer to make the necessary purchases, and some of them shop together for the food. For three or four days the dining room is bustling with activity. Officers drop in to see that things are proceeding on schedule and are usually asked to open a window or adjust a table. They linger about, discussing the upcoming events or some church news. The men josh the women, the women tease the men. This is often accompanied by occasional bursts of laughter and friendly pats. Members who are not concerned with the preparation drop in to gossip and assist with decorations as well as to "see how things are coming along" and joke with one another. Children accompany their parents and romp about the corridors spying on teen-agers who come looking for opportunities for romancing or "rapping with the fellows" in the empty areas of the large building. The food and decorations are prepared during vivid, loud, and varied discussions which are occasionally interrupted by whispers of a more lurid nature. This activity continues into the early hours of the morning, when the last of a dwindling group filter out. These late hours require that the men escort unaccompanied women home and provide opportunities for reported extracurricular intimacies.

After two or three days of this type of preparation, the day arrives to serve the "saints." The children and lay members arrive early and are required to wait until the officials filter in with an air of patient circumspection and receive the deference appropriate to their offices. The officers are seated first, in the choice seats, and are served first. Often the children and some of the lay members must wait until the first group has eaten because of lack of space. Much conversation and laughter fill the room as the "saints" eat heartily.

After the meal the officers, their wives, and guests can remain seated to converse; lay members are asked to give their seats to others who have not eaten. Most of the members mill around after the meal talking with one another and subtly ascertaining whether, on one pretext or another, they can secure some of the food to take home. Those who have prepared the dinner reward themselves and their friends with their leftovers. This necessitates much discreet communication, as one tries not to seem greedy or needy, or to become the object of the wrath of an authoritative "sister" who will "loud talk you." Those with good connections in the kitchen move in and out with their bounty, while others slink about attempting to beg with tact. The officers and important guests are offered food to take with them, but children and lay members are denied this privilege unless their contacts in the kitchen are excellent.

This patronage system of the leftovers, as well as the guarantee of dinner (as much as one can eat in private because one works out of view) and the general opportunity for fellowship, ease recruitment of help. The leftovers create many more workers to clean up than participated in the preparation. The clean-up is accompanied by lively social intercourse. Again the departure of the workers (with their food wrapped and secure) allows liberal opportunities for friendly relationships, and officers and the elite are in demand. Expressive activities such as anniversary dinners expand the participation in Zion beyond sacred activities.

During state meetings and often on Sundays (when members are expected to give large sums of money) the members supplement their giving capacity by earning profits in the kitchen. Two or three families rent the kitchen for the ten days of the state meetings, which they use solely for profit.

The kitchen is a room on the first floor of the building with two windows with counters opening onto the main hallway. One is used to serve take-out items when the kitchen is overcrowded and the entrance to it is blocked. It is also used by the cooks and waitresses to observe who is going into the church and to greet and delay those whom they choose. The other window is used for hat checking as well as for the sale of small confections during large meetings. The kitchen is divided into a 150-square-foot area for dining and a 75-square-foot area for cooking and preparing the food. When it is open there is a sign outside on the sidewalk: "Delicious Home-Cooked Meals Inside at Reasonable Prices." This instrumental effort to raise money provides hoards of opportunities for expression; church intrigue, seduction, courtship, friendship, fellowship, and gossip flourish.

Food has a special meaning in Zion (discussed in chapter 6), and the presence and consumption of food are always catalysts for interaction among the members. When the kitchen is open, many members spend most of their worship time there and listen to services through a loud speaker. If something is signaled (a favorite speaker is introduced, a large emotional "shout" occurs, or a preacher begins to overwhelm), aprons fly off and patrons rush upstairs to witness, often neglecting to pay for their food. The kitchen is the "crossroads of the state." All are seen here at one time or another. Children and new members have dignitaries pointed out to them here where they can see them in a rare, informal disposition. State and local officials are surrounded and treated to free food by less fortunate lay members. The cooks and waitresses pay homage to these officials by all sorts of extra services. They keep their personal diet drinks in the refrigerator where space is scarce; keep their special foods off sale in spite of demands; give them side dishes refused to other customers; allow them in the cooking area to wash their hands, a practice which is strictly prohibited to others; take their food back to cook or season it more to their satisfaction after they have sampled it; lend dining tables for their personal business though

they are in demand; and grant the very special privilege of forgetting
to pay often large bills after they have treated groups of their financial
supporters in grand gestures. These officials have come to use such
homage as reinforcement of their positions.

Back in the cooking area the cooks and waitresses discuss various
patrons as they work busily. "That sister has diabetes and she eats
everything the doctor told her not to." "Now look at her, that's her second plate and now she wants pie and she's so fat now she can hardly
walk; no wonder she has trouble with them legs." "Look, she can set
that preacher up but she can't buy her kids school shoes; next month
she'll be asking the church to pay her rent." "He can treat those young
girls; watch what he buys his wife." "Who paid for that, the bishop or
Sister Joseph?" "There is Elder Jones again, he always wants something
for nothing; I have already given him some cake, anything else he gets
he'll have to pay for it." "Isn't that the sister who had the baby for Elder
Sax?" "There is Brother Meeks; he is wasting away to nothing, give him
a little something if he doesn't have any money."

There are no written menus. For each inquirer the fare is spelled
out verbally:

> We have fish sandwiches and fish dinners, chicken sandwiches and
> fried chicken dinners and roast chicken dinners, or hamburgers
> or ham sandwiches or hot dogs; with your dinners you get greens
> and potato salad or cole slaw and dumplings with the roast
> chicken. For dessert we have ice cream, watermelon, cake, and
> pies, and pop and coffee to drink.

For many this enumeration is not necessary, for the meals do not
vary that much. But there are those who use it to start a conversation
and then walk out saying, "I'll get something later." Often the dialogue
continues between the patron and client:

What kind of fish is it?   *Black Bass.*

Who made the pies?   *Sister Munsey.*

How much chicken do you get on a sandwich?   *A leg or a breast.*

How much is a chicken dinner?   *$1.25.*

We need you up in service.   *I'll be up a little later.*

You shouldn't charge the saints that much for food. *You try to buy it.*

Before and after the services the kitchen is a grand meeting place. Some spend more time here than in the regular worship services, and many flock here during the "change of services" when offerings are being taken. Some get up and march around to the offering table and give, and then, tired of sitting through the long services, go to the kitchen to socialize and refill. The kitchen is first to open and last to close, and on Sunday night or at the end of a state meeting, one sees again the leftover food ritual. Employees are paid partially in wares or, in the case of raising money for a special event for the church, totally in food. The kitchen workers and an officer who stays behind to lock up are the last to leave after an exciting day of intense work and expressive interaction.

REHEARSALS AND CHURCH PLAYS

Instrumental activities, too, have their expressive features in Zion. The members manage to structure most occasions into opportunities for social expression, for this underlies their solidarity.

Choir rehearsals are a good example. The choir rehearses at the church once a week (more often for special events). The president of the choir contacts the church deacon, who is in charge of the building. He meets the choir there and opens the church. He then either remains until they leave (if he becomes engaged with one or another), or leaves and gets the president's assurance that the doors will be locked securely. The choir members trickle in by carloads and on foot. They stand inside or outside (if weather is suitable) and engage one another in conversation about recent events. Women who seem very fond of other women find opportunities to embrace and affectionately touch them in the course of emotional conversation. All sexes and all membership status groups are greeted with a holy kiss which can be either on the cheek or on the mouth. Men take the opportunity to interact with other men and women.

After this social intercourse, when most of the members who are coming have arrived, the choir begins the rehearsal, during which there are some disputes about whose time it is to solo. Each week the president of the choir has to assign a certain number of solos, and she sometimes uses this power to reward for favors. The rehearsal takes place in a playful atmosphere in which the choir members frequently kid one another about their voices in a particular song. After rehearsal, social intercourse begins again. Older members discuss church affairs; younger members attempt to convince one another that they are wise to the "latest happenings" in spite of being "sanctified." They seem to take pains to assure one another that they are as worldly as the next one. Of course, there are more timid souls who exclaim in shock over the course of the conversation, but who smile and laugh and enjoy it all immensely.

After the excitement of rehearsal has waned and the hour approaches eleven, the members begin to start home in groups of two to five. After standing outside the church, continuing their talk and watching to see who drives up to pick up whom and who can "bum a ride" with whom, they leave. These last moments are often sources of lasting gossip, as all the members know when and where choir rehearsal occurs, and many will drive casually by about the time it has ended to see "what they can see" or "what's going on." This practice, which occurs after most such small group meetings, often culminates in intimate relationships. These groups may leave the church at eleven and not arrive home until two or three in the morning. Car and street conversations last for hours among these members who rarely visit one another's homes. It is here that much of the integrating and intriguing gossip flourishes, second only to the telephone network.

Christmas and Easter are celebrated with plays put on by the "young people," who vary in age from twelve to thirty-five. The drama must be rehearsed once or twice as the holiday approaches. One of the deacons is contacted as to the time, and he opens the church and uses this opportunity to interact with the members of the drama group. Officers are held in high esteem by members, and few of their advances are rebuffed by female members. For rehearsal the pastor's study and the officers' room are open for entrances to each side of the pulpit, which serves as a stage. In these rooms, teen-age petting occurs, and many of the members are anxious to come to rehearsal for this very reason. The members are lighthearted and gay, and even the director, who tries to keep order, smiles and laughs at some inept actor or actress or someone "cutting the fool." After rehearsal, the social intercourse continues.

The church is noted for these plays, and they occur on a nonservice night so that many of the members of other churches in the state organization can attend. There are one or two stars in these performances who are noted for their dramatic ability, and they make the otherwise amateur plays very exciting to the viewers. Both of these are males, one about sixteen, the other about twenty, and they participate in all the plays.

For their audiences, who are not permitted to attend any kind of "worldly" entertainment (movies, boxing, ball games, etc.), these plays are a real treat. To see King Herod knock down his inferiors and jostle his servants in violent gestures raises the church in laughter. Members talk of these plays from performance to performance.

The best actor and the star of one such drama was the sixteen-year-old boy, who is very talented and famous in church circles for his acting. The young girls and the old women and men greeted him after the show when he strutted out from the stage, fully dressed now in his suit and tie and ready for the reception that he knew was waiting. He was vain but tactful, and he knew well how to handle his admirers. The other players also received acclaim from their relatives and friends, who made no attempt to distinguish between their bad acting and the overall performance of the group. It is a gay and pleasant night for the "saints."

CHURCH TRIPS

As state overseer, Bishop Jackson is obliged to travel about western Pennsylvania to support his scattered pastors on special occasions— dedication of a new edifice, installation of a new pastor, money raising to prevent a foreclosure, celebration of the anniversary of a pastor, a pastor's funeral, or state meetings. He even goes out of the state to celebrate a fellow overseer's anniversary in reciprocity. Most such meetings are intended to be a "financial blessing" for somebody, and Bishop Jackson takes with him as many of his members as he can to increase that blessing. He announces the trip several times during worship services and emphasizes that he expects his members to "hold up my arms." The church bus and all available member cars are pressed into service. The writer has traveled with the church to Monessen, Indiana, Clairton, Coraopolis, and Aliquippa in western Pennsylvania, and to Clarksburg, West Virginia. One of these trips is described in detail below. In this descriptive sketch, the behavior is characteristic of the fellowship described earlier.

The members of Zion take several trips a year by chartered bus, the church bus, automobile caravans, commercial travel, or a combination thereof. Most of these trips are a means of intensive social interaction, although the end is usually financial commitment. During such trips, in which the members travel together in large groups, they are encouraged to "get to know each other and have fellowship with each other." This form of activity is stressed as a means of executing Zion's constant theme—fellowship. These events generate tremendous excitement among members, whose social activities are otherwise critically curtailed, as the reader will see.

One of the many trips the church members take each year is to Clarksburg, West Virginia. This is a reciprocal relationship, as the bishop of West Virginia has come to Bishop Jackson's church and preached for him to raise money for his anniversary. Since this kind of reciprocity is very important in the entire organization, Bishop Jackson is obligated to go to West Virginia, taking with him an offering and as many members as possible to augment the offering.

Prior to the particular trip described here, the bishop in West Virginia had brought a busload of his members to Bishop Jackson's anniversary, and these members not only made their presence felt but also contributed to the offering to make that day a large "financial blessing." Thus, plans were made by a committee chosen by the bishop to charter a bus and to collect fares from enough members to fill it. After a month of soliciting by the committee, encouragement from the bishop, and his criticism of those who were not buying, all the seats were sold.

The group was scheduled to leave on a Saturday at three in the afternoon for evening services that night, and they were scheduled to return after the services. The members began to gather at the church at about noon on this May day, and the sidewalks around the church were cluttered with lunches, pillows, coats, sweaters, and small handbags. There was an atmosphere of great excitement among all the members. The adults were laughing and joking about the possibilities on the road. Some were discussing church affairs. Others were conjecturing about how many in certain families were going, and some were discussing their anticipated seating arrangements. The children were running about on the hillside adjacent to the church.

At 2:35 P.M. the bishop arrived and began to inquire of the officers present about the arrangements and any problems before leaving. The officers stopped talking to each other and other members and immediately approached him to give the information they knew he would request. The bishop continued to talk to the officers and to greet other members as one by one they made an effort to greet him. He repeatedly said, "Glad to see you," "Nice to see you're going," "Ah, you going too, huh?" The bus was scheduled to arrive at three. It did not arrive until quarter to four, and for forty-five minutes the worried members paraded back and forth to the officers and the bishop to express their anxiety and be reassured. The bus finally arrived, to the relief and joy of all. The members boarded with smiling faces, laughter, and loud admonitions to their companions, "Don't forget the bag." There was considerable excitement about seating arrangements. The officers and their wives had to be in close proximity to the bishop and his wife, who sat at the front of the bus. Missionaries wanted to sit together. The ministers chose seats together. Certain single and widowed females were trying to get seats with eligible bachelors and widowers. Children wanted to sit in the back of the bus, and teen-agers were attempting to get as far away from the adults and children as possible. Most of the teen-agers seemed to be anticipating some romantic activities during the trip. Officers in charge, anxious to show their own importance, were counting passengers in an effort to see who had not arrived yet. Six different officers checked all the passengers at six different times. The last passenger arrived at 4:05 P.M., and the bus, along with seven private passenger cars, was ready to go. A total of 107 people went on the trip, some of whom were members not of Zion but of other churches in the Pittsburgh area. The bus departed at quarter past four, after the officers decided that the cars would follow the bus and in what order they would line up.

The members conversed as the bus traveled through the city, but once it hit the open highway they began to sing church hymns (see J. and J. Johnson, 1940; Odum and Johnson, 1925; Thurman, 1955). Everyone was enjoying the ride. Some were singing, some were talking, some were courting. Suddenly, about ten miles from the West Virginia line, the bus developed trouble with its transmission and had to pull to the side of the road, to the dismay of some and the joy of others. The teen-agers and children were glad to have a chance to get out and romp in the countryside on a spring afternoon. Some of the adults were anxious about the resolution of the mechanical problems, and the bishop and officers were making a feeble attempt to make crucial decisions. The driver decided that the bus could go no farther and set out to find a phone to call another one. The replacement arrived in thirty-five minutes, and the group was on its way again.

When the group arrived, they were greeted by the Clarksburg members with embraces and kisses. Many knew one another from former interstate get-togethers and from international meetings. The Clarksburg members led their guests to the basement of their church, where meals had been prepared for everybody. Pittsburgh members were seated according to official hierarchy. They were served stewed chicken, dumplings, candied sweet potatoes, collard greens, cornbread and butter, and rice pudding. After the meal the bishop from West Virginia welcomed the members from Pittsburgh, and the bishop from Pittsburgh responded.

The group then proceeded upstairs to the main auditorium, which was the first floor of a large home from which the partitions had been removed. The auditorium was crowded, with standing room only. Most of the teen-agers remained outside to court the others they had come with and flirt with those they had recently met. The service here was very similar to that in Pittsburgh, and the Pittsburgh members had no trouble becoming an integrated part of it. There was testimony service in which several members gave praise to God "for bringing them over the highways safe and sound," "for providing a way in a time of trouble," "and for delivering them from the hand of the devil who was trying to prevent them from reaching Clarksburg."

Next the main offering was taken. Bishop Jackson stood and explained to the congregation how faithful Bishop Timothy had been over these fifteen years, how much he had contributed to the state of West Virginia, and how deserving he was of everything that could be done for him on his anniversary. He asked that one of his members stand at the offering table and collect from his members only, "for I want to show these West Virginia saints how sweet the saints in Pittsburgh are. I'm starting this offering off with twenty-five dollars. I want all the members from Pittsburgh to stand. Everybody who's gonna give me ten dollars or over come forward with your money in your hand. Where's my deacons, and my trustees, and my missionaries? Don't be shame, come on up. Now everybody who didn't have twenty dollars, ten dollars, but got five, you walk to the table. Now all those who didn't have five you bring what the Lord has blessed you to give." The Pittsburgh members filed up to the offering table in impressive numbers, for Bishop Jackson had already organized them. As they marched by the table he remarked, "Look at these Pittsburgh saints, aren't they sweet?" The director of the program for Bishop Timothy then stood and asked all the West Virginia "folks" not to be "outdone" by Pittsburgh. "After all he's our bishop."

After the offering, Bishop Jackson was introduced as the speaker for the evening. He spoke on "Respect for Leadership," one of his frequent themes. After an exciting message, a song, and a shout (dance), an "after-offering" was taken for Bishop Jackson. After that offering was "lifted" it was announced how much had been received for both offerings—for Bishop Timothy's offering, $370, and for Bishop Jackson's offering, $74. Services ended with a benediction given by one of Bishop Jackson's accompanying ministers. The members spent an hour and fifteen minutes giving each other a warm farewell, and at 12:30 A.M. the bus and seven cars pulled out of Clarksburg. The adults and children immediately went to sleep, leaving the teen-agers alone to enjoy one another's company. The trip back to Pittsburgh was nonstop, and upon arrival the sleepy passengers began to negotiate their rides home from the church.

Such instrumental activities provide ample opportunity for members to reinforce their group identity. They broaden their range of interaction into situations that are outside formal services and tend to validate their conception of themselves as a sacred and secular community.

A PICNIC

The members of Zion receive tremendous satisfaction from interacting with one another in informal situations, and this interaction and its rewards are one of the significant attractions to membership in Zion. Much of this interaction takes place before and after regular services. But there are certain events that Zion organizes, outside its regular services, which allow its members to enjoy this kind of informal interaction for the sole purpose of social fellowship. Among such activities is a picnic.

A picnic allows the manifestation of fellowship among the members of Zion without the clear demarcations of elite, core, supportive, and marginal membership that occur in Zion's church services. It is a means of waiving the social distance that members of Zion make such efforts to deny. Outside the context of formal worship, the members exploit the opportunity to reinforce their ideal that "every child of God is equal in the sight of God." The marginal, supportive, and core members have a wide berth for informal contact and fellowship with the pastor and the elite. And the pastor and the elite make every effort to demonstrate that love and fellowship are due the "poor, the outcasts, and the despised few" for whom Zion is established. The picnic is an opportunity to intensify the meaning of Zion as a community with a unique range of tolerance for the varied statuses of its membership.

One of the church auxiliaries is always competing with the others in the pecking order for the pastor's favor. This results several times a year in various outings sponsored by the president of one of these auxiliaries. Picnics, dinner outings, teas, home invitations, and banquets are sponsored by various groups to impress the pastor and other officials of the church. The pastor, his wife, certain officials, and sometimes the entire congregation are invited to take part in these events.

For example, the president of the pastor's aide announced in July that her group was sponsoring a picnic for the church at South Park. She invited all the members to come "and bring something." Thirty-two members participated. Certain members got together and decided on foodstuffs cooperatively.

The picnic was scheduled for ten o'clock on a Saturday morning. Members began to arrive at about half past ten in the predesignated grove. They came with baskets of fried chicken, bowls of potato salad, quantities of rolls, fruit, sliced ham, baked sweet potatoes, cole slaw, hot dogs, and watermelon. Each time a member arrived he would greet the other members with a handshake, a warm embrace, or a kiss, depending on their social and hierarchic relationship. There was much discussion about who was coming, who was not coming, and why, what time certain members would arrive, and what they had promised to bring. The picnic was well organized. The president had a list of all the members and who was supposed to bring what. As they arrived they were recruited to bring picnic tables and benches together, to wipe them off and spread newspaper over them, start a charcoal fire, make the punch, prepare the coffee, and spread the food out in an orderly manner. During all this time the members were laughing, talking, and joking with one another.

By 12:20, twenty-nine members had arrived and the picnic was going full force. There was constant humor concerning who brought what, how it looked, how it tasted, and the quantities involved. Sister Holiday received an abundance of praise for her cold, sweet watermelon, and members constantly remarked, "This is about the best watermelon I've ever eaten." The watermelon was good, there was plenty of it, and it stole the show. Sister Holiday really enjoyed the constant praise throughout the day. Other members received proportional praise for their contributions.

The conversations gradually turned to a mixture of church affairs, members' plights, and food quality. There were swimmers and ball-players on the scene that day, and the members enjoyed observing these activities, which most of them rarely see. The members themselves engaged in no activities other than food preparation, conversation, walking, and observation. The pastor and his wife were paid deference throughout the day, being served, seated, and greeted in a preferential manner. At half past four, one member had to leave for work. This marked the beginning of clean-up and the eventual end of the picnic. By six, the last members were leaving, all exclaiming, "What a fine outing this has been. I really enjoyed myself."

MOVING

The church members rely on one another for most of their needs. When they are sick, a sick offering is taken up for them. When special needs arise, food baskets are arranged for them. When they have legal problems, the pastor goes to court. When they need a residence, church property is made available. When they must move their furnishings, volunteers are solicited. And when they die, the funeral is arranged according to their wishes, and volunteers are solicited as pallbearers, soloists, and those "to have words." The church clerk is in charge of arranging all the funerals, and the pastor does all the preaching.

Taking care of the needs of members is an expressive activity. It gives the joy and satisfaction of demonstrating love and fellowship to one another and receiving the same in return. This idea of love and fellowship is strategically reinforced when it can manifest itself outside its sacred context. It is especially meaningful to the poor and "unimportant," the ones who usually require this assistance, to have such vivid demonstrations that somebody cares. This caretaking reinforces the fabric of security that is built into Zion, and it elucidates what members mean when they say, "I don't know what I would do if it wasn't for this church." Food baskets for holidays, flowers and telegrams for funerals, monetary "love tokens" in times of financial crises, character witnesses in legal scrapes, electric heaters rushed to a house whose gas has been shut off—all fall into this category.

If a member is going to move, he may have announced in the church that he needs a truck or a car or other members to help in the moving. Several members will raise their hands and volunteer after some discussion as to the times they will be available. Often the member will tell a deacon or a trustee who will, in turn, organize a moving party. These moving parties are a source of great enjoyment. During and after the moving there is much joking about how weak, lazy, or hungry one or the other is. Coffee is usually prepared by the person who is being moved and is drunk during rest periods and after the moving is completed. Much of the moving is done at night when the men are available, the neighbors' view is obstructed, and the absentee landlord is ignorant of the event.

One September day it was announced that Sister Brown's son and daughter-in-law needed help to move their furniture to a new residence. Neither is a member, but the request was made as a favor to Sister Brown. The pastor asked for volunteers who would be available that evening (of nine moving events that I witnessed, eight occurred at night). Six of the brothers volunteered to help, and I made seven. Two of us had cars, so after the services we arranged to pick up the other volunteers at a scheduled time at their homes. We met at the Hill District residence at eight, and we did not start to move the furniture until after dark. A truck that Sister Brown's son had rented arrived about quarter to ten. Sister Brown's daughter-in-law was putting small items and clothing into her father's car while we men were moving the furniture. Sister Brown had prepared coffee and fried apple pie for us to have while we worked. The men enjoyed the moving activity, for it gave them an opportunity to cajole one another and interact in a special informal atmosphere.

There was a great deal of teasing about the poor quality of furniture that the Browns were taking the time and effort to move. It appeared that the next piece was always worse than the last. Even though Brother Brown was not aware that such snickering was occurring, he was embarrassed by the state of his son's household. He spent the entire evening trying to convince his son and daughter-in-law that there was no need to take most of the furniture. But this was to no avail. We continued to take out furniture which seemed to get worse and worse. The climax came when we moved a refrigerator that had not been in use for several months. Sister Brown's daughter-in-law warned us not to open it, but one of the men inadvertently allowed the poorly latched door to come open in the moving. Such a foul stench burst forth from the open door that the men set the refrigerator down and backed away without thinking to close the door again. In the three minutes that elapsed in chaos and confusion before the door was closed again, the entire three-room apartment was filled with that foul odor. Sister and Brother Brown's embarrassment was aggravated by this, and they both began to insist strongly that the rest of the furniture need not be moved. Sister Brown's daughter-in-law had received much of her furniture from one of the religious social agencies. A few pieces had been purchased new, and the remainder had been given to her. She was adamant that she was not going to leave her possessions.

The moving only took about an hour and a half. We had more help than we needed, and we all had fun. When the truck was loaded the only thing left in the apartment was old newspaper, large quantities of rubbish, a plastic bag full of garbage, and a day bed that had fallen apart completely while it was being moved. No one felt any obligation to the landlord to leave the apartment clean. Sister and Brother Brown brought the coffee and pies over to the new residence in Manchester, on the North Side of Pittsburgh. After all the furniture had been moved out of the truck into the four-room apartment on the second floor, we sat down to the food and a discussion of church affairs. The son and daughter-in-law ignored us and went about the business of straightening up their apartment.

LEGAL PROBLEMS

Sister and Brother Stokes have a son who has had several scrapes with the law. He is a reputed dope pusher in the Hill, where they live, and he has been suspected of other criminal activities related to drug addiction. Sister and Brother Stokes have always gone to his aid in legal crises. Like most of the members, they request the pastor's assistance in matters such as these. For substantial financial supporters like Sister and Brother Stokes, the pastor can never refuse. Thus he writes letters to appropriate people, visits probation officers, testifies in court as a character witness, and solicits favors from assistant district attorneys. He visits local magistrates, makes peace with angry plaintiffs, and finds jobs for incarcerated relatives who seek parole.

Sister and Brother Stokes asked the pastor to appear as a character witness when the boy was being tried for possession and sale of narcotics. The pastor had a conference with the officers of the church about the matter, because he was not sure what he could do in such a circumstance. Eventually he met with the defendant's lawyer and they agreed to what kind of testimony he could offer. He took the stand in criminal court wearing a clerical collar (he never wears one for his church services) and testified that he had known Sister and Brother Stokes for over twenty years, that they were fine church members and fine people, and had a fine family. He told the jury that the children were all raised in the church and had "good upbringing." The son in question came to Sunday school and Young People's Willing Workers, and took part in the children's days and programs. He pointed out that it would be a heavy blow to the family and his church if this young man were sent to jail. His testimony seemed to make a good impression on the jury. I am not able to say how much effect his testimony had on the verdict, but the jury ruled the boy not guilty. Two weeks after the verdict was announced the pastor made use of it in his sermon by pointing out the advantages of being a good church member, paying tithes, and being faithful. "It means something to be a good church member and to be able to have your pastor to speak for you, and some of you know that when your pastor speaks for you, it counts for something."

A Funeral

Sister Backler, an elite member, had been a member of Zion for thirty-three years. She sang in the choir, handled all the funerals, and had special influence with the bishop, based upon her membership alliances. Many of the female members who had been in the church over twenty years resented her influence with the bishop and on church affairs. Several of the members related to me that they had been "moved" (demoted) by the bishop because of her whims. Sister Backler became sick and died suddenly. (It was at this time that the duty of arranging funerals fell to the church clerk.) The funeral date was set, and pallbearers were chosen from volunteers. Three soloists were selected to sing Sister Backler's favorite songs, a missionary was chosen to read the telegrams, and several cars and drivers were solicited to participate in the funeral procession. Nine people were designated to have "words." Sister Backler was well known, and it was difficult to limit the people who wanted to have words about her. The funeral was set for one o'clock on Wednesday afternoon.

Immediately after the death, the members began to take food to Sister Backler's home so that her children, whose father was dead, would not have to prepare any during their grief. Sister Backler had several grown children who came in to look after the younger ones (the

youngest was fifteen years old). They had the company of church members, who remained at the home around the clock doing whatever
"their hands found to do." The night before the funeral was the official
wake night, and the house was full of members who had brought food
and were prepared to stay all night. The immediate family of Sister
Backler was put to bed after repeated persuasion that "they needed
their rest for tomorrow." The members sat up all night, eating and discussing church affairs. It was a very pleasant gathering in spite of the
circumstances.

The next day the church was packed when the cars bearing the
family arrived. The closed casket sat in the front of the auditorium
before the pulpit. The front rows of the church were reserved for the
members of the family, and after they were seated the services began.
One of the soloists sang a song that set the mood and brought tears to
most eyes. Forty-one telegrams were read, and they came "from far and
near," many from out of town. Another song was sung, the clerk of the
church read the obituary, Sister Saxton read a scripture, the nine members, five of whom "broke down" in the process, had their words. The
pastor was introduced by his helper, and he preached the funeral sermon "to the living, not the dead." His theme was that Sister Backler
"had lived the life and had gone on home to see Jesus, and we don't
have to worry about her. But it's you in the audience that don't know
the Lord that this passing is a warning for."

After many admonitions to "sinners" and much praise of Sister
Backler, the pastor ended his sermon, the last soloist sang, and the
church prepared to see Sister Backler for the last time. Two assistants
to the funeral director went to the casket, opened it, and arranged the
interior lace in its appropriate place. Then they stood on either end of
the casket while two other assistants, accompanied by a church nurse,
took each member of the immediate family to view the body individu-
ally and back to his seat again. After all the family had viewed the
body, leaving the members of the church distraught by their emotional
outbursts, all the rest of the congregation stood and formed a line and
marched around to view Sister Backler. They touched her, kissed her,
embraced her, and frequently had to be restrained in their emotions.
Some of the church members were more emotional than the immediate
family. After the last person had viewed the body the assistant directors closed the casket, pallbearers took their places around it, the nurses
and certain designated members took up the flowers and left the
church, followed by the immediate family and then all the remaining

church members. Outside, in front of the church, the hearse was loaded; the flower cars were loaded; and the members went to their designated cars to accompany the body to the cemetery.

WORSHIP

No discussion of church activities would be complete without some mention of the nature of regular church services held at Zion. The regular church services are Zion's major activities, and they provide the most significant drama that takes place in this Church of Holy Christ. Worship is the predictable social interaction that rallies the membership into this social community, Zion. The service means to the members not only the consistent order of worship that occurs every week, but also the pomp, ceremony, ritual, public display, and recognition in which they participate. It means the fellowship before, after, and (despite the pastor's admonitions) during the formal program.

I will briefly describe a typical Sunday morning service, which is the most important one, and a regular Tuesday night service meeting, which is next in importance because it is the evening on which the core and elite members engage one another without the presence of the marginal and supportive membership or visitors who are usually present during Sunday and Friday services.

On Sunday morning Deacon Stokes arrives at the church at about nine o'clock to open the building and let the worshipers in. If the kitchen is open that day, the cook wants to be in early to prepare the food. Sunday school books are usually locked in the office. The main auditorium is locked and must be opened for Sunday school. As the officers, Sunday school teachers, Sunday school superintendent, adult Bible scholars, and children arrive, there is usually spontaneous conversation about the week's events. Various church services elsewhere and at the home church are discussed, and one brother will tell another, "Boy we had a time last Tuesday night at Elder Boxer's church; you sure missed it," or "Where were you Friday night? Elder Johnson sure preached; we had a church full of folks," or "I didn't see you Monday at prayer service." The dead, the hospitalized, and the injured of the membership and of sister churches are mentioned, and the details of the latest political church gossip are whispered. The conversations grow as more members arrive, and finally talk has to be curtailed by the Sunday school superintendent, officers, and teachers who clear the corridors with, "All right let's go in now, it's time to start," or "Sister Joyce, aren't you coming in? We are waiting for you." The children playing in the halls and out in front of the church, and the teen-agers courting outside have to be rounded up and herded in for the beginning of services.

After the majority have entered the main auditorium the services are opened with prayer by the superintendent (or his assistant if he is absent). The lesson for the day is then previewed, and a short discussion ensues about its meaning. Subsequently the members break up into classes, roughly divided by age, and the lesson and its relevant Scriptures are discussed, often heatedly, by the adults. Classes begin about ten o'clock and end about half past eleven, when the teachers take up the offering from their classes, each attempting to collect as much as possible so his class will have the largest amount or at least make a good showing. After collecting from the class members, teachers solicit from their close friends and other members who are arriving for Sunday morning church services. In the classes the children who give a quarter, fifty cents, and above are praised and the others chided for having perhaps spent their money on refreshments. Outstanding children are made assistant teachers, allowed to collect the offering, or requested to "review the lesson" when the entire group convenes again at the close of Sunday school. Thus children learn early that substantial giving, as well as serious interest in the Scripture, is rewarded in this community. After the offering has been taken (during much of the time the corridors, choir room, chorus room, kitchen, and outside areas are filled again with conversing members), the classes are dismissed formally and the Sunday school convenes again as a group. In this group formation the children are asked to stand and recite a portion of what they learned in class. After the children's recitation, the adults begin to discuss and often argue scriptural relevancies to the lesson.

At about half past twelve the superintendent closes discussion, summarizes the lesson, announces the offering, and dismisses Sunday school. Now everyone is formally dismissed to convene in the other areas of the church auditorium for "fellowship." Some members discuss church programs. One of the church elders or his appointee conducts testimony service (a period for minor officials and ambitious members to be rewarded by having charge of the service), in which each individual is given the opportunity to address the church about his personal life. Testimony service is closed about one o'clock and an offering is taken, after which another minor offering is taken for the "poor treasury." There is not much coercion to give to this minor offering, which is a fund for needy members when they request help. Most members use it to rid their purses of pennies. The elder asks the choir and chorus each to sing a selection. When they conclude these two selections, announcements for the week are made, during which time members are invited to services throughout the week, special programs are announced, and the sick, the dead, and funerals are announced. These announcements are made through a public address system by the church announcer in the bishop's office, where she can read and not be seen. A special request is made each week that all announcements be given to the announcer, but each Sunday morning the church mother and the chairman of the deacon board make their own announcements immediately after the request, when the announcer concludes.

Members know what is likely to occur at any service. Certain members exhibit particular behavior syndromes. Deacon Paint, for example, will "nod" through most of the service. Some members seldom become spiritually possessed (Deacon Paint, Mother Jackson, Elder George, the teen-agers), while others usually precipitate a "shout." Certain members prophesy—"woe, woe, wrath, wrath, pray for your deliverance, destruction, pray for your deliverance." Some members have prescribed duties: the nurse puts on the bishop's robe after his sermon while the order of service awaits this ritual; Deacon Paint and Mother Chips have time set aside in each service for words; a special announcer makes the announcement, and Sister Roach is called up for a solo.

About quarter past one, the elder in charge asks the choir and the chorus to sing another selection each and adds, "The next voice you hear will be that of our own Bishop Jackson." After the choir has sung, and while the chorus is still singing, the bishop emerges from his office to the pulpit in his black full-length robe with an attaché case in one hand and the Bible in the other. He goes to his special chair directly behind the pulpit and kneels to pray. After his private prayer he rises and greets with a handshake the other ministers on the pulpit. He then returns to his seat and moves conservatively in rhythm with the singing chorus. After the chorus concludes, the bishop may ask Sister Roach to sing. Whether he does or not depends upon the lateness of the hour, whether the chorus has sufficiently put him in the spirit to preach, and whether he feels it necessary to reward Sister Roach at the time for her ardent support of his Sunday morning message. Sister Roach consistently encourages his preaching by standing at high points and waving a large, bright colored, lace handkerchief, walking slowly around the church in the spirit, occasionally hollering, and frequently moaning. Her husband, an elder, usually accompanies her by jumping and hollering and otherwise moving in the spirit. Her songs and those of the chorus are usually accompanied by the happy participation of the members who clap, sing, and dance as the "spirit hits them."

After Sister Roach finishes, the bishop steps to the pulpit. For about fifteen minutes he talks to the members about various events of the week, and during that time he scolds those who have angered him and praises those who have "found favor in [his] and God's sight." He usually does not mention the names of those he scolds, but all the members know who they are. If he has visited another church or city, he shares his travel experience with those who could not attend by describing the details of the trip and the church services as well as his reactions. The closest attention is paid to these "fireside chats," for here the members get the lowdown on how the bishop feels about the week's events, about which they have till now heard only gossip. These chats likewise generate the gossip for the next week. All members who did not attend will inquire about them, as will the officials from around the state. So important are these sessions to the members that after the bishop has taken a trip to confer with policy makers in the international organization, the members flock to the church in large numbers on the subsequent Sunday to hear his report. This is especially true when there is significant organizational infighting. The atmosphere is such that the members hang on the bishop's every word, and when he is going to be away on Sunday morning to preach at another church within the city he never announces this, for fear that his members will not come to their own church but will stay at home or follow him.

The bishop takes a text, states a subject, and preaches by explaining, through "parables," the Scripture his reader reads. These parables are often rich with references to his boyhood experiences on the farm and in the city as a laborer. They are always full of lessons concerning the proper conduct of the members.

During the singing, the offerings, and at most other times except during the sermon and prayers, two or three members are walking around soliciting funds for a special project, greeting other members, socializing with officers, or discussing meetings. During these times there is always motion and conversation in the church.

Members have various ways of accentuating their roles. The nurse who places the robe on the bishop after each sermon makes a point of sitting so that she is required to rise and walk through the audience to the pastor's study to get the robe and then onto the pulpit to robe the bishop. This gives her considerable exposure before the entire congregation, and exposure is considered an important ingredient of mobility.

As members walk through the prayer line they often converse with those administering prayer (usually elite or upwardly mobile core members), holding up the movement of the line as well as indicating that they have significant relationships and business with those praying within the sacred inner space. The church mother attempts to fulfill the role of "mother" for all the members by showing concern for the sick, the poor, and the "slowful," and presiding over the Father's Day service for the bishop. All members who have positions publicly praise the bishop during service, for loyalty as well as financial support is a basis for mobility. For example, Deacon Paint says, "Mean something to have a man who knows how to meet people. . . . Like a person they can give respect and who commands his respect." Deacon Paint, an elite member and chairman of the deacon board has built his power upon the ability of the average member to identify with him (alliance) and his constant pleading for financial support for the pastor (loyalty).

When the choir gets new robes, the choir leader's robe has a distinctive design. When a member testifies, she relates prestigious experiences such as a plane ride or an important invitation. When a member prophesies, she can warn the pastor about his "transgressions" or threaten her adversaries. She can admonish the entire church, and at the same time she gains valuable exposure. Well-dressed Sister Roach parades before the pulpit during every sermon the bishop preaches. Her motions are "in the spirit" but never awkward. She is a regular part of every service, and at the same time she gives visual support to the bishop's message.

Certain members are consistently moving about the church outside the sacred inner space discussing church business of one sort or the other. These are the ushers, church officers, missionaries, captains, and the presidents of the various auxiliaries. All these, together with the children who move about the building and outdoors in the summer and the members entering late and leaving for the rest rooms, provide a constant flow of traffic which is of interest to the audience.

Several times during the service the pianist moves between the pulpit piano, used for the chorus and choir, to the grand piano which sits in the main auditorium. From the chorus and the choir, who are dressed in their distinctive robes, there are always two or three members who must leave their seats and walk through the auditorium to the rest rooms or the choir and chorus rooms and then return in full view of the audience. The officers place the offering table in the front of the auditorium and remove it at least twice in every service. The ushers, dressed in distinctive uniform, accompany the members to their seats and carry messages all over the church. The pastor makes several trips to his study during the service to insure his immaculate appearance. Two or three officers always have something to whisper to the pastor and must move onto the center of the platform where he is sitting to do this.

A member is "happy" (possessed of the spirit), speaking in tongues, or prophesying. A financial report is given. An announcement is made. A visitor is asked to say a word. The minister is preaching, the congregation is singing. One, two, or fifteen members are "shouting." Sister Roach, dressed in an attractive outfit, is walking back and forth in front of the pulpit waving her handkerchief as she reacts to the spirit. Sister Dankins is running around the entire auditorium. Two or three sisters are walking around in the front of the auditorium in the spirit. A brother is shaking violently in his seat, and several other brothers are holding him so that he does not hurt himself. A constant drama is being enacted here, and the members are a part of it and understand both the players and the scenes.

The pianist leaves the pulpit piano for the grand piano in the audience after the minister has finished with the Scripture and is ready for the emotional portion of his sermon ("coming home"). When the minister begins to work on emotions (repeating emotion-packed words like Jesus and God and synonyms for them, and asking the people in various ways whether they want to go to heaven), the pianist plays moving chords at the end of every phrase, and the audience responds by repeating what the minister says or other words of praise. This builds up into a frenzy of emotion and culminates in a "shout" (dance). The ability of a minister to bring the people to this peak of emotion is one criterion for judging his preaching.

To induce the audience to participate in the offering, as well as to reward members for their cooperation, the pastor selects certain ones to stand in the prayer line on both sides of the center aisle in front of the offering table. The pastor walks through first and allows those selected "to rub him down" (massage the chest and back simultaneously) while praying for him; and then, as the chorus sings, the entire congregation walks through this prayer line, being rubbed and prayed for, and then on to the offering table to give. This physical contact adds potency to the prayer, and to touch the leader, the symbol of the group, is itself a value. After the offering some late announcements are made, and then the congregation is dismissed with a prayer. Thus comes the end of a long and rewarding day.

On Tuesday evenings various instruction groups meet at about eight o'clock—Young Women's Christian Council, men's Bible class—as well as the church officers. The purpose of these meetings is to analyze the Bible and determine how it instructs the particular age group and sex. One of the officers arrives early to open the church doors, and the other officers arrive shortly thereafter. They engage in discussion of predicaments about the building or some church policy that is of current interest, until other members begin to arrive and the discussions take on a wider range of subjects (how well the pastor preached on Sunday, impressions of a visiting minister, subsistence or health problems of various members, the time they had at a district meeting, etc.). These informal communications continue until enough members arrive to form the various classes.

The leader of a class stands or sits facing the class and conducts it very informally. Anyone can offer a subject for examination, and all discussions try to answer the questions: What does the Bible prescribe? How do you resolve the conflicting interpretations? The bishop, with his wife, usually attends on Tuesday. He does not participate in any classes but spends his time in his office resting, grooming himself, or meeting with someone. He may sit near one of the classes to hear the discussion (often the class led by his sister, who is a college graduate), but he does not sit in the class or participate. Later he may mention or comment upon one of these class discussions during a sermon. The classes meet for about an hour, and then an offering is taken by the class leader for the class treasury, which is presented to the pastor as a token of love on one of the many occasions for giving.

After the offering the classes disband, and all the members come to the front of the church for prayer which opens testimony service. During this period most of the church officers drift to the back room as do the bishop and the church secretary. They spend the remainder of the evening there, supposedly discussing church business. The bishop may leave if he is concerned about the person who is giving the message that night, and the officers and secretary may leave intermittently to confer with a member, go to the rest room, or just to take a break. Much of the time in the back room is spent in informal gossip and relaxation, to break up the monotony of the service. Entrance to it is one of the privileges of officers, who have a wider range of available activities and accessible rooms in the building. They may frequent the bishop's office, and they have keys for the choir and chorus rooms, the third floor, the utility room, the telephone, and the balcony. They often flaunt their privilege by holding an informal discussion in one of these places.

After the testimony service, a speaker may be "put up" if there are enough members present (about twenty is sufficient). This night is used to give the missionaries, young inexperienced preachers, and old ministers with little status in the church hierarchy an opportunity to preach and to obtain an offering, which is necessarily small because of the crowd. After the sermon an offering is taken for the church and then for the speaker, and the members are then dismissed. The formal task of dismissing church is conferred upon someone by the bishop, as another mode of recognition. Informal discussions begin again after dismissal, as rides and future meetings are arranged and members attempt some communication with the bishop. After all have left the building, an officer and those riding with him remain behind to lock the building.

Such activities have given Zion's membership the security, support, identity, and feeling of significance that make them willing to devote their time, energy, and financial resources to perpetuate this church. The intensity of the interaction among the members during such activities warrants appreciation of this group as a small community.

† 6 †

SYMBOLIC EXPRESSIONS

The character of interaction in Zion—intimacy, conflict, fission, competition, mobility, and political alignment—is expressed in symbols peculiar to its members. These symbols revive past experiences in the rural South, yet they vividly demonstrate the dynamics that make Zion a vital and different community in the context of urban society.

This chapter describes some of the distinctive features of symbolic expression within Zion. Religious belief, world view, and language are discussed in an overview of Zion's verbal expressions of its symbol system—one basis of communication within this group. Many of these expressions are couched in Zion's religious belief system; others are a part of wider systems of beliefs shared by the group.

My approach to describing these symbols focuses upon some mainstream American values—money, achievement, education, physical beauty, power, and progress—and shows Zion's particular version of these as they impinge upon this little community (see Warner, 1953). I then take some of the major ideological themes that operate within Zion—food, animals, death, human anatomy, the physical world, the supernatural—and attempt to demonstrate how Zion interprets the world and codifies messages to create solidarity with meaningful categories borrowed from the past in the rural South (see Wilson, 1965). Thus what I describe here among the members of Zion is their distinctive mode of creating, manipulating, and participating in selective verbal symbols that reflect their world view and belief system. This distinction reaches a level of integration in Zion that clearly delineates it as an identifiable group in the urban context.

Looking at Zion as a phenomenon of manipulated categories of meaning or world view allows us to identify, delineate, and appreciate what is Zion. The categories as well as the terms are standard American, but the peculiar constellation and varied shades of meaning comprise a unique style which is one of the bases for Zion's existence as a community. The symbol system is integrated by consistent and meaningful themes that pervade Zion's behavior patterns and conceptualizations. The members of Zion interact with one another most of their available time. They shop and travel together, have teas, prayer meetings, picnics, pageants, and classes. They identify with one another and conceptualize their way of life as distinctive, valuable, and rewarding. It is a life with a purpose, a mission.

One of the forms of symbolic expression in Zion is a communication code that serves constantly to create images of the biblical story and the traditional life style in the rural South. Sermons, testimonies, prophecies, songs, and casual conversation are rich with images with which the members can identify and which reinforce the cohesion of their religious community. The foods they eat and conceptualize are traditional. The animals they use in examples and analogies are reminiscent of life on the farm, and the idioms expressed in human anatomy, the rural landscape, death, the physical world, and the supernatural are subtle codes with which the members of Zion constantly confirm their underlying values. They believe they are different, a "despised few," "poor folks," and "outcasts" in the perspective of the wider society, but they use this perspective to validate their own existence in relationship to familiar things. Thus, perceived pressures from the wider society culminate in a self-conception full of traditional idioms, which they constantly express. Any stranger attending a service in Zion or listening to a conversation among its members misses the subtle communication or codified messages that are usually expressed by references to traditional categories of farm life synthesized with religious terminology.

RELIGIOUS BELIEF

Theology is a major rallying point of Zion. The relationship between the "saints" and God is of primary importance. This unique relationship helps to determine the nature of separation and isolation that characterizes Zion and influences Zion's peculiar frame of reference for wealth, achievement, ambition, beauty, power, and progress. This, as well as the use and manipulation of meanings for food, animals, death, human anatomy, the physical world, and the supernatural, reinforces group cohesion. Within the context of these manipulated meanings there is an emphasis on water, fire, and gossip. Water and fire are available and useful resources for manipulation; gossip is a pervasive theme and activity among the members of Zion (see Hannerz, 1967).

The members of Zion believe that God is the Father of Christ, who was conceived by the Holy Ghost and born of the Virgin Mary. Jesus died for the sins of man. He arose on the third day after his death and eventually ascended to his Father, leaving with man a comforter, the Holy Ghost, while Jesus was away preparing a place for man in the kingdom of heaven. On the day of Pentecost the Holy Ghost descended to the apostles, giving them "quickening powers" with the speaking of tongues and other manifestations of spiritual possession. The ministers of Zion believe in a literal interpretation of the Bible "from cover to cover."

God is a personal friend, "a mother, a father, a sister, or a brother." He is perceived as a human figure: "He has big feet"; "He uses the earth for a footstool"; You can put your hand in God's hand; God has a "supernatural eye"; "He can see what's in your heart"; God is a "big God"; He has the "world in his hand." He is a wealthy God: All the wealth of the world belongs to him; He is a wealthy farmer and has "cattle on a thousand hills." He is "a miracle worker." He is a companion if you are alone. He is a friend when you are desperate, "at midnight."

God in Zion is a flexible phenomenon, changing with your needs and your problems. His power and image are often not distinct from those of Jesus and the Holy Ghost. The members of Zion have a "private line to God," and nothing in the tangible universe can be equal to the power and status of having the "mainline." They can call him at "midnight" when all else has failed. When "trials and tribulations" of life are "overburdening" and your friends have deserted you, Jesus is a friend for the friendless and he satisfies (see G. B. Johnson, 1953).

The members refer to themselves as the "despised few." They have learned to live with their distinctive behavior (glossolalia, prophesying, self-denial, and other expressions of spirit possession; see Dalton, 1945; C. H. Johnson, 1969; Kelsey, 1964; Mischel, 1958). They perceive of themselves as outcasts, yet they invite you to join their "way of carrying on." They are convinced that their way of life—"this thing"—is rewarding, and they "wouldn't take anything for it." Their in-group cohesion insulates them from out-group disdain, which merely reinforces their solidarity. They have their "hand in God's hand," and the outside world ("sinners") cannot judge them. The Bible is their "map," and only Jesus is their judge. They have categorized, classified, and interpreted some of the major values in the mainstream symbol system according to the ideals of the Zion idiom (see G. B. Johnson, 1961).

ZION ATTITUDES TOWARD MAINSTREAM VALUES

Money

The members say you cannot buy friends, love, or salvation. You do not put your trust in material things. "The love of money is the root of all evil." And even if "you get money in the bank" or if "you own houses, you stink like everybody else" in death and if unclean. They say that "you can put that money in the bank and don't live to write a check." You can have tattered clothes but a beautiful Holy Ghost, and they "used to think the more ragged your clothes, the more religion you had." This perspective underlies the practice of "giving until it hurts." It is the rationale for meeting your Zion financial obligations though you may require a special offering to pay your rent.

Achievement

Achievement in this world is of little value, for this is a temporary home to determine who shall be saved. The members are working for that "city on the hill." The promotion of "self" is a sin, and you must get "self out of the way if you want Jesus to come into your life." Ambition is problematic in Zion. There are few financially rewarding positions since most of the financial efforts are designed to support the pastor. The members complain privately that a "promotion" only means that you must "work harder and raise more money." Zion is a self-sacrificing organization of workers whose primary reward is the pastor's praise, a prestigious title, and the "kingdom of heaven." The pastor expends much of his time and energy keeping ambition in check, and extolling the virtues of the "down and out."

Hardship is a meaningful component of Zion's system of expectations, but in the "afterwhile and by and by things will be all right." You will be "sometimes up, and sometimes down, almost level to the ground," but "just a little talk with Jesus makes it right." You are going to be "overlooked and pushed aside." You will have trials and tribulations. Your friends may desert you. Expect this. "We are poor folks, suffering folks, and burdened folks." This is a legitimation of the majority of Zion's members, who are poor, uneducated, and economically immobile. God gave you a place, so stay in your place and don't interfere with leadership. Use your own talent, which never interferes with the leader's "program." The ideal saint is meek, "sweet," and loves everybody. Even the leader expects to be "kicked around, ignored, pushed aside, talked about, and his name plastered on every sign post." "Working in the mill is hard but preaching is harder." There is nothing "like fooling with a lot of contrary folks, grumbling and mumbling." You have "to carry your cross if you want a crown, so take up your cross and follow Jesus down through the valley, for in the end every crooked knee, every arthritic knee is going to have to bow down before Jesus." If your need and desperation become unbearable, you belong to an association, social and supernatural, that is capable of solving all your problems. These themes justify lack of status for the *supportive, marginal,* and some *core* members, as well as those who are hopelessly immobile. The efforts of the pastor to extol those deprived of status continually demonstrate to the members and visitors the range of tolerance that exists in Zion.

Education

God uses the "weak" to confound the "strong," the foolish to confuse the wise. He works in mysterious ways. Education is trivial: "Jesus chose common men, everyday men, men used to the sunshine, men used to the rain, not seminary men or college men"; "You may be trained but not have the Holy Ghost"; "You just educated." Any educated person can put a sermon together and tell a good story, but he is not "in touch with God." You are a university because "you got a university on the inside." "Don't go to school, don't go to college, go to Jesus." "Put no trust in man or worldly goods" (see Thurman, 1949). The members say God takes the ridiculous, the insignificant, and the ignorant and creates his servants. Congruent with such a perspective, the chairman of the deacon board, who speaks haltingly and with little standard White English grammatical structure ("We's done begin us's program"), is a recognized influence in Zion's affairs.

Physical Beauty

Zion's standard of physical beauty is partially determined by its own symbols. You are pleasing to the eye if you look like "you been bred on cabbage and cornbread stirred with water." "You don't see many sanctified folks slim, most of them are fat and fleshy," but you can weigh ninety-seven pounds and have a "heavy Holy Ghost." A "twenty-dollar sister" will always "look so nice" whatever her phsyical features. Most men like women with "flesh on their bones." The women like men who have a "way about them," who hold a recognized position in Zion and are interested in women. Any potential member is a "fine looking sister, a fine young man, a fine brother to have."

Zion has traditionally prohibited most cosmetics and persists today in open criticism of false eyelashes, painted eyebrows, and all blatant use of facial preparations. This is another dimension in which Zion has attempted to insulate itself from mainstream standards of physical beauty. Up until approximately 1940, Zion was successful in this effort. The women wore floor-length black dresses, black shoes that covered the ankles, white turtleneck blouses with black ties, and black head coverings. They used no make-up whatsoever. After 1940 variations in clothing became more accepted, and today the young women use all the cosmetics, but sparingly.

Power

The concept of power has been translated into the Zion idiom. The powerful are those who have the most intimate relationship with God and Jesus Christ. Power emanates from God only. There is no need to be concerned about the influential person because he does not have "a heaven or hell to put you in." Power in the worldly sense is contradictory to the ideals of Zion, for the Holy Ghost represents the means to reach the peak of status in this church. "Bishop Hightower" is a derogatory term used to denote the evil power in church leadership. "Bishop Lowtower" is contrasted in the vernacular to mean the average God-fearing saint. Criticism is heaped upon favoritism that accrues to a "Bishop Hightower" to the detriment of "Bishop Lowtower."

The only power overtly expressed in Zion is that of the leader, who derives his power from God. He stands in a favored position with God, for he directly receives the religious "program" for God's people. He expends much of his time and energy attempting to legitimate his exclusive power. He is the "eagle that can fly over the storm." The eagle is "a powerful animal that flies high and looks low." He is strong, and the rabbit and the chicken are at his mercy. He is the only bird that can look directly into the sun. The leader is the shepherd of his sheep, who are devoid of power. You must lead sheep, not drive them. A good shepherd will die for his sheep and protect them from the wolves of contrary doctrines and creators of fission. The sheep must be kept segregated from the goats (sinners and backsliders). The leader has supernatural vision. He is a "seer and a foreseer." He is above the influence of witchcraft, and only he knows God's "program," that is, the direction and procedures for the church's organization and function.

In contrast, the follower is meek, docile, passive, "sweet," and humble. His relationship to his fellow followers is an ideal sibling relationship, and the only power he seeks is that of the "Holy Ghost and fire." Any follower seeking power is committing sin. Followers must always beware of "anything rising." The ambitious follower disturbs the peace of God's people and is dangerous. His "program" is that of the devil and must be shunned at all costs. He is "fighting the pastor under the cover." The follower must "line up right" or be a "misfit." He must not "be set up in his own way" but "lined up with the program." "To undermine, to get a top spot" is evil. There is no need for God's people to "scratch to get on top," for "what God's got for you you'll get." This perspective of Zion is encouraged to combat the constant threat of fission from each member who may feel that God has called him to establish his own church, attracting friends and relatives who are members of Zion.

Progress

Progress in Zion is made merely by living. There is a special value attached to the behavior, expressions, and age of the "old folks." "The race is not to the swift, nor the battle to the strong," but to those who endure to the end. There is a special value attached to the length of one's membership in Zion. The material progress of a high-ranking minister, the bishop, is ridiculed:

> A shack is all you had and you used to eating grass and now you in the cornfields, you greedy dogs. You got appreciations, anniversaries, hot dogs, tithes, and more and more. You making a slave out of the people. You been building for years and you don't have a chicken coop [a reference to the bishop's plan to build a church].

"Religion is mostly for poor folks. Rich folks ain't got time for Christ." The rich churches may have more members than Zion and possess more beautiful edifices, but they do not have "the Holy Ghost and fire." The members of Zion have had their economic plight redefined for them rather than solutions proffered. The solutions lie in the supernatural future.

IDEOLOGICAL THEMES

We can focus upon the subculture of Zion with themes other than major values of mainstream America. Human groups wherever we find them have a propensity for creating the complex, the intricate, the maze, whatever the available resources may be. The anthropologist has traditionally discovered this phenomenon in kinship, but in Zion the available resources include items such as food, animals, death, human anatomy, the physical world, and the supernatural. The needs of the members of Zion are ministered to in terms that harmonize with their life experiences, their training, and their levels of education. The farm, the landscape, the body, and the Bible provide a reservoir for symbol manipulation. The subtle codified messages expressed by references to traditional characteristics of farm life and familiar features of the human body, and synthesized with religious terminology, are critical for the solidarity characteristic of Zion.

But these are not mere manipulations of terms, phrases, and sayings; they are a critical attempt to revive and perpetuate certain acceptable and distinctive aspects of their native southern rural life styles in the face of northern urban pressures to change. As Linton (1943:233) explains:

> Rational revivalistic nativistic movements are, almost without exception, associated with frustrating situations and are primarily attempts to compensate for the frustrations of the society's members. The elements revived become symbols of a period when the society was free or, in retrospect, happy or great. Their usage is not magical but psychological. By keeping the past in mind, such elements help to reestablish and maintain the self-respect of the group's members in the face of adverse conditions. Rational perpetuative nativistic movements, on the other hand, find their main function in the maintenance of social solidarity The elements selected for perpetuation become symbols of the society's existence as a unique entity. They provide the society's members with a fund of common knowledge and experiences which is exclusively their own and which sets them off from the members of other societies. In both types of rational nativistic movement the culture elements selected for symbolic use are chosen realistically and with regard to the possibility of perpetuating them under current conditions. [See also Barber, 1941; Clemhout, 1964; Devos, 1972; Hill, 1963; Honigmann, 1964; Park, 1919; Wallace, 1956, 1959; Willems, 1970; Worsley, 1957.]

Food

Food is a pervasive theme in the conceptual framework of the membership. One of the familiar pleasures of rural surroundings, food is incorporated into their new way of life. Zion has salvaged the values of "good food" of the rural South and recast them into a new symbol subsystem. Food is accordingly fashioned into a symbol of communication and solidarity. It is to the land of "milk and honey" that they all aspire, in the "sweet by-and-by." Even the ruler there can cook: "Jesus can cook, not just preach and heal. He cooked for Peter and fed five thousand." He is a "sweet Jesus." "Taste him and see that the Lord is good." Jesus Christ is "bread in a starving land."

One of the criteria for identifying an in-group is the food they traditionally consume. It is constant reaffirmation that "we are different; we are unique; we know about food." The outsider "don't know what I am talking about"; "he don't know about that." Even the young and the "city folks" "don't know about that." Certain items are persistent symbols of identification. When you are criticizing the sale of food in the church as a sacrilegious activity, you emphasize that "hot dogs" are being sold in the church. But when you are encouraging the congregation to spend the entire day at church and have "fellowship in the kitchen," you emphasize the sale of fried-chicken dinners, stewed-chicken dinners, fish dinners, fish sandwiches, chicken sandwiches, collard greens, cabbage, cold watermelon, chocolate cake, and sweet-potato pies. They say, "Nobody can cook fish like Mother Jackson," and this distinguishes her in the group. They believe that stomach disorders can be healed "through cooking." They say "a lot" of their members "can smell a pot of beans and tell how long they have been cooking." A person gets his strength from having been bred on "collard greens and drinking the pot liquor." The pastor may tell the congregation, "I know you love greens, Kool-Aid, pork chops, and black-eyed peas," which is his way of emphasizing that he knows the nature of his membership and the leadership they require. Members say, "you can look at them and see they're used to eating cornbread and cabbage," thus attempting to validate their "fleshy" physical appearance.

References to food pervade the conceptual framework of the group. They describe some of their fellow members as being "so sweet that honey is falling out of their mouths." Someone has a "butter-mouthed tongue" if he practices well Zion's themes of love and fellowship. Solidarity is expressed in terms of reliable members who can digest "strong meat," "cornbread," and "black-eyed peas at night." A "strong" sermon, one that has a chastening effect on the congregation, is equated with ham hocks and contrasted with ice cream, which is "smooth and sweet." Members are told to "stay out of the kitchen if you can't stand hot grease" ("don't come hear me preach if you can't endure a strong ser-

mon"). A pleasant or "weak" sermon, one in which the preacher entertains the congregation and they "shout off" (dance), is characterized
as a "sugar tit" sermon or a "sugar-coated message" in contrast to "pork
chops and beans" that will disturb one's sleep or a "spoon of hot soup
that will burn all the way down. You don't need a bowl." And the trials
and tribulations of life are described in terms of "drinking your cup
of vinegar."

Styles of behavior among the congregation are exemplified by foods.
A "sweet dumpling" or "pumpkin pie" is an agreeable sister who goes
along with the leader's program. Such terms characterize a dependable
member who causes no conflict, in contrast to the "sour peach" who is
disgruntled and dissatisfied. These sweet dumpling members are considered vulnerable as well as valuable, for there is a fear that some
other pastor may attempt to persuade them out of this church into his
own. This fear is often expressed in supernatural terms, and thus
dumplings, the food, are frequently the object of potential witchcraft.
This fear is a reaction to the extreme anxiety, stress, and tension that
are created by a threat of schism in Zion or even the loss of a few of its
dependable members to another church.

A sour peach has its animal analogy: It is said that a sour peach looks
"like a toad frog when you put salt on his back." Such a member is perceived as being disruptively ambitious. Temptation is exemplified by
crabapples. One's personal qualities, abilities, and achievements are
often identified with apples; hence the expression "don't pick apples off
my trees" to mean "do not exploit my assets for your own ambitions."

The preacher (who is anyone "called" by God to reveal his will) is
sometimes called a "chicken eater" in a derogatory sense in reference
to his expropriation of members' resources. The description "tender
meat," in contrast to "strong meat," alludes to youth and all those who
have not been in the membership long and cannot endure open exposure to conflict in the church. Thus food is a basic theme in the idiom
of Zion—as nourishment, as an instrument of identity, as a mechanism
of communication, and as a means of solidarity.

Animals

References to animals, too, provide a consistent theme in the communication among the members of Zion. The eagle, for instance,
described as "a powerful animal that flies high and looks low," is used
as a symbol of leadership. As mentioned previously, it is said to be the
only animal that can look directly into the sun and fly so high that it can

get above "the storm." Foxes and their dens (referred to as "foxholes")
are conceptualized as threats to the task of leading "contrary people."
The behavior of geese is utilized to validate leadership in the pastor's
analogy: "When I was a little boy down in Kentucky and geese would
go back, there was always one just a little ahead of the rest. That was
the leader." The members of Zion consider the faithful and dependable
among them as sheep and the "confusion-makers" as goats. They say,
"Where there are sheep there is always a goat around," or "A goat is the
only animal that will *eat* dry paper" (an indication of inferiority and
gullibility), and this is especially significant when you consider that
what the members of Zion eat is both literally and figuratively well
defined. A goat "sits up in church and sleeps." A goat will lead the gul-
lible sheep up on a mountainous stump where the wolves can get them.
"The goat smells like a polecat; he's a stinky thing." The goat is
frequently associated with "worldly" people. The members of Zion
describe the harsh initiation ceremonies in the fraternities of sinners as
"riding the goat." In short, the goat is the epitome of evil in contrast to
the sheep, an analogy drawn from the New Testament (Matt. 25:33).

The wealth of the Lord can be measured in terms of cattle. The
members say, "My God is a rich God; he has cattle on a thousand hills."
The nature of evil is described in its many varieties by the use of animal
references. Persecution by the agents of the devil is "being beat up by
crocodiles." When the agent of God persecutes you for interfering with
his program or his leader who administers that program, "God has
turned his bloodhounds loose on you," or "That's why you in the
hog pen."

The pastor explains contrary members with the example of the pig
litter. In his sermons he sometimes tells this story:

> When I was in Kentucky we use to raise pigs. You all know any-
> thing about pigs. The mama would have a litter of ten or twelve
> little pigs. They would all grow normal but one. Wouldn't noth-
> ing grow on him but his head. He had a great big head and a
> little body and he would be gruntin' all the time. He would eat
> all the time but he would never be satisfied so he was gruntin' all
> the time. Down in Kentucky we used to call him a runt. You
> couldn't sell him because you couldn't fatten him up like other
> pigs. The only thing that would grow on him was his head. So we
> would kill him for hog head. Everybody doesn't like hog head.
> We've got runts in the church. We've got people in the church

who are just like runts. They mumble and grumble all the time. No matter what you do for them they are never satisfied. They don't grow in the spirit. Nothing grows on them but their head.

The members illustrate humility by the example of the dog who lies on his back with all four feet up. Failure is described in terms of one who fishes all day (to win souls, or natural fish) and does not even catch a bullfrog or a tadpole. The pastor reacts to division amid the congregation or a threat of fission in the church with this animal analogy in his sermon:

> You can get someone in the church to go along with you no matter how wrong you are. You can be killing someone's influence and someone will say, "You can count on me." You didn't even catch a bullfrog or a tadpole. It looks like a fish but if you give him time he won't be a fish, he will be a frog. I'm talking to those Mississippi, Louisiana, South Carolina, and Virginia folks. You city folks don't know what I'm talking about. Some folks want to put on airs, a front, and ain't got two dollars. I never did like this front business. I was raised where a shirt was so stiff it looked like a fly would not be able to hang on it. But if you take that coat off there was nothing there but a front with strings to tie it down. You'd be surprised at the folks you think are wonderful ain't nothing but a front. You ought to be a sound minister and not trying to act like somebody else. You will just pick up his faults. . . . Launch out in the deep. Get away from these folks who can't go where the clean fish are.

A wolf in Zion is a "church buster." He has canine teeth to tear the flesh of the sheep, and he is always hungry. He does not heal and comfort but isolates and destroys. If you are not careful the wolf will teach you his language (how to create division in the church). Even the discussion of men suitors in Zion is described in animal terms. The pastor tells his congregation, "I am going to bark at these foxes in my chicken pen." He rationalizes this action by telling the members that any good hen will take her roost under her wings when there is danger about.

Finally, the Holy Ghost and fire that one must have in Zion are described as a house aflame with heat so strong that the spiritual rats and roaches who would otherwise be attracted by the trash, garbage, and rubbish (gossip and other sins) cannot dwell therein (see Leach, 1972).

The members of Zion have integrated the images of familiar animals and foods into a distinctive perceptual field (for a statement on urban study using this material see Williams, 1973b). The nature of this familiarity in Zion determines identity and enlivens communication. Moreover, it affords the potential for the organization of, participation in, and manipulation of rural symbols within the context of contemporary urban life. Such distinctive symbolic expression underlies this group's solidarity and defines the nature of subculture and community as useful concepts for understanding the interaction in this church.

Death

The concept of death, too, is a standard vehicle for communication among the members of Zion. A familiar human crisis out of their past, death is sometimes exploited for the solidarity of Zion. It is the chasm that must be crossed by every member of Zion to reach the "land of milk and honey." When death occurs, it is an opportunity to demonstrate loyalty to a member of one's alliance, category, or church; or to demonstrate one's love and fellowship with the survivors by one's presence, labor, and food. Death is the final, full, and complete exposure proffered a member of Zion. The members organize the funeral as a final tribute of membership and as a rite of intensification of Zion's values. Thus the members will praise the financial support, the loyalty, and the alliances of the deceased while giving him his final exposure. It is an earthbound reward for one's services in Zion. As the chairman of the deacon board put it, "I has done much that will only be told when I is dead."

Death has a character all its own, as indicated by the phrase "death is still riding" used to admonish anyone who opposes the pastor's program or a particular member's self-interest. The members are warned periodically by the pastor that "death is still calling folks in. You got to go when God gets ready."

Death is a time of fear, and that fear is used to coerce loyalty and financial support from the members. These admonitions are designed to bolster the humility that fosters solidarity in Zion. Death is made a frightening phenomenon, contrasted with "blood running warm in your face." The members say, "You don't know when God is going to move; you don't know when we're going to be shot down in the street"; "you don't know when bombs are going to fall." The pastor proclaims, "I am scared of hell." He warns the members,

> You may have cancer now, you don't know. God is a killer. He'll kill you in your home. He'll kill you on the operating table. . . . My wife worries about me because I fast a lot. Some of us leaders will have to give our life. Some of us are going to lose our life. Times are going to get worse. You don't know when God is going to call you on the carpet.

In this way death and the fear of death are used to mitigate against potentially disruptive conflicts in Zion. Death is a sanction threatened against unruly members and those in conflict. The members testify, "I see somebody [dying]." After the timely death of his adversary (Elder Jodie), who was plotting to split his state after splitting his church, the pastor attempted to vindicate himself: "I didn't plot and plan how to overthrow anybody. I didn't pray and ask God to kill nobody. If God wants to kill 'em, he knows how to do it."

Death is a time of victory if the deceased was your competitor, as in this case. The pastor exclaimed that God was "on my side." He explained that he had "let God fight my battle." This can have the effect of demonstrating the supernatural power of the victor, especially after a long struggle between two adversaries such as Jodie and the pastor. This indication of supernatural power adds significantly to the victor's charisma, and thus to the loyalty of his followers. One of Elder Jodie's close associates reacted thus to such an indication by the pastor:

> There's no TV time here. Elder Jodie's time was not cut off because of his controversies. Don't sit in judgment here. There's only one umpire in this game and that's Jesus. It is better to have fellowship with men than to lead men. Don't get so excited over leadership that you lose fellowship. Drink your cup of vinegar. Accept someone you can't accept. Love someone you can't stand. Discuss, argue, fuss, but stay together.

Death is a time of practical adjustments in the system of ranking among the members of Zion, especially if one dies holding an important position, and there are always those "who can't wait to move to the head of the class." The emotional intensity of these prospective adjustments make death a powerful symbol. Even the pastor expresses his anxiety about events that will probably occur after his death.

> After I leave some grievous workers will come in among you, will rise up among you, speaking perverse things; watch everything rising. When I am laid out don't have all those folks who didn't support me having something to say over me. Let the folks talk who supported me, who stood by me, who worked with me. I want to be laid out in the new church. It makes me vexed to see all these folks talking over you at the funeral who helped to kill you and couldn't stand you when you were alive, who did every thing they could to make things hard for you then get up talking about sleep on, sleep on, we love you but God loves you best. . . . People put you in a way-out cemetery so they can forget about you. You live in Homewood but they don't bury you in Homewood; that's too close.

The pastor and the members make frequent references to "this life" in contrast to "when I am gone off the scene." They believe that some of their ambitious enemies pray for the Lord to take them. But they assure these enemies, "Don't think I'm going to flunk. You can't look me down to the undertaker."

Death is used to motivate lethargic members. They are told to "get up and get in the prayer line cause it might be your last chance." The congregation is often rebuked and intimidated by the pastor with "those old saints, the end is near." Death is the life crisis that Zion frequently uses to proselytize the living before it is "too late," for it is that moment in Zion when one's soul is either saved or damned. But Zion is the answer to death, for through its membership one can have everlasting life.

Even love and fellowship are reinforced in terms of death. You must be careful not to kill a man's joy or influence, for "he that would kill a man's spirit commits worse than suicide." Members are queried about their lack of enthusiasm during the services: "What you doing all week that you come to church dead." Members say they don't like a dead church. Leadership is explained in terms of the good shepherd who will give his life for his sheep, while a hired servant on salary (Zion's pastor does not get a salary) will flee when the wolf comes. The members assure one another that death is God's remedy for "contrary" members: "These folks grumbling and complaining, many of them you won't see no more." They believe that death is one of God's instruments for punishing: "I want to live so God won't put his bloodhounds on me."

The concept of death pervades Zion's ideological framework. It is a sanction for misbehavior; a threat for social control; the entrance to eternal life; a ritual of solidarity and intensification; and an idiom of communication. Death is a familiar phenomenon to all, even Zion's wide range of membership. It is a secular and sacred life crisis with a prescribed place in Zion's scheme of things.

Human Anatomy

Components and features of human anatomy constitute another rich source of symbols for the members of Zion. The human body seems a distinctive focus. They want it to survive after death so they can "walk the streets of heaven" and are obsessed with its being crippled and diseased, "bent over" and "crooked." The sexual potency of their bodies is a concern, for it may lead to "evil" or distraction from keeping their "whole mind and body" in Zion. This concern is expressed in constant references to the anatomy and demonstrated in body actions that are permissible in Zion's services—running, jumping, hand-clapping, singing, dancing, screaming, swaying, foot-tapping, rapid shaking, "speaking in tongues" during spiritual possession, and feet-washing. The constant response to the minister as he delivers the sermon often includes waving one's handkerchief in the air as a symbol of solidarity in Christ. Bodily expression is important for these people, and the restrictions imposed upon this expression by their religious code result in a concentration upon these expressions of body position, conditions, movements, and features which are acceptable within the doctrine of their church.

The members believe that the body and all its parts are unclean. Concern with the body and its needs, desires, and pleasures is evidence of a "carnal mind." To be rid of this unclean body one must be "born again," for this is a denial of the "old" body with all its sins: the "new" body has been washed clean with the blood of Jesus. The members believe that all of man's troubles arise from his "interest in bodily pleasures" instead of his being motivated by the Spirit of God. This concern with the problems of the human body in relation to its propensity for evil spreads to verbal symbols rich with references to anatomical terms. Obsession with a human body that is forever threatening one with evil activity (illicit sex, illicit conversation or gossip, smoking, intoxication, swearing, and competitive behavior) compensates for the body's cultural deprivation, and becomes a continual rite of intensification for the commitment of self-denial and an effective form of social defiance. This body orientation is a built-in mechanism for intense excitement among the membership when the "backslider falls away" because the temptation of "worldly" pleasures is too great. The member will be forgiven when he subsequently returns to the church, but his reputation, packed with vivid images of sin, will never be forgotten. He will be referred to with considerable delight as "that devil" for his susceptibility to temptation, yet he will be a validated member in Zion, especially if he is among the elite or core members.

Human anatomy is ripe with vivid images that can be called up even in the context of religious services in the form of religious themes couched in anatomical terms. The verbal accounts of Zion's development are rich with stories of the transgressions of present and past members; periods of time are marked by such events. There is no animosity, but an excitement even in the recollection. A missionary informed me that a trustee, "that old man," would teach me "bad habits." "He's done more than you've ever thought about." She seemed to be able to document it with personal experience, and she received considerable delight in recalling escapades of his past life in his presence. Thus the notions of pollution related to the human body seem more complex in Zion than what Lessa and Vogt (1972:196) describe: "Notions of pollution and taboo are no more than rules which protect men and societies from ambiguity and dissonance; they create and preserve boundaries by which moral and social order may exist." These notions provide evidence that in Zion ambivalent entities have a potency which may be both worshiped and feared. "Whatever is taboo is a focus not only of special interest but also of anxiety" (Leach, 1972: 211), and anxiety, kept within tolerable limits, is a mover of men.

The pastor and members frequently refer to parts of the body, body positions, and conditions of the human body. Some of the old members remember Elder Baxter, whom they described as a "rough" preacher who referred to women's "backsides" and their "hind part." Elder Jodie was later called a young Elder Baxter because he made constant references to females' "thighs," "miniskirts," and "sweetheart" relationships. His sermons were usually full of anatomical symbols:

Big folks are hiding in the mountain. The devil's got folks with a downhill drag. Deacons are sitting in a corner with the bishop's wife, and the bishop's in the corner with the deacon's wife. Nobody's mad but the devil [mad because of his biting criticism]. Burn off the miniskirts, God. The more I talk about miniskirts the higher they get, but God's going to burn them off. People lay on their hair so much it won't grow. Get up and go to church. You stay at home looking at naked women on TV, but miniskirts is gonna put TV out of business. Women, hide your thighs. When you get married, then look at the thighs and anything else you want. Mother, you are going to hell if you don't put that little girl's dress down. I didn't get a chance to say much, but a spoon of hot soup will burn all the way down. You don't need a bowl of soup. Words fall from my mouth and hit folks right here [pointing to his heart]. You should leave any church that's not going to give you this word of God. Stop laying home on your lazy self. If you're mad, tell the usher to give you your hat. If you got a robe on [in the choir], take it off. No, you better not; you might have a miniskirt on under it.

Wigs and miniskirts are frequent subjects of conversation in and out of the pulpit.

Many texts are taken on the subject of homosexuality. The members often refer to the fact that there were not two men or two women "in the garden [of Eden]." The pastor preaches, "It's not natural for a man to be *burning* for another man." There are frequent discussions about sissies, women-lovers, men who "burn" for other men, and women who "burn" for other women. In a congregation where it is the ideal to greet members of both sexes with a holy kiss and a hug, this insistence on appropriate sexual "nature" creates some problems. As one male member put it, "When a man hugs me I want him to hurry up and turn me loose." The pastor advises his congregation that there are two places to look if you want to know a person's sex, and he quickly adds (in his timidity about that subject) that his wife told him that.

He uses analogies that consist of references to nudity: "When you're naked you're not comfortable. Time the door moves you jump. But if you got your clothes on you say come on in. Some people are naked spiritually and they're trying to hide it, they don't want folks to see them." The Bible is referred to as the "naked word."

Many descriptions of preachers are couched in anatomical terms. When a preacher "preaches hard" the members say he "rared back, laid his head on his shoulder." A preacher suspected of illicit affairs is referred to as a "common law, slipping around, lopsided preacher."

The symbols of mobility in American society concentrate on disguising or manipulating the features of the human anatomy. These disguises and manipulations are designed to create appearances that fit into the schemes of American standards of beauty, poise, and polish. But the members of Zion take the opposite approach in their verbal references to the human anatomy. They emphasize the frailty, disease, inadequacies, and common features of the human body. In their references to human anatomy, they make no effort to disguise or manipulate physical features to adhere to some standard of beauty. On the contrary, the Zion membership uses the human body to demonstrate the fundamental equality of its members, who must "carry around with them" a frail and troublesome body. These references to human anatomy are successful idioms of solidarity. They are persistent messages to the membership that Zion is for "common people," the "despised few," and a Zion mechanism to combat the social distance which results from a ranked organizational structure.

Even their religion is translated into concepts of human anatomy. The members say that God knows everything about you, your "down-setting and your up-rising." The power of the Lord is symbolized by "His mighty hand," and his ability to "blow you away" (kill you). He can "wash you on the inside," and his ability is described by the saints with an analogy to "natural cleanliness": "Some people don't wash good. They're in too big a hurry. They jump in the tub and jump out, but God starts on the inside." They remind one another that "you must get your eyes off one another and see Jesus." Praising the Lord is referred to as "lifting Him up." Members are taught to "turn your face toward heaven and tell God what you need." The power of God is described as "His mighty hand," and he is said to have "scooped the [Red] Sea out with the palm of His hand." The pastor describes God for the members:

> God's so big there's just enough space in heaven for Him to sit down and use the earth for a footstool. He's got big feet. You can lean on God. He won't give way. He's a sturdy crutch. He's a good leaning post. He has a voice like thunder and when He open His mouth lightning comes out.

The members say, "I want to be so much like God till I walk like Him, till I talk like Him." They conceptualize communicating with God as "breaking through to God."

The pastor advises the members about the church doctrine in anatomical terms:

> Some people say my mother always told me I was born with a hot temper. She said I came here kicking and fighting. But you suppose to be born again. When Bishop Jenkins left me at that old antiquated church, they wouldn't believe you were saved unless you rolled on the floor [in possession]. But you can be saved by faith. Only faith is necessary. You don't have to hit the floor.

A "knock-down" sermon is one that "hits" (criticizes) most of those present. The members distinguish between an "honest-heart sinner," who makes no secret of his actions, and a "sneak church sinner." The latter are described as the "half-handed, eagle-rocking church folk" (note that the eagle is used to represent the leader).

Conflict in Zion is frequently described in anatomical terms. A reaction of anger is characterized as "having rocks in your jaw," to "puff up," "swell up," "get hot," and "blow your top." The pastor says that angry members "draw up like a knot and if you don't get your way you look like you're sitting on a spoke." The members say that they have "no confidence in the flesh; some folks can't see no further than their nose; and a lot of folks have forked tongues, they can talk out of both sides of the mouths." The pastor often uses the family to make analogies to relationships within Zion, and these relationships, too, are described in physical terms. The marriage ceremony is "jumping the broom," avoiding the finality of being swept away forever, by means of potential offspring. But "a wife means more than rubbing your head." "A whole lot of folks just rub your head when they want something." The pastor continues:

> Sometimes you can't believe your own folks calling you honey bunch and pie today and tomorrow they got a club for you. Make all the friends you can but don't try to buy 'em. Don't try to buy me. You make me think, you think I'm soft. Give me all the gifts you want, but don't try to buy me with gifts.

The members are often admonished by the ministers not to "put their mouth on the leader," that is, gossip about him. They are told that if they make their "bed hard they are going to have to turn over in it";

that you should not come to church to look at one another; that there is no little toe in the church, there is only one whole body; that you should have clean hearts; that you should greet your sisters and brothers with a holy kiss and hug instead of "backbiting" (note reference to body and teeth). The pastor explains:

> You can wear yourself down dealing with contrary folks. The spirit is willing but the body is not able. When disease is upon you, it is sin 80 to 90 percent of the time. These ulcers, cancer, and opium are from sin. Self can be dangerous because to exalt in self is sin. You must get self out of the way if you are to receive the blood of Jesus. Folks pat self on the chest so much and really think they're somebody. I have no confidence in the flesh. You don't have to pull no strings, pay nobody off, slide nothing under the table to advance in this church. On February the fifteenth, I came into the church. I didn't ask to be ordained. I didn't ask for any office. But I got it anyway. Somebody tried to block my ordaining. I lean on God, not them.

Members who create "confusion" are described as having "something wrong with their heads," "their heads not functioning right," or being "confused in the heads."

The problems of daily living are described in terms that refer to the human body. The pastor advises the members:

> You need supernatural help because some men will desert you. But God will be with you though all men forsake you. Peter said, "I don't know the man," when asked to speak for Jesus at the cross. This is happening today, and the days are hard with all the odds against you. Everything seems to be going against you. The waters won't behave themselves and the sun won't shine. All the leaning posts are falling away. But you must trust God. Everybody is looking for you to fail. Nobody is expecting you to make it, but you are advancing through handicap. You battle with the adversary day after day, year after year, wear yourself down, and you get weak physically but stay strong on the inside. They have done me wrong but I'm not bound. I haven't upset the city, but they are accusing me. All I have done is preach Jesus.

The members describe anger as feeling "something moving on me." The trials and tribulations of a member's life are described thus: "Saints are knocked and buffeted about in this life, but hold on with your little strength." Persecution is described as "being stoned to death." Stubbornness is "being hardheaded," and education is something that "swells your head." Members of Zion are "walk-around folks." Humility, meekness, and passiveness are Zion ideals, but in actual relationships they recognize that

> being saved don't mean to let folks walk over you all the time. God gave you five senses and there's a time when you should stand on your feet and speak up. You can be too soft. You got to know when someone's on your territory. Jesus said if you're going to be my disciple you're going to have to deny yourself. You got to know the differences between Jesus and me. Ourself is our greater hinder. It is like the tongue. No man can master the tongue.

The pastor describes the women who do day work thus:

> Men are the head. They may be a weak head, but he is the head. God didn't intend for these women running around catching these buses. If she helps you to get out of the hole, you ought to call her in afterwards and say you can sit down now, honey. A whole lot of people don't want to sweat. The book says by the sweat of your brow. They want their hands clean. They want a sweetback job [note reference to taste and anatomy].

All the ailments of the limbs are referred to as "being crippled" and "bent over." The sick are "shut-ins." A saint testifies, "When my bronchial tubes were stopped up and I could not breathe for myself, I needed an artificial respirator and Jesus got in them tubes." Another testifies, "I had a sore throat yesterday. God is a throat specialist." Body deformities are frequent themes of discussion: "This old flesh gives us a lot of trouble. It wants to peak out on you. It takes a lot of care." But you do not need to get a "hand" from a "hoodooer" (a voodoo practitioner). You do not need to "run somebody down; you don't need to lay somebody out." "Keep your hand in God's hand and you will get what's coming to you."

Spiritual growth of the saints is described with anatomical vividness:

Some children are born, and this ain't no reflection on nobody, with a head bigger than their body. And mom says, "Come on Hon, come on Hon," and Hon can't come because he's unbalanced. You got to have a big head with a big body, big feet, and big hand. . . . Saints suppose to grow, not just their head. It is easy for your head to grow, especially if God is blessing you.

Saints are supposed to close their "weak and watery eyes so they don't see too much." They are supposed to hold "their tongues so they don't talk too much." Their arms are "too short" and their strength "too weak." They need the Lord. Stubborn members are characterized as "stiff-necked folks," "carnal folks with carnal minds." They "will take your head off."

The pastor slows the pace of his Scripture reader by saying, "Don't carry me too fast, let me hear what you're saying, don't carry me too fast." The members describe lethargy as "looking funny." Members are consistently described as being spiritually "weak":

We need a tarrying meeting because all of us are weak and some here need the Holy Ghost. Somebody helped us. Tarried at midnight until sweat ran down. Brought me out of the muck and mire. [Note reference to nature, midnight, and moisture.]

Membership recruiting can even be described in anatomical terms: "Just before you break is there any among you who is not a member of the church? [Four people acknowledge, and the pastor leaves the pulpit and comes down into the congregation.] I want to shake your hand. Now I'm not trying to shake you in the church."

If dissident members are allowed to come back into the church without "humbling themselves," they are characterized as being allowed to "come strutting in." To give organizational support is verbalized as "to stand by me." Not only does God talk to his "chosen few," but he even whispers to them at midnight:

Some folks put forth all the grand plots they can think of to put people against you. God is the one that whispers in your ear, sometimes late at night, and tells you to live on when the doctors have given you up.

Success for the members is described as being "lifted from the dunghill and set on high," or being removed from the "muck and mire."

Even geographical references can be translated into body features. The immediate Pittsburgh metropolitan area is described as "this neck of the woods." Leaving the church before the sermon is over is termed "running out on me." A capable minister is described as being able to "walk around." When the membership is not listening, the pastor chides, "When people turn a deaf ear to you, you have to have enough grace to keep your feet on the ground."

The members' conception of Satan is couched in terms that suggest he has a human anatomy. The relationship between members and the devil is sometimes seen or described in pugilistic terms. Thus they caution one another to "hold on," when the devil is getting the best of them, and to be aware that with all their prayers the devil is "still hitting you below the belt." The pastor says, "I fight hard not to let nothing get in my heart against those trying to hurt me." The devil has a body which the Lord can "bind." The devil can also enter a member's body and "bind" that member's spirit, in which case the devil is told to "Loosha, Loosha" ("Turn loose the body and the spirit of this child of God"). You have to "shake yourself loose from the devil." The devil is ordered to "get behind me," and the Lord is beseeched to "go before me."

Some saints who have been "saved" and return to the "world and sin" are called backsliders; they are said to be able to fall on their face and "get up in the morning and we're somewhere talking our way into hell," that is, they ask for forgiveness and are forgiven while members are gossiping about them. The members refer to those who participate in gossip as "busybodies." Those who are in need of prayer are told to "get on their knees." Those who come out of the baptism pool frightened are described as having come out "kicking." The act of praying for someone is "laying your hands on them." Unpleasant experiences are bumps or knots on the head from which God can teach you a lesson. According to the members, all such communication harks back to a period of rural life in the South where such expression was common, accepted, and valued; one who used them was "a good talker." It is revived in Zion to express and identify the dynamics of interaction that occur there.

Thus human anatomy is pervasive in the membership's conceptualization. It was an available resource for conceptualization in the rural South. It is the subject of ritual pollution in Zion's religion (see Douglas, 1972). The members have contorted it into a unique symbol system for communication and codified messages which underlies their solidarity.

The Physical World

A familiar reaction to disenchantment with the urban American competitive way of life is the extolling of the virtues of "mother earth" and the search for some means of "going back to nature." The sun, the sky, the trees, the grassy landscape, running streams, wide-open, spacious expanses of hills and valleys are used to conceptualize the purification of man's soul. This orientation is especially appropriate for the members of Zion who have migrated from the rural South. They are very much aware of these natural features of the landscape and have no problem creating in their minds vivid images of a pure and wholesome nature.

The features of the natural world are symbolically integrated into the conceptual framework of the members of Zion. The use of nature is a constant reminder of the migrants for whom Zion was established. A system of values habitually expressed in a given arrangement of landscape phenomena has been violated through migration. Nostalgia for the hills, flowers, and land in the rural South is manipulated with symbols that reflect these past values and identify the group that is Zion. The members have successfully integrated their religion with the natural surroundings of their rural southern past. Thus their religion becomes a validation of their past. It legitimates them as a group and identifies those for whom this religion is designed—"men who are use to the sunshine," "men who are use to the rain," "country folks"; "you city folks don't know about that."

The members say there is a place in God's vineyard for everyone. Heaven frequently is conceptualized as a land where milk and honey flow. It is water in dry places, bread in a starving land, and a way out of nowhere. Jesus is the lily of the valley, the bright and the morning star, cool (not cold or refrigerated) water in a burning land, the rose of Sharon, sunshine on a cloudy day. Heaven is a place where the sun is always shining and the clouds have "passed over" forever. There, those who have never owned a house or even a "foot of ground" will "get their share of ground," "their portion of land." Jesus is the solid rock upon which "the church is built," and neither the winds nor the flood shall move it. He is a stone hewn out of the mountain and shall not be moved. Faith can move mountains; it can stop the wind and the flood. Faith can "divide the seas so that children of God can cross on dry land when threatened from all sides."

Members of Zion constantly refer to hills as a locus of the good and as an expression of value. As one member explains it, "I met Jesus in the hills of Kentucky," or God has "cattle on a thousand hills." In times of trouble the members look "to the hills." God "stays" on the mountain. Even the substance of the mountain or hill is valued. The members say, "lead me to a rock," which is their symbol of stability, security, and the substantial. When the chorus or the choir has stirred the congregation, the members say "they took us to the mountain." In contrast to the hill, the valley is perceived as a "lowly place." The valley is symbolized as the existential persecution.

In contrast to the favorable connotation that is attached to the term "hill," there is the idea that mountains are symbols of the obstacles of existence. The members say, "I have climbed many mountains through God." They recognize that sometimes "you have to endure the mountain instead of asking it to move." The Lord is recognized as the one who is able to move mountains, and when there is "no way out," one is between two mountains where "Pharoah is behind you and the Red Sea in front of you."

Thus Zion's religion is distinctively structured for its membership— migrants from the rural South. The integration of the rural scene into their religious ideology with emphasis upon that landscape is critical here. Some of these are biblical references, but they are selected for constant use in secular and sacred communication. They are images with which the members identify, and the fact that they are also in the Bible further reinforces their group validation.

Of all the features of the southern rural landscape, water is the most pervasive in the Zion symbol subsystem. Cool spring water is a remedy for all the problems of this life. The pastor confesses:

> I want a room in heaven with nothing but cool water in it. You can push a button and water will come gushing out. I want to live so God won't put His bloodhounds on me. I've been pastor since 1932. They've been digging ditches and setting the gallows for me ever since, but God is looking out for me. If you want God to look out for you, come while the blood is warm in your face.

A watered-down sermon is one that has been diluted and is thus weak. You water down a Christian with money and compliments. The desire to have "water on hell" is the wish to have the pastor treat "damnation lightly." Cornbread "stirred with water" is somehow a stronger nourishment because of the water. To participate overenthusiastically in the service is potentially to "drown out the sermon." When everything is "going against you," it is said that the waters won't behave themselves. Members who don't come to church in "wet" weather are "fair-weather folks." Leadership is compared to swimming: "There are too many people launching out without learning how to swim and there's nothing for them to do but go to the bottom. I can swim a little bit." The old members once believed that a person was not converted until "sweat ran down" in a tarrying meeting. "In those days," conversion was measured by the amount of perspiration that came from one's body, evidence of the commitment and purging one brought to sanctification.

God talks to the devil and tells him, "Do your stuff, show yourself, and the devil gets in the wind and the water." The bishop distinguishes between those who would create fission, the "isms and schisms," and the "mainstream," which is the legitimate church organization. "Souls for Christ" are conceptualized as fish in deep waters. The quality and quantity of one's religion is described in terms of how "shallow or deep" one is in "living water." The pastor explains:

We are drawing water here and the only way you can do it is with joy. This is living water. Some folks set in this Holy Ghost water and you don't get a drop on you. You are a dry bone in the valley. This aspired few, this holy bunch, make you clap your hands, throw up your feet. [Note references to body parts.]

Members who are "cold and indifferent" will be cold when they participate in the service and thus will put "ice cold water on the fire" of spiritual enthusiasm. "Good times" and "bad times" are described in terms of the elements:

Thinking people try to make hay while the sun is shining high. Don't wait until it's raining and the weather is bad to try to make hay. Thinking people try to make a nest egg. They put something aside—that's if they're making enough to do that.

Even in a mundane sense a violation of water makes a sharp impression:

A man in our church who is a pest, disturbs the service, hair not combed, won't shave, won't clean self, look like lice might be on him, I'm afraid to tell you to throw him out because God might take my blessing from me. You can't have respect of persons. He went so far as to spit in the pitcher of water.

The Lord "rains" his blessings on the "temple," and the members fear that unless they "do right" God will "shut up" his heaven and won't "rain no more." Rain is also a symbol of God's purging of the church. Unresolved animosity is explained thus: "Fire in the wall will burn until the roof collapses, but out in the open you can take water and put it out."

Conflict and the threat of fission and competition in Zion, and the anxiety inherent in all of these, are constantly expressed in the Zion idiom of the features of the natural world. The pastor reacts to the threat of fission:

We are too long discovering a false individual. It's not the real thing, it's the chaff not the wheat. . . . When you stand up for truth you will lose friends but God will give you new friends. I stood in the middle of the road and didn't take sides with confusion.

People talk about hurry up and do something. Do something overnight. Build on sand. You didn't build a church but got a church out of a church [a reference to Elder Jodie's schism in Zion].

The ship is rocking, the wind is blowing, but we've got to hold on.

Potential leaders are warned of their ambition; they are told that if you keep going somewhere you don't "get nowhere; a rolling stone don't gather no moss." Saints who are not supportive in the service are referred to as "setting up in church like a knot on a log." Competitors refer to the inferior status of newcomers by statements such as: "A shack is all you had and you used to eating grass and now you in the corn fields, you greedy dogs." The competitor's sweethearts are criticized as having been in the relationship so long that they've gotten "rusty." In the days of adversity, the times are expressed as "a thick cloud," "a dark cloud," but there is hope eternal for "a bright day somewhere."

Members of Zion are admonished not to allow the sun to "go down on your wrath"; don't "die mad." When "contrary winds" are blowing, one has to be careful. Anger is described in terms of the roots of trees being shallow in the soil rather than deep enough to endure the storm of life. The members say if you are "settled" in Zion, a little wind can't blow you across on the other side of the hill to another church or into the "world," or "you been eating short grass too long; you need to get out in the green pasture and eat green grass and drink still water" (become totally committed to Zion). Status is expressed in terms of acting as if you are on top of a mountain when you actually "only have two dollars."

There are other references to nature in the integration of Zion's system of symbols. Praise, congratulations, and compliments are described as "pinning flowers where flowers are due." It is even recognized as a value to "pin flowers" on people while "the blood is still running warm in their face," in contrast to presenting flowers to the dead. The members have periodic ceremonies (Mother's Day, Father's Day, pastor's anniversary) in which flowers are pinned upon appropriate members. The concept of flowers is even extended to the pleasantness of the rose in the expression "don't try to rosey hell up," or make it seem less harsh.

The preacher is obligated to preach "in season and out of season" (what the people like and what they do not like), and one of the bishop's annual state sermons is known as the "annual spring message." Even God is an "in-season God," a "right-now God," an "on-time God." (Note the reference to time among Black people, who are supposed to have a distinctive conception of time.)

There are even some mundane descriptions of people which embody symbols that have meaning in the natural world. Men who believe in their physical prowess are referred to as "hard-rock Charlies," and there is an admonition that there are some "hard-rock Charlie" women too. Small children are referred to as "little stumps."

These are references to human behavior expressed in the Zion idiom that the members believe is peculiar to them. They exemplify how they see the world and express what they see. If a member travels to other churches in the Church of Holy Christ, he expects to interact within the same sphere of conceptualization. He feels at home in other churches and in state and international meetings because the world view is the same and is expressed in this familiar vernacular. It is part of his evidence that "we are a peculiar people." He is steeped in the same expressive tradition as his hosts, and the symbols have the same basic significance. He communicates, identifies, and interacts.

It is thus that the peculiar way of seeing and manipulating the natural world contributes to the integration of Zion and to my conceptualization of Zion as a subculture. I suggest that it is this subculture which helps to define and reinforce Zion as a community in the urban context.

The Supernatural

The supernatural is a significant component in the structure of Zion's theology. The members believe in the Father (God), the Son (Jesus Christ), and the Spirit (the Holy Ghost). They believe that God reveals himself to chosen ministers whom he has "called to preach" and to his chosen lay members, upon whom he has bestowed the Holy Ghost. He reveals himself directly to his ministers and through dreams, prophecies, and visions to his lay members who have acquired the Holy Ghost. Thus the supernatural has a legitimate place in Zion's religion. But supernaturalism has expanded in Zion from this structured position to such an extensive proliferation that the supernatural has become one of the distinctive ideological themes that help to integrate Zion into a cohesive group.

The members of Zion have a distinctive conception of good and evil spirits. A disgruntled, temperamental, or obstinate member is described as having an "evil spirit." One who insists on behaving in opposition to the program of the pastor and elite members is labeled as possessing an "evil spirit," as being "a slave of the devil," as operating the devil's "program," as having the same spirit as the devil, or as propagating evil plans. "The devil can beat the saints shouting, singing, and testifying."

There is something ominous and evil about midnight and the "damnable" dark. It is most advantageous to be able "to get in touch with God at midnight," because midnight is the hour when one is most alone in the world. It has special significance that Jesus is a friend at midnight. The midnight hour can be perceived as the final opportunity to make a decision for the good or evil side, the time "when one is in the valley of the shadow of death." But "early, early in the morning" is associated with the good and the Godlike. The evil that women do is described as what they have done in the dark. Frequent references are made to behavior which must be consummated before sundown. Sundown, like midnight, is perceived as a final hour of decision.

The members refer to dark clouds, dark days, and dark times. "We are living in a dark day, perilous times." Gossipers can "darken your name," and "cloud your program." And religious conversion is being called "out of the darkness into the light." Evil lurks in the dark. Here again one hears constant images of dark, overcast nights reminiscent of a rural South without electricity. The members recall sitting around a coal oil lamp and telling stories of strange occurrences that have been passed down for generations in the South. The members perceive the South (especially Alabama and Louisiana) as the geographical source of witchcraft.

Some members can see "things" or "somebody" in the dark. Others can "hear things." One member explains her fear of the dark: "We who know the country carry a stick at night to beat the weeds. You can see a snake in the day but not at night." Another member recalled having worked one evening in the summer of 1951 rehabilitating a dilapidated house in the lower Hill to allow his family of eight to move out of a three-room apartment. He had worked on this house for two weeks and was attempting to finish on this particular night by working late. He was tired, and the hour seemed later than it was. When he went into the dark basement to get a tool, he heard his mother who had been dead for sixteen years speak to him, "Son, you have done enough, now it's time to go." According to him she spoke in such a way so as not to frighten him. He did as she commanded. The pastor recalled, "My mother use to say that when you see chickens walk at night, it's not chicken." Other members have recalled similar experiences for me. These bits of evidence and others lead me to suggest that midnight and the dark have special significance to the members of Zion; that common significance seems an important ingredient in the cohesion of the membership (see Brewer, 1958; Puckett, 1926, 1931).

Most of the members believe in witchcraft, couched in the peculiar symbols of Zion. They believe that the devil has agents operating in and out of the church. These are characterized as having a "bad spirit." It is explained that often when you "hate a man" it is not he who is mistreating you, but a demon inside him. These agents are frequently described as the aforementioned "slaves of the devil." Some of their activities consist of "fighting the pastor under the cover." They are told that a psychiatrist cannot help them; "you've got a demon in your mind." Agents of the devil sometimes ask God to kill somebody. They are able to "read folks" as well as God's servants can, but they get "theirs" from the devil. They are described as "dirt diggers," "trick workers," "gossipers," "root workers," "stuff workers," "bewitchers," "hoodooers," "soothsayers," "rascals," and "half-handed folks." The pastor tells the congregation: "Lot of people don't get concerned until somebody dies, then they fill up the church. The dead can't help nobody. Get that out of your mind that somebody can call the dead up."

The members of Zion believe that agents of the devil will "get you through your stomach if you're not careful." This means that supernatural forces can be put into operation through one's food and water. One of the favorite foods for the process is dumplings. The members frequently state that one must be careful that someone does not "put something in your dumplings."

You've got to watch these folks fixing a big meal for you, especially if you like to eat. They're feeding you for a reason, to get you through your stomach. You need the Holy Ghost power for these folks. A real message will make their hair stand up on their head.

You can also be attacked by external manifestations. Someone can "sprinkle down powder" around your door, around the pulpit, or around your gate. This will result in bodily harm. The devil's agents can cut off a dog's tail, put it in a paper bag, and burn it as you leave your shelter, and you will "bark like a dog." The devil can bewitch you. The pastor tells the members:

You can go through this persecution if God is with you. They may be killing you, stoning you to death, you're being stoned, lied on, persecuted, because you won't take sides with confusion. Many people don't know what they're doing. Their heads are not functioning right. They say they stand for right, but their deeds are evil, they're confused in the heads. I don't believe all sick people have sinned. Some people will bewitch you. But you can't bewitch folks and go to heaven. Some people are working stuff, taking Louisiana trips, and I'm watching all these trips to Alabama. Some believe in root work. You can fool around and they can put something on you. An' I'm not sure they can't unless your hand's in God's hand. [Note there are particular geographical areas that abound in witchcraft. It is there that one goes to get his "hand," or supernatural power; see Whitten, 1962.]

The devil has a program all his own, and various members are carrying out that program at various times. These members are able to use "little balls of roots" to inflict physical and mental harm on their adversaries. They have devices and instruments to deceive and manipulate others. They have "dice that won't pass, thumb in the deck, and a voo-doo curse." They can "look you down" to the undertaker. They can "work stuff, put disease upon you, read folks, put down white stuff, and sift stuff around." Even God sometimes works with the devil to punish the righteous for their evil. The agents of the devil will "cross" you. They will wish you bad luck. They will wish you would die. They can concentrate evil on you. They can "put evil on you." The pastor admits:

> I carry a piece of cheesecloth in my billfold all the time [a blessed cloth to ward off evil]. . . . But hold on just a little while longer, afterwhile and by and by you won't see your enemy anymore [God will kill him]. God has a way to protect his people. . . . The devil puts imps on your trail when you decide to live right.

God will help to defend you against the devil. Members explain that God will "move" their enemies. Problems, controversies, and fissions will be resolved if you only wait on the Lord. He will prevent your enemies from "slipping up on you" and will give you a supernatural eye to detect the "evil ways" of the devil and his agents. He will give you the ability to interpret dreams which provide insight into future phenomena. These abilities are most necessary, because the devil is always present. He is not an "ugly" person; he looks like an angel and thus deceives even the "very elect." But the preacher has all the necessary capabilities; he is a "seer and a foreseer." The righteous can feel the presence of evil. The minister knows that if God rejects you, you go looking for a witch: "When Negro men and women have home troubles or say they have no husband, the root workers tell them, 'I see a husband coming.' A person can bewitch you so you think they are right when they are wrong." The preacher is aware that both God and the devil have similar powers, instruments, and techniques for manipulating the affairs of humans, the distinction being that God is more powerful. This powerful ambiguity is fraught with potential supernatural sanction to control behavior in Zion.

CONCLUSION

I have provided above some brief examples of the distinctive use, participation in, and manipulation of symbols among the members of

Zion. I perceive this unique subsystem of symbols as a significant component of the perpetuation of Zion. It is the foundation, the idiom, the identification, and the means of gratification of Zion which lead me to postulate that Zion is a community. The members perceive this symbolism as the heritage of "this despised few," their unique conception of the world, "our way of carrying on." It is upon this evidence and the resulting social boundaries I perceive that I define Zion as a subculture.

This population, whose nucleus is migrants from the rural South, have created a way of life which reestablishes their lost values and recasts their most precious symbols into a system of communication and solidarity. The world and the urban environment represent chaos, and their conception of order is couched in their southern rural images of what is good and lasting. The outsiders only see and hear the obvious, but those who are affiliated sense complex cues of identification. Even the intonations, emotions, and grammar reinforce this. As one member expressed it when four visitors from West Virginia "testified" in the familiar idiom, "they're talking our language."

The dualism of intimacy and organizational competition is made tolerable; the chasm between doctrine and practice is made acceptable; the contradiction of loving one's enemy and wishing one's "brother" dead does not create dissonance; because most of what the outsider perceives as cognitive disjunctions have subtle resolutions for the members of Zion couched within the symbol system discussed above.

THE PHYSICAL SETTING

The *communitas,* or sense of brotherhood, within Zion is created to some extent by the members' being both performers and audience in their services. Most of the members contribute to the worship and are important officeholders with titles and responsibilities. But the setting in which they interact also contributes to solidarity by incorporating, consolidating, and mobilizing the membership. Not only do the members of Zion have a special relationship with one another, but they also have an abiding association with the physical setting in which the community congregates.

I have tried to describe the special meanings that various areas of the church building have for the membership. The kitchen, dining hall, rehearsal and dressing rooms, even the contiguous areas outside the building are important staging places where certain acts of the Zion drama are performed. But the auditorium where worship services are conducted is the main stage. It is here that every place has a distinctive meaning and every member has a unique place. These relationships of place, people, and meaning resemble a life-sustaining ecological system.

As I pointed out in chapter 3, the nature, extent, and duration of strategic visibility in Zion are one mechanism of membership mobility. Therefore, exposure plays a significant part in the interaction of the members within the church setting. The musical director sits at the highest point in the church auditorium (see figure 3), and in that position she is the most exposed person in Zion. Her visibility is enhanced by her need to move periodically from the piano near the choir and chorus to the grand piano on the main floor of the auditorium. She takes her position at the grand piano during the "coming home" portions of the minister's sermons (the finale) and during congregational songs which are sung to arouse the membership before and after a sermon. Because of the mechanisms for mobility in Zion, this critical exposure adds significantly to the congregation's admiration of the musical director. This phenomenon is reinforced by the fact that the musical director is also associated with the church songs, which most of the members identify with and love. Her exposure is to some extent

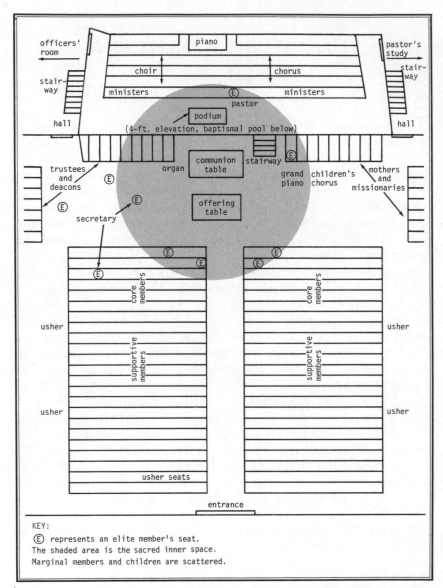

FIGURE 3. *Seating Chart of Zion's Auditorium*

diminished, however, because when she is in her primary seat, high atop and in the center of the stand for the choir and chorus, she has her back to the membership. She has a mirror which enables her to see into the main auditorium and in which she can partially be seen by the congregation. Because of her exposure, the musical director has never been given an important title in Zion. It is as if the leadership, aware of her access to exposure, has been very circumspect about aiding and abetting her rise in Zion. As a consequence, the musical director is one of three salaried employees (the secretary and janitor being the other two) whom the pastor can hire and fire. The pastor thus controls her strategic visibility in Zion and maintains a close relationship with her (see figure 2, p. 35).

The choir and chorus also sit in elevated positions. Their seats begin behind the ministers and rise to their maximum height at a point adjacent to the seat of the musical director and the piano. Thus, the members of the choir and the chorus share maximum visibility with the musical director and have access to tremendous exposure mobility. Their visibility is accentuated by the fact that they march in procession into the auditorium and to their seats at the beginning of the services and during offerings, and march out at the end of services. In contrast to the musical director, the members of the choir and chorus do not have any formal checks upon their exposure mobility. It comes as no surprise, then, that some of the most powerful women in Zion have been groomed and entrenched in the choir and chorus.

The musical director and the members of the choir and the chorus are a cohesive clique in Zion. Because of rehearsals, traveling engagements, and singing programs, these members spend even more time together than does the general membership. This is evident during the services. Teen-agers in the chorus trade gossip about recent events and, since their hands are hidden behind the backs of the chairs in front of them, distribute chewing gum and candy among themselves. They admire one another's finger rings, hair styles, apparel, and trinkets (afro combs, necklaces, hair ribbons, coins, dress pins, writing pens, etc.). They display their money competitively and share in the amusements that occur during the services, like comical dances or wigs threatening to fall off. The adults in both groups can be seen quietly laughing and conversing before and after their songs. They compliment one another's hair styles and apparel and quietly discuss church business, musical arrangements, and singing itineraries.

The members of the chorus are staunch and enthusiastic supporters

of the songs sung by the choir and of solos sung by its members. They
enjoy reciprocal support from the choir. When a member of the chorus
or choir is possessed by the spirit, it is likely that others in the groups
will also become spiritually possessed. When a member of the chorus
or choir avidly responds to a sermon, other members are likely to follow. A verbal attack against any one member of this choir-chorus-
director triad will often antagonize them all.

It is thus significant that the president of the choir, the member
closest to the pastor in Zion, sits directly behind him. The exposure and
participation of the choir and chorus are increased by their locations
adjacent to the back room and the pastor's study, from which they are
separated only by a partitioned stairwell. The choir and chorus see the
visitors who enter and leave these rooms during the service, many of
whom stop and converse with members of the group.

The ministers, who sit on the pulpit, and the pastor, who sits in the
center of it near the podium, must walk past the chorus or choir to
get to their seats. This creates an occasion for warm greetings before,
during, and after worship. The officers of the church not only move in
and out of the back room, but also go on and off the pulpit to converse
with the pastor and various ministers sitting there. Thus they, too, must
pass the members of the choir, and this heightens their visibility. It is
interesting that of all the seats on the pulpit and elevated platform of
the chorus and choir, only those of the choir president and the pastor
fall within the area designated in figure 3 as the sacred inner space.
Thus, even though the president of the chorus sits adjacent to the president of the choir and the ministers of Zion are positioned around the
pastor, the circumference of the circle of the elite excludes them.

The sacred inner space, surrounded by the circle of the elite, seems
an appropriate name for the space in Zion which seems most exclusive
and protected and where the most sacred activities occur (communion,
feet-washing, baptism, group prayer, sermons, "tarrying for the Holy
Ghost," initiation to membership, dancing, possession, solos, and healing). It is the space where visibility is at its maximum because of both
the sacredness of the space and the access to the congregation's vision.
The concept of inner space (see Erikson, 1968) is associated with
womanhood and is most appropriate for Zion, which was founded by
a woman and receives its greatest support from its female members.

The seat of the pastor and the podium from which he preaches are
positioned over a concealed baptismal pool which is exposed when the
chairs, the podium, and the flooring are removed. The pool has a stair-

case at either end so that baptism candidates can enter the pool through one staircase, be baptized by the pastor and an assisting minister, and leave the pool by the other. This process allows the candidate who has been "cleansed" to avoid touching the staircase he had used to enter.

Two staircases lead to the pulpit, and a third, located in the center of the pulpit, leads directly to the podium (within the sacred inner space) and is used only by a minister giving a sermon. The entrances to the first two staircases are on the opposite sides of the main floor of the church auditorium. The missionaries and church officers are strategically seated at these entrances—the missionaries at the entrance leading to the pastor's study and the officers at the one leading to the back room. Thus, the officers and missionaries have easy access to the back room and the pastor's study, respectively, and to everyone proceeding to and from the area of the pulpit, choir, and chorus by these stairs. They use these positions well, greeting all who pass them and moving in and out of the respective rooms easily. These positions place the officers and missionaries close enough to the source of the sermon that their verbal support can be heard by the preacher or teacher (who stands at the offering table), whose confidence and motivation are determined by such support.

In front of the seats of the missionaries and mothers, near the grand piano and within the sacred inner space, is the seat of the pastor's wife. She sits in a position of maximum visibility, near the missionaries and mothers and in an obvious supportive position to her husband. She is strategically located to observe the reactions and actions of the members and to be observed by her husband, who can "read her face." She gives him facial cues about his statements, which he often acknowledges and then disregards her advice: "Wife is looking at me. . . . Wife is looking funny, but I'm gon' tell the truth no matter who don't like it." The pastor and his wife try to keep a constant vigil over the services, so she usually leaves the auditorium only when he is in his seat. When both are absent from the worship, a confidante informs him of all behavior, for the pastor believes that Zion requires that "you watch everything and everybody." Mother Jackson is a sensitive person who is very light-complexioned and whose flushing is visible. You can observe her discomfort when her husband says something that might antagonize some of the members. But Bishop Jackson is a "plain man," and he often says things that are potentially offensive. So, as the members say, Mother Jackson "sits on pins and needles" throughout most of his sermons. This relationship between them is often the focus of attention of some of the members, who watch her "every move," and her motions are later the subject of face-to-face and telephone conversations.

In the center of the sacred inner space is the offering table, where the money is collected and blessed. The pastor or "minister in charge" (note the impotence of this temporary title) selects two officers to stand to "take the offering." This is a prized appointment because those officers always "have something to say" about the offering and often, to the dissatisfaction of some, about matters that have nothing to do with the offering. These are moments of high visibility, and most members singled out to "come before the people" take the opportunity to "talk and talk." But this is tolerated because most of the members praise the pastor, "keep his name before the people," praise his wife, and justify the monetary efforts in their behalf.

One's seat in Zion is more than a place to sit; it is an expression of one's status. Most members have been sitting in the same seat for so many years that their seats are informally reserved for them. (The only person I have seen violate this unwritten rule is the pastor's brother, who is "unsaved" but a familiar figure in Zion and has a unique status as a sibling of the leader.) A position within the officers' or missionaries' section is a badge of distinction in Zion. The pastor expects to find his "strong" members in their close and familiar positions, and he may comment upon their absence. When the pastor invites members of the congregation to accompany him when he preaches in other churches, he makes it known that he expects his familiar faces to surround him for emotional support. Most churches affiliated with this international organization have somewhat the same ecological systems, and the members are cognizant of the visiting pastor's need for support. Furthermore, officers, missionaries, and mothers in other churches in the organization respect reciprocally recognized statuses, and when an official enters their services they take pains to see that the visitor is seated appropriately.

Supportive and marginal members would never sit in sections occupied by members of higher status and are often reluctant to move closer when asked by the pastor because of poor attendance. There is an atmosphere of sanctitude around the sacred inner space, a feeling of visibility, and an obligation to participate actively with which none but those most socialized in the cues of the Zion idiom feel comfortable. A new face in these intimate surroundings is observed at once as evidence of newfound zeal or as a clear indication that one does not know "what he is doing."

In the first two pews within the sacred inner space sit the elite members of the pastor's immediate family. The seats in the first two pews outside the inner space are occupied by staunch and upwardly mobile core members. On the right side of the auditorium, this group consists of members who have not reached the age of thirty (two of whom direct the children's chorus positioned directly in front of the first pew) plus older members who identify with the younger members. Behind them sit the teen-agers who do not participate in the chorus and young adults who have not made a firm commitment to Zion. On the left side of the auditorium in the first two pews outside the inner space sit the wives of officers, along with other older women who are widows of former officers or have long associations with Zion without having become missionaries. The secretary sits here, when not engaged in official duties, to reinforce her official association. This group also includes marginal and supportive members who have been in Zion for many years but have remained in those categories. They have an indisputable place in Zion in spite of their lack of official status. Their seating often extends back for several rows, depending upon the attendance. The remainder of the auditorium is occupied by children and visitors, who are uncomfortable under the watchful eye of the congregation if seated near the front, but who enjoy observing others from the rear.

The ushers are posted strategically near the visitors and supportive members, and their reactions during the services encourage these otherwise reluctant participants. The ushers not only accompany all who enter the auditorium to a seat (making a special effort to get them as near to the front as possible), but also sing, clap, pray, move with the rhythm of the music, become possessed, and encourage supportive members, children, and visitors to take part in the service with smiles and encouraging gestures. The ushers also keep order among the children, who frequently become so involved in their own play that they forget where they are or become overly rambunctious in imitating dancing or possessed members or in reacting to the services. They protect possessed members from hurting themselves, their possessions, or those sitting next to them. Adept members who are activated by the spirit find their way out of the pew into one of the three aisles and into the inner space, but those who are not so adept are assisted. The ushers are aided in these duties by the church nurses, the missionaries, the mothers, the officers, and core members.

The secretary has an official seat within the inner space where she collects money designated for specific funds and records contributions according to the intentions of the donor. She also stands here or near the offering table to read various financial reports, but no one remains in the center of the sacred inner space during the sermon. When new members decide to join, the secretary records their names near the offering table in the center of the inner space. (This procedure means that there are often people on the rolls who were motivated by the services and exposure but thereafter fail to return or participate.) The secretary's stylish apparel, her movement to and from her official seat and in and out of the pastor's study and the back room, and the parade of visitors to her official seat are a pageant in themselves. Many members make it their business to talk to the secretary because of the visibility and apparent importance of such conversations. The pastor and other elite members also have a parade of visitors as soon as they take their seats.

Sister Roach, when called to sing, leaves her seat in the missionary section and moves to the inner space. During her song she moves around the circumference of the inner space with graceful gestures that accompany her song. After her song she may spend three to five minutes reacting to the spirit she has generated, all within the sacred inner space.

Most ministers, including the pastor, remain within the sacred inner space when they are preaching, but many move all around within that space to arouse the congregation and in reaction to their own arousal. Both the grand piano and the organ which are used to accompany high points in sermons are located within the inner space, establishing "church music" as an important ingredient in the Zion way of life. It is so important that it often competes with the significance of the preaching, and the minister or pastor must remind the congregation that "singing won't get you into heaven." The musical director is herself a focus of attention. She not only plays the piano, but reacts to her music, sings along with the congregation, and is often overwhelmed with the spirit as she plays. She displays tremendous skill by playing every note accurately while she is so stimulated that it is difficult for her to remain in her seat. Such displays are contagious and inspire others to react and participate, especially those who identify and interact closely with the musical director.

Communion takes place within the sacred inner space. The church mother and her female lieutenants, with their white uniforms and towels, silver pitchers and goblets, and solemn demeanor, aid the pastor and officers in this ceremony. Ritual feet-washing takes place within the inner space to demonstrate the humility of Christ and the Zion elite vis-à-vis the lowly.

All the basic behavior of Zion occurs within the inner space. This area is so sacred that many members hold a hand up in reverence as they walk through, and no one enters during a sermon except in emergencies or spiritual possession. Children who accompany their parents to seats within or near the inner space must be rigidly controlled so that they do not become a disturbance. Babies near this area who begin to cry or otherwise interfere with the service are hurried out of the auditorium by their mothers, friends, or the ushers. Teen-agers seldom sit near the inner space, for it represents a degree of involvement for which few of them are prepared. The only exception I have seen is a drummer who was persuaded temporarily to sit near the organ to play during a service. This was copied from a competing church to insure that Zion's "young people" would not feel slighted.

The church officers are the official caretakers of the Zion community, but they must continually validate, legitimate, and reinforce these positions. They must create meaning within the context of their roles in relation to the members who comprise their reference group. Thus the officers can usually be seen around the auditorium adjusting windows, propping open doors on hot summer days, adjusting fans, determining lighting, replacing light bulbs, checking the temperature of radiators, and adjusting them. The offering table is frequently moved to the side for group prayer, healing services, feet-washing, communion, and other rituals. Then it must be returned to its original position for the next collection. The officers are constantly adjusting the microphone of the loudspeaker for different users. During large meetings they can be seen providing extra chairs for dignitaries, taking their hats and coats, and giving each a warm welcome and the assurance that his comfort is their concern. They repair locks, check the furnace, look for children who may be avoiding worship, and secure the building at night. They supervise the cleaning of the grounds, the repair of kitchen equipment and plumbing fixtures, and the general maintenance of the building and other church property. They leave no doubt as to their authority and responsibility. Any problem that develops in Zion at any time is sure to be referred to the church officers—even by the pastor during an interruption of his sermon.

The missionaries have their place in Zion too. They take the responsibility and authority for the decor in Zion and see to it that all rituals and ceremonies are "carried out properly." The ministers must have drinking water. The pulpit must have flowers. Certain women must have corsages on various occasions, and the pastor and certain officers must have carnations for other occasions. The pastor must have a new robe occasionally. The pastor, his wife, and outstanding members must be presented "love tokens" during organized appreciation ceremonies. The church must be decorated appropriately for Easter, Palm Sunday, Christmas, and every other day. The missionaries take this charge, and like the church officers, they make it clear at all times that this is their responsibility.

The ecology of Zion reflects the group dynamics that operate in the church. In the arrangement of chairs around the pulpit, the ministers who sit closest to the pastor usually have the highest rank and degree of support for him. Zion ministers do not usually enjoy as friendly a relationship with the pastor as some other core members (see figure 2, p. 35). If they are able preachers and organizers, they are a potential threat to the pastor's leadership, and if they are not able they are an aggravation. They must be allowed to preach and officiate periodically in spite of their awkward methods of conducting services. Ministers are needed to relieve the pastor of preaching duties for minor occasions, to fill vacancies throughout the pastor's state jurisdiction, and to demonstrate that the pastor has the ability to attract even those who have been called by God to preach. The pastor often boasts about the number of ministers he has in his pulpit. Of all the members in Zion, the ministers especially must exhibit constant loyalty, often to the point of obsequious devotion, which is obvious and ridiculed by the members. But such behavior is rewarded by frequent opportunities to preach and otherwise officiate, especially if the minister is able.

The deacons in Zion are closer socially to the pastor than are the trustees (see figure 2, p. 35). This is evident during most church services, when the deacons make more contact with the pastor and are referred to more often in the course of his sermons. The trustees are responsible for church business operations and have traditionally had differences with the pastor about such operations. The chairman of the trustee board must often lead the opposition to business policies which he feels are not in the best interest of the church—a peculiar function when one considers the absolute authority of the pastor. The result is the traditional social distance between the pastor and the trustees. The deacons, on the other hand, usually have the same concerns as the pastor—keeping Zion viable, with harmony and general membership welfare demonstrated in their community. This parallel effort brings the deacons and the pastor closer in their interaction and their feelings toward one another. Within the scope of the deacons' responsibility is the obligation to keep the pastor content with his financial rewards and prestige, so that he will remain at the helm of Zion. It is thus easy to understand why the deacons have a much greater opportunity for social proximity to the pastor than do the trustees. This is borne out by the nature of their social interaction and by the ecological relationships in Zion.

Not only does each member of Zion have his part in the religious drama acted out here, but he also has his cues, stage positions, props, and mutual expectations of fellow actors. The setting of Zion is a strategic part of the community that interacts there. The pastor can convert the sacred inner space instantaneously into an area where all the members and visitors are welcome, for he represents a tremendous symbolic power to the membership. If he invites the "sick and crippled" up to the altar for prayer, before he has anointed four or five with healing oil the entire congregation will have formed a line for such ministering. I have seen the pastor leave the pulpit by way of the center stairway after preaching his sermon in order to shake the hands of some of the members who wished to congratulate him on such a "fine message." Before he could complete the few handshakes he intended, most of the congregation had decided that they should participate, and the pastor had to be rescued by another minister who took him by the arm and led him back to the pulpit. The many well-wishers left behind understood that the pastor could not endure an extended ordeal of handshaking after such an exhausting sermon.

There is versatility in the Zion ecology. When the auditorium is converted into a theater for the Easter and Christmas plays, the pulpit is used as a stage, and the pastor's study and the back room are used for dressing rooms. At these times, as during baptisms and children's pageants, the members take the best seats available. At Christmas time there may be a decorated Christmas tree within the inner space with "love tokens" and gifts under it, and on Tuesday and Friday worship nights the small turnouts often result in an informal gathering which operates outside the formal system. But when the system described is in operation, the guidelines are rigid, although not explicit. For instance, once a trustee decided to give two twin evangelist missionaries who were "running a meeting" at Zion a "going-away love token." But this trustee likes a "good laugh," so he told the members several days in advance that if anyone could guess what he had in the package he would win twenty-five dollars. The presentation took place on a Sunday morning between the Sunday school service and the regular service. The trustee presented the package, which was about four feet square, to the congregation for them to guess its contents. The striking feature of this event, besides its demonstration of the variety of interaction that occurs in Zion, was that for no explicit reason the trustee presided over this affair entirely outside the inner space. He intuitively recognized that this event was not appropriate for the inner space on Sunday morning. As the presentation progressed, it was evident that no one would guess the contents, and the trustee began to open the package. It turned out to be twenty-one packages all neatly wrapped inside one another. Finally two writing pen sets emerged whose total value was less than the twenty-five dollars promised to the winner of the guessing contest. The members took this in good humor, and the event was the talk of the members for several weeks.

On each side of the entrance to the auditorium an usher stands to assist people as they arrive and to greet everyone with a handshake, an embrace, or a kiss, depending on the inclination of both parties. The ushers at the entrance also solicit an offering from anyone who appears to be leaving before an official offering is taken. Greeting rituals and ceremonies are common in Zion, as I pointed out earlier. But after each worship or other official gathering in which the members have been required to be attentive for a period of time, and especially after a well-attended service in which many of the members have not had an opportunity to greet one another, the auditorium becomes a tumultuous social gathering. The members greet one another as if they had been parted for years, even though it may only have been two days since their last meeting. They often spend hours after such worship and other services hugging, kissing, back-slapping, firm shoulder-gripping, arm-holding, laughing, and talking with one another. These ceremonies can be embarrassing for those not familiar with the idiom and comforting to the lonely and isolated; they are a small part of community life for the members of Zion. This kind of interaction is one of the primary techniques used in these familiar surroundings to recruit new members and to solidify the cohesion of the group. It is explicitly described as "fellowship," and the pastor often advises the congregation to exhibit this behavior with new and old members.

The Zion auditorium has a balcony on three sides, and during large state meetings and other such occasions it is open to members and visitors. The children especially enjoy the use of the balcony because it means that they can be some distance from their older siblings, parents, and core members who maintain order. The balcony also offers a vivid picture of the pageant that is Zion. The bright colors of wearing apparel, especially the hats, the movement around the auditorium for business or as part of the worship, and the reactions of others can be seen from a different perspective. It is especially intriguing to look down upon a large group of ministers in the pulpit during state meetings and watch their interaction. There are antagonists and protagonists, patrons and clients, the powerful and the weak, all committed to a philosophy of love, fellowship, and brotherhood, sitting on a common stage where they are obliged to act their parts regardless of personal allegiance or opposition. To a lesser extent the drama is the same with cliques within the general membership. The enterprise of Zion must go on in spite of personal antagonisms.

As one walks into this large auditorium (approximately 70′ x 40′) with its balcony and high ceiling (approximately 35′) on any day when it is empty, it seems to be a great theater where important human dramas have occurred. To the members of Zion I am sure that this is far more than a mere impression. Man incorporates his setting into his patterns of life so that the two become inseparable. So it is with Zion.

The setting of Zion is familiar and elegant to most of the members, who have few material possessions. It is a place where rituals and ceremonies transform and transcend the natural state of man and give meaning and hope to the future, even to his ultimate destiny. It is a partnership in material wealth for those who disavow the larger materialistic society in which they live. But it is even more, for it is the context for membership interaction and is thus arranged and utilized to give meaning and structure to the Zion community, a community that transcends the rhetoric "I am somebody," though Black, poor, and "on welfare." It is in this sense that the setting is inseparable from the behavior that takes place within it and thus can be called the Zion ecological system. But a member explains it better. When I asked him, "What is there about this church that you love so much," he answered:

> I don't know, son. Its just home to me. Its just like I live here. These church folks are my family. I'm closer to them than I am to my own people [family of orientation and procreation]. They mean me well and I mean them well even though we have our fallin'-outs. I can't wait to get here and see who's here.
>
> You got to live for somethin'. You can't just act a fool all your life [like worldly people]. I know when I close my eyes the saints will talk over me and tell what I's done in this church. Then I know my life's counted for somethin'. I's helped a lot of saints. I's

helped this church grow when there was stumbling blocks every-where, and when we old folks die we'll leave the young people somethin' to carry on with.

The people in the world don't know the secret. They look all their life but they don't find it and they don't know why. But we've found that secret [fellowship, brotherhood, and community]. Its like they got a coverin' over their eyes and can't get it off and the secret is right here in front of them but they can't see it. So they look for it in dope and wine and bad women and stealing and fighting, and even killin'. But when it's all said and done they's worse off then they was before they start lookin'. This life ain't no plaything. It'll mess you up if you're not careful. There's all kinds of snares out there and if one don't catch you the other one will. Most things that look good is bad for you. You got to put the devil [temptation] behind you or he'll lead you straight to hell [trouble].

People is tryin' to jump over the moon [achieve large suc-cesses] when they could have joy inside and peace in their minds if they just got their thinkin' right. I don't claim to be smart, but if people who supposed to be get in the fixes [troubles] they do, then, I don't want to be smart. So this [the church] is my life. These is my kind of people. And it may not be much to worldly folks, but it's all I need. It's just where a few people come together with a pure heart [good intentions] that you find Jesus [the "secret"].

And so it is that the Black peasant in America has brought the ethos of the rural South to the urban North protected within a bounded eco-logical niche.

† 8 †

COMMUNITY

Many of the groups in the Black ghettos of Pittsburgh are in competition with Zion, especially for those who were born and reared in the urban ghettos of the North (see Keiser, 1969). This competition requires that Zion recruit its members without restriction as to neighborhood, social, or economic criteria and exhibit great tolerance for a wide range of human conditions among recruits. The Zion members must depend upon a social network of relationships that extends across neighborhood and subcultural boundaries to reach potential recruits wherever they can be found, as well as to nourish them as members once they are committed to the church. These relationships and the way they are linked make Zion a community (see Leeds, 1968).

If it is possible to consider community as a social construct and a network of social relations without its traditional geographical limitations, then we can conceive of Zion as a small community. On a structural and cultural level, the characteristics of Zion's interactional social network and its distinctive symbolic idiom suggest a community.

"A community is a cluster of people . . . who share a common way of life" (Green, 1968:290). It is "the localized population which is interdependent on a daily basis, and which carries on a highly generalized series of activities in and through a set of institutions which provides on a day-to-day basis the full range of goods and services necessary for its continuity as a social and economic entity" (Smelser, 1967:95). "A community is the total organized social life of a locality" (Ogburn and Nimkoff, 1968:291; see also Arensberg, 1965; Henry, 1958; Nisbet, 1969; Redfield, 1955, 1956; Stein, 1960; Warner, 1941).

Zion is a huddling place where members take refuge from the world among familiar faces. It is a source of identity and a matrix of interaction for the members it recruits. It is a subculture that creates and transmits symbols and enforces standards of belief and behavior. It allocates social status, differentiates roles, resolves conflicts, gives meaning, order, and style to its members' lives, and provides for social mobility and social rewards within its confines.

If one can define a community as patterned interactions among a

157

delineated group of individuals who seek security, support, identity, and significance from their group, then Zion is a community as well as a church (see Gustafson, 1961). The members of Zion consider themselves a "despised few" surrounded by a hostile urban "world" of many. They describe their position as "sheep among hungry wolves" and distinguish themselves as "sanctified folks," "outcasts," "a queer people," "walk-around folks." Fellow members are those who "speak our language" and love "this carrying on." They contrast themselves to "worldly folks" (see Jones, 1939).

When members of Zion describe others in the urban context as "worldly folks" and "hungry wolves," they are referring to the competitive nature of other groups in the urban setting. Drug, "hustler," religious, and street-corner subcultures in this urban Black ghetto contend for the available human energy, commitment, and resources (see McCord, 1969). These subcultures, too, make a concerted effort to integrate their own members into meaningful life styles that allow escape from the alienation and lack of belonging that characterize those unattached and uninvolved in the modern urban scene. Each of these other groups, like Zion, expends its major efforts combating social distance among its members as a formula for achieving integration among them in spite of the pressures toward mobility in the wider urban society. One of the means Zion uses to accomplish this is a network of membership communication in which the members of the church as well as those in a wider group outside the church are treated distinctively.

THE SOCIAL NETWORK WITHIN ZION

The members of Zion have clusters of social and communication networks. Zion is a significant part of the members' lives, and news about the church or its members can be a source of great anxiety until it is shared with someone who is similarly concerned. Positions have to be taken on various issues within the church even by those who are powerless to make changes. One must know which opinions lie with which group to take the proper stance with one's closest friends, with the power structure, or with the opposition. Often it is necessary to discuss rumors with several members of one's social cluster in order to achieve some degree of clarity about an otherwise puzzling event. The pastor will often only hint about a tedious situation or problem, and if he goes into detail he seldom gives the full background. The social network is the only other source of church communication. The looking-glass self (one's identity as determined by a reference group) applies to emotions and feelings as well as to opinions of self. In situations that produce emotion, one's feelings may be ambiguous and require some social interaction to determine or identify them. The range of ritual behavior in response to the spirit within the church context is not rigidly determined, and one needs others for comparison and interaction to determine such limits. The social network serves these many functions.

This network is composed of clusters of individuals who gossip, face to face and by telephone, about the total range of church affairs. The pastor, his officers, and the church secretary combine to form one cluster. They discuss the church business in the back room and delegate authority for performing needed tasks. They telephone one another regularly to discuss problems and procedures for performing administrative tasks. In these interactions, the pastor and his officers often express their personal frustrations, anxieties, and motivations about church activities and the specific members involved. These conversations are confidential and are designed to remain within this social cluster. But each of the members of this cluster participates in another social cluster, and this radiation of cluster members forms the church social network.

The pastor has an auxiliary called financial captains, which consists of nine people in charge of fund raising for the pastor each month and for a large "appreciation" each year. The leader of this group, Sister Ulrich, is a big money raiser, and her influence with the pastor is very great. She often "calls the shots" about decisions in the church because the pastor cannot afford to antagonize her. The pastor spends considerable time with her discussing church affairs, and much information channeled through her subsequently filters down through four of her "close workers" in the pastor's aide. All the male church officers in the organization except one (his wife belongs to another church) have wives in Zion with statuses equivalent to "missionaries." Each wife belongs to a cluster of women which includes certain missionaries and acts as a nexus for informal contact and communication of church information. Missionaries have the privilege of "teaching" in all the churches within the organization, and thus they maintain contacts with other churches throughout eastern and western Pennsylvania and all over the United States. There seems to be more esprit de corps in the women's state and international organizations than in the men's. The women raise more money, organize more extrachurch affairs, and maintain the international mission work. Thus, it is largely through the missionaries that intra- and interchurch information is disseminated and informal contacts solidified. The male church officers belong to other auxiliaries such as the usher board, men's Bible class, the choir, and pastor's aide. Their various duties (opening and closing the church, supervising cleaning operations and maintenance, etc.) keep them in continuous contact with other members and thus provide ripe opportunities for communication.

INTENSIVE RELATIONSHIPS AMONG SELECTIVE GROUP MEMBERS

The lay members have an informal buddy system in which two or more members are usually found in each other's company. They come to church together and leave together. They ride together on church trips, sit together, and often join the same auxiliaries. They testify on the same nights and "feel the spirit" at the same times. One can often discern the membership of social clusters by observing the sequence of spiritual reactions during a period of "rejoicing in the spirit." Powerful missionaries as well as church officers and even the pastor cause the spirit to "hit" most of the other missionaries when "it hits them," while the rejoicing of a lay member may only affect her buddy and other lay members. I have seen two such lay members, young men of twenty-five and nineteen, "quicken in the spirit," jumping and exclaiming outside in the street for fifteen minutes before church services began. Each was responding and supporting the other in what seemed to me a display of courage in the presence of members and nonmembers alike outside the normal context of such behavior.

Ministers require support to maintain the emotional pitch of their own voices as well as those of the congregation. They often request this as they preach: "Pray for me," "Can I get an amen," "You don't have to say amen," "Don't get rocks in your jaws," "Don't dry up on me." One can identify a given minister's social cluster as the avid supporters who are emotionally involved in his "message." Supporters within the power structure generally respond without being possessed, while lay members do become possessed. The pastor's preaching receives the emotional support of all the members at one time or another. If he is possessed (always for short spasms), any of the members of the power structure may become possessed. You can often determine the prestige, status, and position of the speakers by the pattern of reaction among the congregation. As one minister of junior status put it, "God's not just here on Sunday night" (when a certain high-status member runs the service). Or as other members say, "You got to be folk's honey today to get an amen." "Amens are running in self not the Holy Ghost. A preacher gets lost for words and shouts and you say 'didn't he preach,' but he didn't preach, he just shouted. God don't have any respect of person."

There are free and fixed channels of communications. Any member can discuss church business with any other member, for the church belongs to all members. But the messages sent and received are determined by the positions in the church structure of those interacting. There are "seasoned" members who can "take" the problems of the church and "unseasoned" ones who would be discouraged.

The back room and the pastor's study are the nerve centers of the social network, and the activity or flow of traffic in and out is a barometer of the intensity of an issue at any given time. There are days when the officers and secretary spend the entire service period in the back room. Each officer has a special interest group, and the secretary informally represents the missionaries and formally represents an auxiliary of women, the Young Women's Christian Council.

The pastor spends much of his sermon time counseling the members about the evils of communication within the social network, especially during periods when such communication carries information about him and his program. He admonishes the "saints" that they can see and hear too much for their own "protection." He advises them to close their eyes to avoid seeing too much to "get through to heaven." The "saints" who have been members for years are cautioned to keep misunderstandings from the young and new members and are chided about failures here. Keeping "unsaved" husbands and wives of members up to date about misunderstandings in the church is a new phenomenon, scolds the pastor: "Old-timers never let sinners know about misunderstandings. . . . Now even some old members can't digest strong meat, cornbread, and black-eyed peas at night [controversy in Zion]. . . . Got a medicine cabinet full of medicine for digestion [in contrast to possessing adequate faith that creates endurance and heals]." He claims that the telephone is damning the "folks." Members do not come to church, but call other members to find out what occurred in the service. According to the pastor, members call him simply to worry him and to "signify," or stimulate gossip. Several husbands and wives of key members in the social network joke about their spouses' dedication to the telephone and the large amounts of time spent using it.

When a leadership crisis develops and the social network gets "hot" with information, the pastor threatens the members with death if they continue to discuss his shortcomings with the usual elaborations and embellishments that accrue from discussion to discussion: "God is going to move someday." The churches are very prone to fission and fusion, and the intrigue and news surrounding these breaks and regroupings are constant subjects of gossip. The nature of the new group, the leader's reaction, how the leader's family is taking it, and which members are aligning where are subjects of the communication network.

The Nature of Zion as a Group

In the Black ghetto of the North there are a few vestiges of the traditional social communities—the village, family, neighborhood, parish, etc.—of the rural South. But the quest for meaningful human interaction is establishing new forms of community life relevant to the residents' present social and economic plight. Responding to the threat of a fraudulent, remote, or incomprehensible social order which is beyond real hope or desire and invites apathy, boredom, and even hostility, these Blacks are creating bounded groups which give them a stake in a social order. The traditional conception of community which applied when there was far less geographical mobility is too restrictive for modern society. Perhaps this church can be characterized as a "cultural device" (Murdock, 1949:85) capable of extending personal relationships beyond the neighborhood, and thus we must define Zion in terms of the nature of this extension. The Zion Holiness Church is a group of Blacks whose residences are scattered all around Pittsburgh, but who have found a new social institution with which to identify. Each member has a function and an allegiance. He is an integrated member in a hierarchy with symbols and norms exclusive to his group. This bounded group is distinctive, small, quite homogeneous, and self-reliant. It is a process or system of human interaction with a distinctive social structure and patterns of behavior, much of which is traditional southern Black behavior. Only in a community such as this can such behavior be retained with meaning and dignity.

This community is not static. There are fissions, disputes, cleavages, and conflicts. But burdened by poverty, ill health, political deprivation, and death (membership is top-heavy with age), the members find meaning in this religious community that enables them to go a little beyond the problems of surviving from day to day. The majority, who have no hope of raising their standards of living, have a way of life in which such aspirations play no part.

"I would rather be here [in the church] than anywhere else I know," said Sister Brown after a brief hospital stay. "I want to thank you for the offering you sent me. It made me feel that somebody loves me." This community satisfies the need for affiliation. The members have needs which are gratified by interpersonal relations—friendship, prestige, approval, and support. These are satisfied by submerging one-self in the church and being represented by it, as well as by perceiving one's individuality through self-evaluation in terms of other church members. Thus, after Elder Jodie's death, when his son became pastor, many of the older members could not identify with a twenty-five-year-old man who associated with the younger members taking over the reins of the church. They could no longer find the approval, status, and help they had come to expect. The majority of them left the church en masse and formed a new congregation.

A member evaluates his own opinions and abilities as he interacts and competes for positions within the church. This is one of the human needs that requires face-to-face interaction in human groups. The members evaluate their performance within the church in relation to others who are significant to them, a reference group, and a symbol of themselves in a satisfying association.

The church provides a setting for the release of members' anxieties (see Homans, 1941). Every church service has a portion set aside for "testimonies" which can be sung or spoken, and everyone can partici-pate. Members use this period to relate all their recent problems and exhibit their faith that the Lord will provide solutions. There are also periods throughout the church service when a member can stand and relate an intense experience: "The spirit just came to me and said, 'Don't worry, the Lord will provide.'" During the singing and preaching, members are expected to have and physically demonstrate emotional experiences. One member will often get out of his seat "in the spirit," go to where another member is sitting, and while speaking in tongues "prophesy" on the other member, often by rubbing him down and repeating a single word such as "wrong, wrong, wrong." These are intense moments of communication and release for the church mem-bers, for they know what personal conflicts are involved and under-

stand the attempted resolution. When I have had a full understanding
of the personal conflicts being resolved, I have been as enraptured as
any member. These episodes of shared communication are vivid rites of
community solidarity and intensification as well as a function of that
community in reducing personal anxiety.

Zion is a stable group whose members have little opportunity to
achieve social acceptance outside it. Therefore, the members interact
intensely within the group, creating complex mutual obligations which
support its cohesion. They visit sick members and offer prayer for them
at home and in the hospital. Money offerings are taken up for the sick,
the needy, and victims of personal tragedy, and food baskets are given
to their poor on feast holidays like Easter, Thanksgiving, and Christmas. Members set up car pools to transport one another, and they help
each other in kitchen responsibilities. They listen to others' problems
in private and in church testimonies and respond when they can. The
holy kiss and embrace demonstrate love and affection. Such obligations
are conditions of membership, because no one can be saved unless he
demonstrates love for his brother. The pastor particularly must meet his
responsibilities to the membership, for he is the symbol of the community. In fact, financial and political support are given to him in direct
proportion to his effective reciprocity. This, of course, is done on a
graduated scale: his most effective supporters must receive his most
effective concern, but every member has obligated him by the simple
fact of membership.

The church is a closely knit hierarchical organization in which people's positions and obligations to one another are defined, recognized,
and predicated. The social organization of the church has little connec-
tion with the structure of the society around it. The members who gain
advancement and recognition within the church would be less likely to
do so in the society outside. The typical member lives in a slum; he is
Black and uneducated; and he has a sense of inferiority vis-à-vis the
symbols of mainstream society. He has effectively abandoned that
society for most of his social needs, and any attempt to influence his
social life must deal with and through his church community.

Considering the general anthropological proposition that religion
serves the central and crucial function in society of supporting social
integration and cohesion, and, further, that every society requires some
consensus on basic values, it is understandable that when these conditions are met within a bounded social group such as this church, we
have the basis for a viable human community. Metropolitan areas are

congested, with overlapping geographical spheres of influence which no longer function satisfactorily to integrate human groups. The Zion Holiness Church is a community of interaction for residents of various Black geographical areas. This strengthening tie of various geographical units to a nongeographical community orients them in important and clearly definable ways which make the traditional model of community less relevant to the modern scene. Their community is not a common geographical locality, but a social subsystem which relates members of a group in patterned interaction. It is an interactional and a process phenomenon. As one of several interactional fields in modern urban life, it integrates the society at large, in spite of cleavages, by creating another interactional field for those marginal Black souls who would otherwise have fewer alternatives to practice the American way.

Sister Sims and her husband illustrate two of these interactional fields. Sister Sims's husband is an alcoholic who spends most of his nonworking hours at a corner bar two blocks from his house. He arrives there from work and leaves from there to go to work. On payday, Sister Sims has to send a friend to the bar early to catch him in a good mood and "get money for the house." This allowance for her is always secondary to his drinking money, and she must do domestic work to make ends meet. When the bar closes on Saturday night he brings his drinking buddies home, where he sells them liquor and gambles under the pretext of earning money to "straighten out some bills." He never makes a profit and never seems to care. These weekend affairs end late Sunday afternoon. Sister Sims and her two daughters stay with her mother during these and other periods of conjugal dispute. Their marriage is very unstable. But she understands his "sinful" life and he, her "sanctified friends." She thinks a "no-good man is better than none." She prays for him all the time, and her church community sympathizes with her plight. His interactional field is the street-corner world, hers is the church; together they are two on the modern urban scene.

MEMBERSHIP RELATIONSHIPS OUTSIDE ZION

The most significant aspect of Zion's extension into the larger urban milieu is its meagerness. The church conceptualizes people outside Zion as sinners, worldly folks, and hungry wolves (note the oral reference). Even the Baptists, Methodists, and Catholics, though worshipers, are sinners because they practice the wrong doctrine. The members of Zion say, "Holiness or hell."

The members avoid relationships with neighbors, social-action people, community workers, and politicians for fear of contamination. They say that "sheep don't lie down with wolves" and "the rabbit don't run with the fox." "We are saints of God; we don't commingle with worldly people." One member who dares such a relationship with his former pool hall buddies is suspected of limited commitment to Zion. Any relationship with the wider urban context is circumspect and situational.

There is a mutual respect between the members of Zion and the police. The members feel that both Zion and the police are combating the same enemy, sin. When the members witness a breach of the peace, they are quick to inform a police officer that they are "members of this church"—deacons, trustees, or missionaries. The police pay deference to the church and its members. They ignore parking violations during times of worship, in spite of massive traffic jams during large state meetings. They are quick to respond (a rare phenomenon in this neighborhood) to a call from the church and are very polite on church premises.

The members believe that politicians are as "crooked as lawyers; they buy you." "But you can't buy God's folks with money under the table." Of neighbors they say, "How can one walk with sinners unless he also sins?" Of social action they say, "Drug programs, youth programs, all these programs are not the answer. Jesus is the answer. All the plans of man will fail; only Jesus can set this world right." Even fashion and styles are "worldly stuff," and the members of Zion are not of this world.

Most members live with their families of procreation or orientation, and rarely do all members of a family belong to the church. This creates frequent occasions for discussions about the validity of the intensive preoccupation and participation of the churchgoers. But the "sanctified" do not expect to be accepted or understood by the "unsaved." Often a sympathetic member of one's family will help to raise money for the church by accompanying one on a soliciting route or by asking his associates and employer for aid. Whether the members of one's family are sympathetic or not, they can often appreciate the church member's need to maintain his status in the church. This can only be accomplished by financial contributions.

Most of the church members work in domestic or other menial labor situations. Their distinctive behavior (restriction of smoking, swearing, modern dress length, movie-going, modern hair styles, etc.) and their conversation (usually rich with church details) make no secret of their religion. This creates an impressive point of departure for soliciting funds from employers and fellow workers, especially during a major fund drive for the church. Often these employers and fellow employees are invited to special functions of the church, to repay them for their contributions, to bring about the opportunities for further solicitation, to create a further financial commitment in the future, and to demonstrate the "fine" religious group in which the members participate. The housekeeper of the chief newscaster of a local television station invited the newscaster to be a judge of a church essay contest. The newscaster attended, along with several other prominent people invited by other church members. Prominent churchwomen make a point of attending the functions of prominent Black women and the newsworthy events of churchwomen in other denominations. Thus, in major church events at Zion, Black civic leaders are frequently announced and asked to acknowledge their presence to give pomp to the occasion.

The members solicit funds in the streets, in bars, and at the entrances to supermarkets and banks. The kinship network of the members is another prime source of solicitations, especially for major financial drives. When the members are serving in the kitchen, they advertise outside to draw people in from the neighborhood, and they make special efforts to satisfy these customers so that they will return.

Not only do funeral-home directors extend aid through hand fans printed with their advertisements, chairs, and financial contributions, but those among them who are prominent in the community are also asked to speak on special occasions. These men are often sought out for business advice by the pastor and the officers of the church. The wife of one funeral director participates in the network of churchwomen and is occasionally seen at Zion.

ZION: A SUBCULTURE AMONG SUBCULTURES

A Black ghetto is a harsh physical environment. It represents the opposite of most of what we cherish in the wider society (see Ginzberg, 1968). Black ghetto dwellers, including the members of Zion, must have mechanisms of adaptability and strategies of survival to sustain themselves here. Exposed to the values of mainstream America via television, radio, employment, schoolteachers, landlords, bill collectors, social service personnel, and other networks that extend into the wider society, the Black ghetto dweller must exert tremendous energies to maintain a viable in-group perspective.

One traditional means of maintaining this group solidarity has been to defy, defile, and deny certain standards of mainstream mobility. Social distance is a pervasive characteristic of social organization in the United States. So one feature of the poor Black subculture, where mobility is rare, is the effective control of disruptive levels of social distance within groups that tend to cohere and persist. Zion is one of these groups, but there are others surrounding Zion, and their style is different at some levels.

In Zion orality is flaunted in the form of food symbols, reference to the mouth, and the blatant exercise of verbal expression during worship. Testimonies, prophecies, speaking in tongues, the holy kiss, and the constant refrain during sermons are a consistent exercise in orality. Such exercise effectively disavows the standards of poise, dignity, and composure that characterize middle-class behavior, especially during worship.

This defiant behavior is also evident in the members' movements during religious services—running, holiering, screaming, jumping, waving arms and hands, dancing, and violent shaking during spiritual possession. This, too, totally disregards mainstream standards of behavior within or outside church. These patterns of behavior are not incidental features of Zion; on the contrary, they are a cherished design of this group. They are meaningful instruments of solidarity. They defy mainstream standards of approved religious conduct and defile the very conception of religion held by most mobile Americans. Relative to other groups in the ghetto, Zion is restricted in the range of signs and symbols it can organize, utilize, and manipulate, but those at its disposal are intensively exploited.

This defiant behavior is not exclusive to Zion, but is the behavior of the Black ghetto within which it exists (see Grier and Cobbs, 1968; Powdermaker, 1967). Any discussion of the alternative groups that surround this church requires some attention to the nature of their solidarity, which is a competitive alternative to Zion's. Black ghetto-specific behavior is rich with evidence that these people are in a fierce struggle to keep social distance among themselves at tolerable levels. Whether rapping, jiving, running it down, copping a plea, signifying, or sounding (Kochman, 1970), poor ghetto Blacks manipulate defiant signs and symbols—oral, anal, and genital—which defy, defile, and deny certain standards of mobility in the wider society.

To protect his redistributive social network from the disruptive symbols of social mobility of the wider society, the poor Black attempts to level any tendency of hierarchy among his group with the use of defiant symbols with oral references—"suck," "sucker," "suck out," "eat," "eat me," "eat my," "blow," "tongue," "kiss," "kiss my," "gum," "teeth" (defiled), "mouth" (polluted), symbolic lips (defiled), and symbolic tongue (polluted)—in his daily unoffensive communication. He also manipulates genital symbols—"fuck," "fucker," "sack," "make," "some," "get over on," "stuff," "cock," "pussy," "hole," "cat," "poontang," "poodle," "a little bit," "grinding"—in the same manner. And anal signs and symbols too—"ass," "asshole," "butt," "sweet," "nice," "punk," "faggot," "girl"—are basic conversational vocabulary (see Gover, 1961).

The poor Black will also nickname his children for food—"Sugar," "Peanuts," "Peaches," "Beans," "Butter," "Duck," "Cookie," "Honey." He will publicly manipulate his anal and genital zones; he will use terms that are polluted and value-laden in the wider society—"mother," "sister," "father," "brother"—as common expressions of greeting and communication as well as verbal games ("dozens"). These are not historical accidents so much as mechanisms of survival and adaptability. Oppressed groups will organize, utilize, and manipulate signs and symbols to defy the values in the symbol system of the oppressor (see Abrahams, 1962; Bailey, 1965; Berdie, 1947; Boas, 1966; Dillard, 1972; Dollard, 1939; McDavid, 1951; Stewart, 1965, 1966). I have found similar evidence in prisons, ghetto schools, detention homes, and among the Black Muslims, where defiance becomes an instrument of solidarity for those whose lives are oppressed.

Social distance is a luxury of substantial economic resources. Conversely, it is a threat to a redistributive social network with a precarious subsistence base. This threat is accentuated among people whose ethnohistorical circumstances have eroded the symbols of solidarity common to viable cultures. Thus, the available resources for solidarity among poor Blacks generally and among the members of Zion specifically are the defiance, defiling, and denial of mainstream symbols of mobility and values. The social scientist must examine closely these dynamics of survival, adaptability, and solidarity to understand the nature of subculture in modern society. I have attempted to do so only to the extent that such examination will help us understand Zion.

In the geographical setting of the lower Hill in Pittsburgh, there appear to be other critical interactional groups. By critical I mean that participation in one or more of these groups appears to structure the life style, social network, and character of the participants. These groups seem to be meaningful alternatives to Zion.

A member of the drug subculture (if we can conceptualize such a group as a subculture) is a participant in a closely knit network of associates whose orientation toward the world is distinctive. The drug addict is not only a marginal member of the wider society, but he is also an accepted member of a group whose reason for being is determined by the need for drugs and the activities required to secure them. Within the drug subculture there is an esprit de corps, a sense of belonging, a significant reference group for self-identity—a cultural and structural dimension that is often overlooked by those who perceive this subculture only as criminal. The members of this group have almost total access to the homes and meager material possessions of the other members—a unique phenomenon in this poor Black ghetto. They share food, cars, clothes, and residences. They pool money for drugs and other exigencies. They understand, discuss, and empathize with one another's political, legal, and economic plights. This is a cohesive group that rallies around the use of hard narcotics and the economic activities attending that use. A member of this group has most of his face-to-face contact with other members, and his participation in that group to a large extent determines his structural and cultural life.

The "hustler" subculture is another important group in this geographical setting (see Polsy, 1967; Slim, 1967). The members of this group rationalize that there are no economic endeavors available and take extreme pride in their abilities to survive outside the framework of traditional labor. A favorite expression of disdain for work of one with whom I am acquainted is, "I wouldn't tell a mule to get up if he was sitting in my lap." The hustler is recognized by his fellow members and the wider neighborhood population. This group has its own system of mobility and ranking. The members who have "made it" view with disdain anyone who works or depends on government agencies for a living. One aspires to the upper class of hustlers, where he will have his own network of relationships in the market for drugs, prostitution, the numbers, and stolen goods. The pool hustlers, gambling hustlers, and the pusher, pimp, and madam are all part of social and cultural systems that exist as meaningful alternatives in the lower Hill.

The religious subculture, of which Zion is part, is also a viable group in this neighborhood. As I stated in the introduction to this work, the lower Hill contains two Catholic churches, two Methodist churches, two Baptist churches, five Pentecostal churches, and several storefront missions of various denominations. Members of these religious organizations to some extent appear to relate to their churches in an intensive interactional style of life. I am aware of some members in other churches who perceive their church as the most significant interactional framework of their lives. I suspect that a participant-observer in some of these churches would find some of the same interactional patterns and distinctive life styles that I have observed in Zion. There would, of course, be variations. The members of the larger churches are often part of a broader economic base than those who belong to Zion. Members of the larger churches have a broader range of education and social status in the wider community. Larger churches attract people who have differing orientations and purposes, whereas Zion is a more homogeneous group of members whose needs appear to be similar.

In describing the characteristics and interactional dynamics of Zion, one does well to remember that many of these phenomena in Zion have counterparts in the larger religious subculture. This subculture recognizes the different churches that belong by means of periodic neighborhood church contests that include all churches in competitive endeavors (outstanding pastor of the year, churchwoman of the year, etc.). Noted churchwomen in the neighborhood perpetuate their images as "great church workers" by visiting the various churches in the neighborhood on special occasions and having "something to say" on these occasions.

Prominent churchwomen throughout the neighborhood have access to the church editor of a local Black newspaper, and their activities are published weekly, often with competitive vigor. These women from different denominations have very little contact, but they have great respect for one another. They recognize the goals and problems they share and actively seek to reinforce one another's prestige.

There are pastors and ministers who also exploit these means of enhancing their social prestige; to be well known is a valuable asset. Funeral directors are consistent links in the church network, as they visit and financially contribute to the various churches in the neighborhood. There are occasional banquets, teas, and other social functions which all the "noted churchwomen" feel obligated to attend.

The street-corner or corner-tavern subculture (see Liebow, 1967) presents another alternative in this geographical setting. The neighborhood taverns and contiguous street corners provide the setting for meaningful human interaction among people whose resources are extremely limited. The members of such groups spend most of their time, money, and energies in this social setting, where they meet friends and associates. A peculiar redistribution of wealth occurs in this setting. Members of the group periodically make substantial "hits" in the numbers game. They receive a sum of money which is too large to integrate into their normal life style but is too small and undependable to change that life style. Therefore they distribute it among the members of their subculture in such a way as to reinforce their ties in that subculture and to create obligations from the other members. This redistribution is couched in behavior such as "setting up at the bar," loans, "rolling" the intoxicated, and "clipping" the inattentive. Income tax refunds, social security payments, inheritances, and criminal exploits are other sources of substantial income for this redistributive system. But on a smaller scale, even a member's normal weekly income finds its way into this redistributive flow. The members form a primary group in which each knows the total economic, social, political, sexual, and physical plight of the other. Each perceives this unit as his social universe. Family, extended family, sexual companions, employers, landlords, bill collectors, and welfare agencies must come to grips with this subculture if they have contacts with those who belong.

As we can see, Zion is one social group of many in the Pittsburgh Black ghetto. Poor Blacks appear to put a premium on the dynamics of social interaction. The rural migrants in Zion created an effective means for establishing such social interaction as well as a means for reviving the intimate nature of church life. The children of these original members as well as other recruits who have felt the need for this interactional community have perpetuated the church. Zion survives today in spite of the other subcultures available to those in the urban ghetto.

But the original members are few in number, and in the next ten years they will probably all be dead. The competition from these other subcultures and the gradual disappearance of one of the original needs (an intimate association for southern rural migrants) have produced a recruitment crisis in this community which may result in its demise in the next few years, unless Zion creates new attractions to recruit the new breed of ghetto dweller.

Regardless of its future, Zion represents a distinctive human achievement. It has reached out across neighborhoods and subcultures to attract its members, and it has maintained its interactional community for fifty-four years. This group is an intricate reservoir of social dynamics that has perpetuated a unique kind of cohesion in the midst of competing subcultures. It is a distinctive little community whose nature and content I have attempted to outline throughout these pages.

† 9 †

CONCLUSION

My specific research has dealt with the Black Pentecostal ghetto poor who migrated from the rural South, but my major concern has been with human behavior. The questions that the research and the concern have generated have not been entirely answered here, but they have been clarified and delineated to some extent.

I have been concerned about the relationship between poor, Black, ghetto life and that of the wider society. I have attempted to examine the nature of interaction that creates viable living in spite of economic and so-called social deprivation. I thought that by trying to merge myself into the experiences of the Zion membership and discovering how they think and feel, I would find some of the clues to why mainstream rewards are not the only avenues to human happiness, and why human subgroups in American society have the potential of determining for themselves distinctive satisfactions in living. Surely the nexuses of communication and transmission of subcultural messages would provide indications of this unique cultural development and social process vis-à-vis mainstream America. Zion does not have a separate system of values. Many mainstream ideals (marriage, stability, achievement, mobility, work, etc.) are shared. The organizational hierarchy and the system of deference based upon status, prestige, and material possessions are American, but distinctive in their symbolic content. This mainstream perspective and transvaluation, coupled with Zion's own, gave me some ethnographic evidence of what subculture is in modern society.

Directing my attention to the question of what made Zion a community, I felt there had to be a pattern of interaction that supported this group's conception of themselves as unique, "different," "peculiar." I had to find their methods of motivating and rewarding to understand how they had perpetuated this community for fifty-four years. Even after I had collected much of the data, I was doubtful as to how it explained the social phenomenon of Zion. Later in my research efforts I found that I was looking for explanations out of my own experience and system of symbols. The data had to be examined again and again until some of its meaning could be discerned.

The members of Zion interact, but in a distinctive way. They have a saying, a theme, and a parting prayer that they repeat at the end of almost every service—"Keep your mind stayed on Jesus." Translated in terms of its effect, this means, "Remember who you are until we meet again." They talk about, think about, and behave in terms of their membership wherever they are. They are always interacting with one another by one means or another (mental images, self-conception, gossip, etc.). When one commits himself to this "despised few," as they call themselves, he has established a looking-glass self that defies anything but total commitment to Zion. Thus the members' physical patterns of interaction are only part of the picture and do not tell the entire story. We must listen again and again to how and what they perceive in order to understand their community and the nature of its cohesion. Another factor that must be considered is their limited access to the larger society—limited because of language, poverty, race, and lack of ability or willingness to use or manipulate mainstream symbols.

Zion is a religious organization, a human community, a Black group in a Black urban ghetto, and a Black response to the worldwide human phenomenon of urbanization (see Thomas and Znaniecki, 1958, for a Polish response; see also Patterson, 1964; Plotnicov, 1967; Willems, 1970). Zion is an aggregation of southern rural migrants who settled in Pittsburgh and attempted to reestablish the style of life they had known in the rural South. The members perceived this effort as one of excluding others, isolating themselves, and establishing social boundaries. They live *in* the city but they are not *of* the city; or as they would explain it, "in the world but not of the world." They achieved this duality by intensive *solidarity* among the members. But in the urban context, members were more exposed to the struggle for power, position, prestige, recognition, wealth, and social mobility in the larger society. They recognized Zion as an available means for achieving these values within a smaller group. This quest for mobility in Zion is the major basis for *conflict* in this church, and it is perceived as the greatest threat to the members' solidarity. Zion's response to the distinctive nature of its solidarity and conflict is unique, as I have tried to demonstrate.

The critical task of Zion is to assimilate the social distance that usually accompanies social mobility with the love, fellowship, and equality that were to establish and maintain Zion's cohesion. This task requires Zion's persistent effort to combat social distance and promote cohesion among its members.

The system of symbolic expression in Zion validates this church community. The communication code discussed in chapter 6 allows the members of Zion not only to belong to this religious community but also to be carriers of the community content wherever they find themselves in interaction with other members of Zion and those in the international organization of the Church of Holy Christ. The members identify with Zion and one another. They embody the stuff of community. They reinforce, identify, and conceptualize in terms of images of whom that community represents. Thus, their communicative code, full of references to food, the farm, the rural landscape, human anatomy, animals, death, the physical world, and the supernatural, contains messages and is indicative of a system of symbolic expression that validates and identifies these southern Black rural (peasant) migrants apart from the wider society.

This distinctive system of symbols has historically supported Zion. Its members have consistent patterns of expression and communication that were discussed in chapter 6 and an in-group perspective which creates their universe or community. They have utilized available resources—food, animals, death, human anatomy, the physical world, and the supernatural—to establish the intricacy of their system of meaning. In keeping with a seemingly widespread characteristic of human conceptualization, the Zion system of meanings reveals a binary pattern. Their concentration upon and liking for their traditional foods is a form of social defiance of standards of mobility. Their foods are considered inferior by the larger American society, yet they openly cherish them as nourishment and as symbols of their identity and solidarity. Even the animals they value are those they usually eat, while the animals they disdain are not eaten—the wolf, the frog, the goat, the fox, and the crocodile. The members emphasize that the goat eats "dry paper" in contrast to the succulent foods the members enjoy. This documents the goat's inferiority in a group that places such emphasis upon what is eaten. The "runt" eats and "grunts." He is not satisfied even after he is fed. He cannot be fattened and he cannot be sold. If feeding does not satisfy him he is worthless, because feeding is one of the ultimate values; even God "feeds" his chosen few. The dog, which is neither eaten nor held in contempt, works for God (as his bloodhound) or is used to symbolize humility, a Zion ideal; the eagle represents power and leadership.

When the members describe their disgruntled and dissatisfied members as "sour grapes" and "sour peaches," they are translating into their idiom a powerful feeling of antagonism, for taste is tantamount to experience among these members. When they tell you that those members who are verbal experts in love and fellowship have a "butter-mouthed tongue" and honey flowing from their mouths, they are communicating a vivid reaction in their own idiom. These people endow foods, taste, and eating with a range of meaning that demands the explanation I have attempted.

There is also a constant effort to validate the inclusion of the "poor," the "outcasts," and the "despised few" in Zion. This is Zion's reason for being—it is a shelter for poor Blacks from the rural South. This effort takes a variety of forms, some of which I have referred to in this work. As I have mentioned, some of the instruments utilized, organized, and manipulated for this purpose are the terms, expressions, and symbols of orality. Largely denied the verbal manipulation of those genital and anal terms and symbols that demonstrate a defiance for social mobility in other Black subcultures, the members of Zion resort to and compete with these subcultures with other oral terms and symbols which demonstrate the same defiance. The holy kiss, the butter-mouthed tongue, the honey-flowing mouth, speaking in tongues, screaming while possessed, testifying, prophesying, confessing, and eating (all in the association of other members) are constant ceremony and ritual in intimate oral exposure to combat and defy the very social distance inherent in Zion's social organization of elite, core, supportive, and marginal membership. Many of the members' verbal expressions are codified messages of orality—"Don't put your mouth on me" (gossip about me), "God opens his mouth and lightning comes out," one can talk another "down to the undertaker," and one must be watchful of those who "fix big meals for them." A common gesture in dyadic conversation in Zion is to cover the mouth so as not to offend.

Even with rigid restraints upon genital and anal references, the members manage to evade subtly the letter of the law. Thus, references to the genital, the anal, and especially the oral characteristics of members is a weapon against social distance in Zion and a defiance of social mobility in the wider society. This weapon has been a successful competitive instrument for Zion among the other subcultures in the urban Black ghetto. As such, this defiance of social distance and mobility is a means of solidarity for the Zion community. Yet, in spite of it all, the members of Zion are participants in two cultural orientations. They have a subculture, but they are unmistakably a part of American society.

Its social history also helps to explain the nature of Zion's cohesion.

The history of association of most of the members who belong to Zion enables them to have a conception of their group which is ten, twenty, or forty years old. They know one another down to the most minute details of their daily lives. This detail is communicated through testimonies and prophecies, as well as through gossip and conversation. Such familiarity is not incidental to the nature of Zion; rather, it is an intrinsic aspect of the church's design to foster intimacy and combat social distance. After all, this group's primary purpose is to create an alternative life style to the alienation of northern and urban life. Thus longevity has a special value among the members. It usually means that one has "come through the fire, the flood and the flames" (the trials and tribulations), the conflicts, and the fears that are characteristic of Zion. A member is "strong" because he or she has survived it all. It means that there is a leveling mechanism in the form of "old-timers" who knew the leaders and the members of the elite "when" they were first "converted" or accepted into Zion. These "old-timers" are privileged to refer to the pastor, leaders in the international organization, and members of the elite in Zion as "boy" or "girl" without being disrespectful because they were stalwart members of the Church of Holy Christ or of Zion when the others were recent recruits to the faith. The older members are quick to inform others that they knew when certain prestigious members of Zion joined the church. They are anxious to recall their contributions of time and effort that led to the success of such members. They never allow anyone to forget that they know the intimate details of his life and development in Zion. This familiarity even extends to periods before migration when certain members were instrumental in aiding other members and their families to come north. It is in these ways that history is a cogent instrument of the solidarity characteristic of Zion.

The story of Zion, with its striving for a tolerable level of tension and controversy, is a history of only one human group. But it tells us something about the social process of organizing individual desires and needs in all groups. Thus not only is a meaningful way of life created for the members, but the conflicts of such an organization are integrated to perpetuate and vitalize that organization. Zion was born out of interdenominational conflict and has developed and survived with it (see Gillin, 1910; L. L. Haynes, 1953; Leslie, 1960; Niebuhr, 1929; Smith, 1959; Vogt, 1951; Weatherford, 1957; Woodson, 1921). Its idioms of solidarity and the themes that compose it have provided the viability that has allowed this community to persist. Its story is the history of a "despised" Black few who have organized not only for a "Kingdom in the by-and-by" but also for a place in the here and now. The pomp, ceremony, and deference that surround the leaders in the Church of Holy Christ have their equivalent in mainstream society. Yet the leaders of the Church of Holy Christ usually have none of the credentials of validation required in the wider society. The processes of competition for leadership which I described in Zion's history have created meaning and purpose for the members. The church has created a continuity of social purpose, design, and ultimate values for a group of poor Blacks who could never have achieved those rewards as validated in the wider society. Thus I hope the history of Zion tells us not only about the events there but also something about the nature of man.

The activities of Zion also support the group's solidarity. Closely knit human groups must satisfy a range of needs if they are to develop and perpetuate themselves. Zion administers to the psychological requirements of its members through prophecies, testimonies, and spiritual possession. But it goes beyond the psychological to create a viable social context in its other church-centered activities. Any human group that solicits the total commitment that Zion does must provide a range of social involvements. It is my intention that the discussion of church activities in chapter 5 be not so much inclusive as suggestive of the nature of organized activities in Zion that creates community.

The formal organization within which organized activities occur integrates and identifies the membership of Zion as well as the international membership of the Church of Holy Christ. That organization is duplicated in every church in the international organization of the Church of Holy Christ. Organizational relationships structure the Zion community to some extent but by no means determine it. Critical observation of real behavior and actual relationships is required to discover the true determinants of Zion's social organization. Such is the case for any human group.

The formal organization tells us something about the nature of intensive interaction in this church, but an examination of the informal organization helps one to understand even more. Zion has a power structure, the elite, whose members are striving to maintain their positions, reinforce their power, and even enhance their influence in the international organization, and we have some indication of the nature of interaction within this category. We know something about the broad category of members who are not part of the Zion power structure but whose responsibilities and duties are necessary for its survival. Their mobility is perceived in terms of moving into the elite, and their efforts to be mobile are based upon alliances with members in the core group and support from members in the elite. We can also determine that supportive and marginal membership are categories that allow the core and elite membership to identify their positions in the organizational structure of Zion, and these supportive and marginal members constitute a category which helps the core and elite to validate their purpose—saving souls and creating fellowship in Jesus. Thus the formal and informal organizations together give us an analytical view of the behavioral dynamics in Zion.

Within the context of Zion's organization, and permeating much of the activity in Zion, is a quest for status, power, recognition, prestige, and money. This quest is continuous in spite of the ideology in Zion that discounts all such achievement (see chapter 6). This abiding quest for a distinctive kind of mobility based upon charm, exposure, money, and loyalty results in conflict that is characteristic of Zion. Schism has occurred in Zion, and there is a constant threat of further fission. Influential members who have considerable influence pose the potential threat of leaving Zion and "carrying" other members with them. There are many such members in Zion who perform the necessary operations of such an organization. These members are frequently frustrated in their individual competitive bids for more status. Thus there is a constant fear among the membership of schism, or conspiracy to split the church and undermine those in strategic power positions. There are times when such threats have been imminent, and the pastor and the congregation seemed filled with anxiety. At other times such threats have temporarily diminished, and the pastor and congregation expressed their relief in intensive emotional releases like dancing, singing, and prophesying. The competition in Zion supports a level of anxiety in all the core, elite, and supportive members which utilizes their energy, commands their interest, and provides a basis for their interactional system.

Social ranking and social mobility in Zion are also a basis for the solidarity of this group. The status and recognition achieved in Zion are adequately supported by the ceremony and ritual to make such achievements rewarding. When the pastor, ministers, captains, elite, and church officers perform their duties and take their appropriate seats during church services, they are functioning within the enormous prestige of the Zion idiom. All members are relatively isolated from the values of the stratification system in the wider society. In this group the pastor represents the pinnacle of success, and he is accorded the appropriate deference. These members' social mobility is completely within the Zion frame of reference, and their relative status is determined within it.

The members perceive and interpret the world in similar terms. No legitimate attempt can be made to understand their problems, joys, pride, values, and aspirations without due consideration of the Zion charter. During a series of meetings about plans for building a new church, several city officials, wealthy benefactors, and corporation executives experienced the ambiguity of their own relative positions in the midst of the Zion elite when the members, keenly conscious of their own status in Zion, required the deference of those who possessed higher status and recognition in the mainstream society. Thus the social organization of Zion is a strategic component of the members' looking-glass self and places a meaningful separation between them and the values in the larger society.

The efforts to achieve social mobility in Zion account for much of the interest, energy, and drama, as well as the conflict, in this group. It is enlightening to discover that what first appear to be small details of mainstream behavior eventually can be discerned as important characteristics of the Zion behavioral system. This is illustrated by the interest in hats worn by the female members described in chapter 3.

The conflict in Zion, if unchecked, would disrupt the church as a group; but it is controlled by the constant demonstration of love among the members. Being a member means that one is expected to think love, talk love, and demonstrate love at every available opportunity. Almost every sermon touches upon that theme, using Christ as a model. You must love the pastor, love those who spitefully use you, love "everybody," or be damned. Testimonies frequently contain the phrase "I love everybody." Members seek the favor of the pastor for opportunities he can bestow upon them, such as appointment to positions or "space to preach" and "teach" with access to an offering. The pastor counts on the favor of members for loyalty and support. Elite and core members seek the favor of supportive and other core members to gain support for their fund raising, which is a prime means of recognition in Zion. Thus love and fellowship are the dominant interactional ideologies in Zion, reinforced by the fear of hell, sin, death, and various other supernatural sanctions; God's disfavor, the pastor's disfavor, members' disfavor; and the loss of status, position, and praise from the pastor and members.

Solidarity is further achieved by means of Zion's standard of physical beauty, its identifying and communicative use of food, animals, human anatomy, and the physical world. All this is the basis for the wide range of tolerance that characterizes Zion.

The networks of social interaction, the competition with other sub-groups in the urban context, the political dynamics of Zion leadership, the viable competition of Zion's membership, the distinctive life style, the structured relationships to outside organizations, the personal satis-factions that members express, as well as Zion's historical process, its church organization, the nature of its membership, its range of church-sponsored activities, and symbolic expressions—all culminate in those premises upon which I conceptualize Zion as a little community. The community I suggest is found in the nature of interaction and the quality of behavioral context in Zion. Perhaps I have described these phenomena sufficiently to win over the reader to a position that I have arrived at by personal involvement. Nevertheless, with any analysis of human behavior there is always the risk of a perspective that does not adequately account for all the variables.

If I am a mother, a missionary, a minister, a deacon, a trustee, or a saint in Zion, I am sanctified because I have a familiar and esteemed pattern of behavior among our members. I have a functional system of symbols at my command. I belong to a delineated group with a distinct way of life resulting from the common social needs of its members. Constant political intrigue stimulates interest, motivates alignment and realignment of loyalties, maintains the gossip networks, and creates the emotional excitement that gives life meaning. All of these shared facets of life bring about the cohesion on which Zion is founded.

The fifty-four years of Zion's existence demonstrate its success at maintaining the equilibrium between conflict and solidarity that is the nature of its member interaction. Its long life is a tribute to the church activities that tend to level social distance among the members and contribute to their cohesion.

The mechanism and process of socialization are the informational cues, rewards, and satisfaction that membership and participation in this design for living provide to members. Mainstream ideals are known and practiced where members' values allow (women's teas, dinner out-ings for the pastor's wife, and other means of competing for status, prestige, position, deference, material possessions, and money) and altered where their design insists (no one drives a more expensive car than the pastor; very few try to impress by entertaining at home). The members are not alienated, although by contrast to the American ideal, their homes are a shambles, their children ragged and ill nourished, their families suffering from promiscuity, mental and physical ailments, criminal activities, slothfulness, or lack of education. As long as they serve the church physically and financially (often public assistance is a source of their giving), they have a place in the design, a node in the social network. This place gives meaning, expectation, and reward to the lives of those whom mainstream ideals seldom penetrate unless reinforced through the Zion subculture. They make their life from the church fissions, disputes, reconciliations, and rumors thereof. They participate intensely in the lives of other members through gossip, envy, competition, and interaction. They are aware of the world outside, but the world does not recognize them; they reciprocate by withholding recognition from the out-group of "sinners" or "worldly" people.

The members receive their life style, direction, and meaning from the congregational community. Their sacred and secular lives are integrated into the workings of this congregation, without which their existence would lose its meaning. Elder Richter, president of the state Young People's Willing Workers, a dignitary who ranks himself with men of high esteem, would seem to the rest of the world an ignorant retired laborer in a poor Black ghetto, a hopeless nobody. But the church has its own rules for mobility. This congregation orders the sacred and secular lives of its members because the church *is* their life, and they expect to find no better elsewhere. The pull of this social network, the attraction of the way of life is documented by Raymond Jackson:*

> The devout member prays and discusses his church on the job [his fellow employees and his employer know he is sanctified by his conversation and his behavior], at home, on the telephone, or in the street. It has become a success approach to this complicated life of Black urban victims in America.

Thus, Zion is one of those social entities created by the stresses and strains of people dislocated from the rural South settling into the urban North. As a dynamic, interactional little community it has been sustained not only by the ability to fulfill the needs of its original members but also by its ability to attract other poor Blacks whose temperament,

---

* International officer in the Church of Holy Christ, personal communication.

character, capabilities, and life perspectives have been more suited to this church than to the other available subcultures in the Black ghetto of Pittsburgh. As I pointed out in chapter 7, most of the original members are deceased. In ten years most of those born in the rural South will have died. The competition of other ghetto subcultures will probably overwhelm Zion when the commitment of these southern members is no longer available. The mainstream society has changed in the last fifty years, and the avenues for Black achievement are not as restricted as they once were. Education is a growing value among Blacks and is becoming more and more available to them. The supportive ideology of Zion—salvation for the "despised few"—is becoming less and less meaningful in an aggressive and often militant age (see *Black Scholar*, 1970). The purpose once served by Zion as shelter for Black rural southern emigrants is becoming less and less important. Considering the recruitment problems it is experiencing today, Zion may disappear within the next ten years. The nature of urbanization itself will probably require very different human responses in the near future from those required in the recent past. Communities like Zion may no longer suffice for an isolated Black population facing new problems in an inner city and yet denied assimilation because of phenotypic stigmata.

Zion is more than a church. It is more than a little community. It is even more than a network of human social interaction. It is a human phenomenon responding to social and economic upheavals. It is a peculiar human phenomenon—a population that is poor, Black, discriminated against, and caught in the throes of northern migration and urbanization (see Rogler, 1972, for a Puerto Rican case). Its responses to such social and economic upheavals are thus necessarily distinctive. Zion, then, is a case of human process resulting from social conditions, and as such, represents a worthy study in the science of man. The dynamics that operate here go beyond the story of Zion and relate something of the human trauma that urbanization creates for man in the threat of alienation and isolation for a social animal who requires meaningful social interaction. This story may relate to us something about the nature of intensive interaction among poor ghetto Blacks who live in close proximity and have learned to derive a high level of human reward from the characteristics of structured kinds of intensive interaction with their fellows. Culture is a system of meanings. Man takes whatever resources are available and exploits them to create those meanings. I have briefly observed that process among these members of a poor Black ghetto church. I suspect that one of the critical components of that meaning, intensive interaction, extends to other groups in the Pittsburgh poor Black ghetto.

Religion in Zion is one available means by which man can create his social reality (see Durkheim, 1961). If he is inept with the symbols that create cocktail parties, debutante balls, lawn parties, country clubs, "sportsmen," "street-corner men," hustlers, drug addicts, or "lodge brothers," man must make himself—with the societal symbols he can use or manipulate. Depending upon the social condition of the man, these may be distinctive enough to create a symbol system—a community. Zion is an example. Further study of Zion and other Black urban subcultures of American society should yield significant data about Blacks, community, subculture, and urbanization in modern society (see Herskovits, 1951).

The values and attitudes of "poor" Blacks in America are far more complex than our analytical tools suggest. These people have fields of perception that operate differently in mainstream contexts than in the familiar surroundings of their Black subculture. They focus on the situational context, and from this comes their perceptual orientation. Looking at the organization of meanings and expectations among this predominantly poor Black group, I think we get a glimpse of how facile the human mind is at creating well-being out of what seems to be cultural flotsam. Despair among these folk is incidental to the main business of life, which is well integrated into a complex pattern of organized meanings and social networks. These individuals are no more desperate or frustrated than any other American regardless of his social context. I am afraid that much of the plight of the poor continues to be a concocted tool of social revolutions, middle-class perspectives, and ambitious social scientists caught up in the culturally competitive academic arena where the myths of poverty are contemporary grist for their publishing mills (see Lewis, 1968; Parker and Kleiner, 1970; Riessman, 1964; Spier et al., 1959; Valentine, 1968, 1969). Knock on any American door and you will find incidents of despair and frustration. I have yet to be convinced that poverty is an independent variable. Thus, little groups committed to a certain life style continue to challenge the authority and attraction of mainstream American culture.

Poverty in the United States and our conceptions of it are institutionalized aspects of American economic life. As such, they are intricate parts of our American way that determine our conceptions of self, perceptions of the world, and orientations toward our daily lives. Without poverty and our conceptions of it (necessarily dreadful in our materialistic society), our society as we know it would collapse. Our ideology of poverty validates, organizes, and legitimates human behavior and values among us all, behavior and values that support the competitive, achievement-oriented structure of our culture and society. Thus we constantly ritualize the poor in symbolic gestures and institutional ceremonies to reinforce and perpetuate the ideology of poverty as well as to sustain the poor who are the mythical evidence that supports the ideology. It is typically American to suggest perpetually that we eliminate the poor with money as we simultaneously exploit them and the ideology surrounding them in one enterprise or another (see Feagin, 1972).

Poverty and its ideology, then, are an intrinsic part of our economic system. And though we all suffer from the social and human ramifications of that phenomenon, we contrive to superimpose all the expressive disadvantages upon the poor. Yet the instrumentalities are grave for a society and culture which assume that somehow the good, the true, and the beautiful are related to one's command over material goods and property rights. The quest for fame, wealth, status, material possessions, recognition, prestige, and power leaves its devastation everywhere. Why only concede those ill effects among the poor?

We must not allow our economic mythology of scarcity (see *Time*, 1972)—in which those with little access to, possession of, and control over economic goods are conceived as underprivileged, deprived, and poverty-stricken—to contaminate our preconceptions of social life among the poor. This mythology will help us to understand why some of the poor deny, defile, and defy the values in the larger society. But poor people throughout the land within organized groups of intensive interaction and complex networks of social intercourse will continue to cherish life—lived in their style and with their own perspectives of the world.

I have provided descriptions of some characteristics of selected members in Zion which allow us to observe the range of tolerance for human behavior that Zion embodies. Perhaps they also tell us something about the nature of human groups which attempt to provide a means of social interaction, a place, prestige, and a role for every human being who has ever lived. This tolerance for the human condition makes me suspicious of any attempt to determine the quality of an individual's life without knowing something of his social network and of the context and quality of his social interaction. It makes me suspect the traditional labeling of men as stricken, as in the term "poverty-stricken," deprived, as in the term "culturally deprived," and miserable. Such categories may be a design within our social system to perpetuate and reinforce motives, ideals, and goals without any regard for the nature and the quality of life of those who are so labeled. The members of Zion, like the members of any human group, discover the meaning of life within the context of their social involvement. For the members of Zion, that involvement is almost exclusively with other members. It is most impressive to discover such complex social organization, meaningfulness, and quality of social interaction among what the wider society would conceptualize as the flotsam of American culture. Thus, a look at the membership of Zion is a look at a human membership and perhaps tells us something about membership in human groups.

Finally, I suggest that the nature of community in Zion structures the quality of life's content among its members. Much of the mainstream perspective on deprivation that we ascribe to poor ghetto Blacks must be examined within the context of our system of cultural values, which creates motivation and incentive for the perpetual striving for economic status, class-determined prestige, financial position, categories of wealth, and material accumulation. Most of the members of Zion are poor ghetto Blacks, but each has a community of intensive interaction, a viable network of social relations, and a meaningful style of subcultural life. They are no more "deprived" than any other American economic, ethnic, or racial societal niche, if one views their world from *their own perspective* (see Legesse, 1973). This is not to propose that economic and social efforts are not required among these people. For if we are to assimilate them, we must provide the economic and social resources that allow them to participate more fully in the mainstream perspective. The logical implication is that we must effectively undermine their subculture. But can this be done with any guarantee that what is substituted will surpass or even equal the quality of the original?

BIBLIOGRAPHY
INDEX

BIBLIOGRAPHY

Abrahams, R. D.
  1962 Playing the dozens. *Journal of American Folklore* 75:209–20.
Arensberg, C.
  1965 *Culture and community*. New York: Harcourt, Brace and World.
Bailey, B. L.
  1965 Toward a new perspective in Negro English dialectology. *American Speech* 40:171–77.
Barber, B.
  1941 Acculturation and messianic movements. *American Sociological Review* 6:663–69.
Battle, A. C.
  1961 Status personality in a Negro Holiness sect. Ph.D. dissertation in anthropology, The Catholic University of America.
Berdie, R. F.
  1947 Playing the dozens. *Journal of Abnormal and Social Psychology* 42:120–21.
Beynon, E. D.
  1938 The voodoo cult among Negro migrants in Detroit. *American Journal of Sociology* 43:894–907.
Billings, R. A.
  1934 The Negro and his church: a psychogenetic study. *Psychoanalytic Review* 21:425–41.
Black Scholar
  1970 The Black church. *Black Scholar* 2, no. 4:3–49.
Bloch-Hoell, N.
  1964 *The Pentecostal movement: its origin, development, and distinctive character*. Norway: A/S Halden.
Boas, F.
  1966 *Race, language and culture*. New York: Free Press.
Braden, C. S.
  1963 *These also believe: a study of modern American cults and minority religious movements*. New York: Macmillan.
Brewer, J. M.
  1958 *Dogs, ghosts and other Texas Negro folktales*. Austin: University of Texas Press.
Brunner, E. de S.
  1923 *Church life in the rural South: a study of the opportunity of Protestantism based upon data from seventy counties*. New York: George H. Doran Co.

Buni, A.
  1974   *Robert L. Vann of the* Pittsburgh Courier: *politics and Black journalism.*
          Pittsburgh: University of Pittsburgh Press.
Calley, M. J. C.
  1965   *God's people: West Indian Pentecostal sects in England.* New York: Ox-
          ford University Press.
Catton, W. R., Jr.
  1957   What kind of people does a religious cult attract? *American Sociological
          Review* 22:561–66.
Clark, E. T.
  1949   *Small sects in America.* New York: Abingdon Press.
Clark, W. A.
  1937   Sanctification in Negro religion. *Social Forces* 15:544–51.
Clemhout, S.
  1964   Typology of nativistic movements. *Man* 64, no. 7:14–15.
Conn, C. W.
  1956   *Pillars of Pentecost.* Cleveland, Tenn.: The Pathway Press.
Cutten, G. B.
  1927   *Speaking with tongues.* New Haven: Yale University Press.
Dalton, R. C.
  1945   *Tongues like as of fire.* Springfield, Mo.: The Gospel Publishing House.
Devos, G.
  1972   Social stratification and ethnic pluralism: an overview from the perspec-
          tive of psychological anthropology. *Race* 13:435–60.
Dillard, J. L.
  1972   *Black English: its history and usage in the United States.* New York:
          Random House.
Discipline of the Pentecostal Holiness Church.
  1937   Franklin Springs, Ga.: Publishing House of the Pentecostal Holiness
          Church.
Dollard, J.
  1939   The dozens: dialectic of insult. *American Imago* 1:3–25.
  1962   *Caste and class in a southern town.* New York: Harper and Row.
Douglas, M.
  1972   Pollution. In *Reader in comparative religion: an anthropological approach,*
          ed. W. A. Lessa and E. Z. Vogt, pp. 196–202. 3rd ed. New York: Harper
          and Row.
Drake, St. C., and Cayton, H. R.
  1962   *Black metropolis: a study of Negro life in a northern city.* New York:
          Harper Torchbooks.
Durkheim, E.
  1961   *The elementary forms of the religious life.* New York: Collier Books.
Elinson, H.
  1965   The implications of Pentecostal religion for intellectualism, politics, and
          race relations. *American Journal of Sociology* 70, no. 4:403–15.
Epstein, A.
  1969   *The Negro migrant in Pittsburgh.* New York: Arno Press.

Erikson, E. H.
   1968   Inner and outer space: reflections on womanhood. In *The Family*, ed. N.
      W. Bell and E. F. Vogel, pp. 442–63. New York: The Free Press.
Fauset, A. H.
   1971   *Black gods of the metropolis: Negro religious cults in the urban North.*
      Philadelphia: University of Pennsylvania Press.
Feagin, J. R.
   1972   Poverty: we still believe that God helps those who help themselves. *Psy-
      chology Today* 6(Nov.):101–11.
Franklin, J. H.
   1947   *From slavery to freedom: a history of American Negroes.* New York: Al-
      fred A. Knopf, Inc.
Frazier, E. F.
   1968   *The Negro in the United States.* New York: Macmillan Company.
   1971   *The Negro church in America.* New York: Schocken Books.
Geertz, C.
   1966   Religion as a cultural system. In *Anthropological approaches to the study
      of religion*, ed. M. Banton. A.S.A. no. 3. London: Tavistock Publications.
Gelman, M.
   1965   Adat Beyt Moshe—the colored house of Moses: a study of a contemporary
      Negro religious community and its leader. Ph.D. dissertation, University
      of Pennsylvania.
Gerlach, L. P., and Hine, V. H.
   1966   The charismatic revival: processes of recruitment, conversion, and behav-
      ioral change in a modern religious movement. Mimeographed.
Gillin, J. L.
   1910   A contribution to the sociology of sects. *American Journal of Sociology*
      16:236–52.
Ginzberg, E., and Hiestrand, D. L.
   1968   *Mobility in the Negro community.* Washington: United States Commis-
      sion on Civil Rights. Clearinghouse Publication no. 1 (June).
Gluckman, M.
   1954   *Rituals of rebellion in south-east Africa.* Frazer Lecture, 1952. Manches-
      ter, Eng.: Manchester University Press.
   1959   *Custom and conflict in Africa.* Glencoe, Ill.: The Free Press.
Goldschmidt, W.
   1947   *As you sow.* New York: Harcourt, Brace.
Gover, R.
   1961   *One hundred dollar misunderstanding.* New York: Ballantine Books.
Green, A. W.
   1968   *Sociology.* New York: McGraw-Hill.
Grier, W. H., and Cobbs, P. M.
   1968   *Black rage.* New York: Basic Books.
Gustafson, J. M.
   1961   *Treasure in earthen vessels: the church as a human community.* New
      York: Harper and Row.
Handlin, O.
   1962   *The newcomers: Negroes and Puerto Ricans in a changing metropolis.*
      New York: Doubleday-Anchor.

Hannerz, U.
　1967　Gossip, networks and culture in a Black American ghetto. *Ethnos* 32: 35–60.
　1969　*Soulside: inquiries into ghetto culture and community.* New York: Columbia University Press.
Hawley, F.
　1948　The Keresan Holy Rollers. *Social Forces* 26:272–80.
Haynes, G. E.
　1969　*Negro newcomers in Detroit.* New York: Arno Press.
Haynes, L. L.
　1953　*The Negro community within American Protestantism.* Boston: Christopher Publishing House.
Helping Hand Club.
　1948　*History of the Helping Hand Club of the 19th Street Baptist Church.* Washington, D.C.: Associated Publications.
Henry, J.
　1958　The personal community and its invariant properties. *American Anthropologist* 60:827–31.
Herskovits, M. J.
　1951　The present status and needs of AfroAmerican research. *Journal of Negro History* 36:123–47.
Hill, C. S.
　1963　*West Indian migrants and the London churches.* New York: Oxford University Press.
Himes, C.
　1965　*Cotton comes to Harlem.* New York: Putnam.
Hoekema, A. A.
　1966　*What about tongue-speaking?* Grand Rapids, Mich.: William B. Eerdmans.
Holt, J. B.
　1940　Holiness religion: culture shock and social reorganization. *American Sociological Review* 5:740–47.
Homans, G. C.
　1941　Anxiety and ritual: the theories of Malinowski and Radcliff Brown. *American Anthropologist* 43:164–72.
Honigmann, J. J.
　1964　Survival of a cultural focus. In *Exploration in cultural anthropology,* ed. W. H. Goodenough. New York: McGraw-Hill.
Johnson, C. H., ed.
　1969　*God struck me dead: religious conversion experiences and autobiographies of ex-slaves.* Philadelphia: Pilgrim Press.
Johnson, C. S.
　1934　*Shadow of the plantation.* Chicago: University of Chicago Press.
　1967　*Growing up in the Black Belt: Negro youth in the rural South.* New York: Schocken Books.
Johnson, G. B., Jr.
　1953　A framework for the analysis of religious action with special reference to Holiness and non-Holiness groups. Ph.D. dissertation, Harvard University.
　1961　Do Holiness sects socialize in dominant values? *Social Forces* 39:309–16.

Johnson, J. W.
  1927 *God's trombones: seven Negro sermons in verse.* New York: Viking Press.
Johnson, J. W., and Johnson, J. R.
  1940 *Books of American Negro spirituals.* New York: The Viking Press.
Jones, R. J.
  1939 A comparative study of religious cult behavior among Negroes with spe-
         cial references to emotional group conditioning factors. Masters thesis,
         Howard University.
Keiser, L. R.
  1969 *The vice lords: warriors of the streets.* New York: Holt, Rinehart, and
         Winston.
Kelley, F. B.
  1970 *Here am I, send me.* Memphis: Church of God in Christ Publishing
         House.
Kelsey, M. T.
  1964 *Tongue speaking.* Garden City, N.Y.: Doubleday.
Kennedy, L. V.
  1969 *The Negro peasant turns cityward.* College Park, Md.: McGrath Publish-
         ing Company.
Kochman, T.
  1970 Toward an ethnography of Black American speech behavior. In *Afro-
         American anthropology,* ed. N. E. Whitten, Jr., and J. F. Szwed, pp. 145–
         62. New York: The Free Press.
LaBarre, W.
  1966 Book reviews of culture and personality aspects of the Pentecostal Holi-
         ness religion and God's people. *American Anthropologist* 68:1549–50.
Ladner, J. A., ed.
  1973 *The death of White sociology.* New York: Random House.
Leach, E. R.
  1972 Anthropological aspects of language: animal categories and verbal abuse.
         In *Reader in comparative religion: an anthropological approach,* ed. W. A.
         Lessa and E. Z. Vogt, pp. 206–20. 3rd ed. New York: Harper and Row.
Leeds, A.
  1968 The anthropology of cities: some methodological issues. In *Urban anthro-
         pology: research perspectives and strategies,* ed. E. M. Eddy. Southern
         Anthropological Society Proceedings, no. 2. Athens, Ga.: University of
         Georgia Press.
Legesse, A.
  1973 Postscript: an essay in protest anthropology. In his *Gada: three approaches
         to the study of African society,* pp. 272–92. New York: The Free Press.
Leslie, C. M., ed.
  1960 *Anthropology of folk religion.* New York: Vintage Books.
Lessa, W. A., and Vogt, E. Z., eds.
  1972 *Reader in comparative religion: an anthropological approach.* 3rd ed. New
         York: Harper and Row.
Lewis, O.
  1968 *A study of slum culture: background for la vida.* New York: Random
         House.

Liebow, E.
  1967   *Tally's corner: a study of the Negro street-corner men.* Boston: Little,
          Brown.
Lincoln, C. E.
  1967   *The Negro pilgrimage in America.* New York: Bantam Books.
Lindsay, R.
  1949   The Church of God. Unpublished manuscript.
Linton, R.
  1943   Nativistic movements. *American Anthropologist* 45:230–40.
Lowie, R. H.
  1922   Science. In *Civilization in the United States,* ed. H. E. Stearns, pp. 151–
          61. New York: Harcourt, Brace and Co.
Lyman, S. M.
  1972   *The Black American in sociological thought.* New York: Putnam.
McCord, W. M., et al.
  1969   *Life styles in the Black ghetto.* New York: W. W. Norton.
McDavid, R. I., Jr., and McDavid, V. G.
  1951   The relationship of the speech of American Negroes to the speech of
          American Whites. *American Speech* 26:2–17.
Mays, B. E.
  1968   *The Negro's God.* New York: Atheneum.
Meier, A.
  1966   *From plantation to ghetto: an interpretive history of American Negroes.*
          New York: Hill and Wang.
Miller, E. S.
  1967   Pentecostalism among the Argentine Toba. Ph.D. dissertation, University
          of Pittsburgh.
Mintz, S. W.
  1960   *Worker in the cane: a Puerto Rican life history.* Caribbean Series II.
          New Haven: Yale University Press.
Mischel, W., and Mischel, F.
  1958   Psychological aspects of spirit possession. *American Anthropologist* 60:
          249–60.
Mitchell, H. H.
  1970   *Black preaching.* Philadelphia: J. B. Lippincott.
Morland, J. K.
  1958   *Millways of Kent.* Chapel Hill: University of North Carolina Press.
Murdock, G. P.
  1949   *Social structure.* New York: The Free Press.
Myrdal, G.
  1962   *An American dilemma.* Vol. I. New York: Harper and Row.
Niebuhr, H. R.
  1929   *The social sources of denominationalism.* New York: H. Holt and Com-
          pany.
Nisbet, R. A.
  1969   *The quest for community.* New York: Oxford University Press.

Odum, H. W., and Johnson, G. B.
    1925   *The Negro and his songs: a study of typical Negro songs in the South.*
           Chapel Hill: University of North Carolina Press.
Ogburn, W. F., and Nimkoff, M. E.
    1968   *Sociology.* 4th ed. Boston: Houghton Mifflin Company.
Park, R. E.
    1919   The conflict and fusion of cultures. *Journal of Negro History* 4:111–33.
Parker, S., and Kleiner, R. J.
    1970   The culture of poverty: an adjustive dimension. *American Anthropolo-
           gist* 72:516–27.
Patterson, S.
    1964   *Dark strangers: a sociological study of the absorption of a recent West
           Indian migrant group in Brixton, South London.* Bloomington: Indiana
           University Press.
Paulk, E. P.
    1958   *Your Pentecostal neighbor.* Cleveland, Tenn.: Pathway Press.
Pipes, W. H.
    1951   *Say Amen, Brother! Old-time Negro preaching: a study in American frus-
           tration.* New York: William Frederick Press.
Plotnicov, L.
    1962   Fixed membership groups: the locus of culture processes. *American
           Anthropologist* 64:97–103.
    1967   *Strangers to the city.* Pittsburgh: University of Pittsburgh Press.
Poblete, R. S. J., and Odea, T. F.
    1960   Anomie and the "quest for community": the formation of sects among the
           Puerto Ricans of New York. *American Catholic Sociological Review* 21:
           18–36.
Polsy, N.
    1967   *Hustlers, beats, and others.* Chicago: Aldine Publishing Company.
Pope, L.
    1942   *Millhands and preachers.* New Haven: Yale University Press.
Powdermaker, H.
    1939   *After freedom: a cultural study in the Deep South.* New York: The Vik-
           ing Press.
    1967   The channeling of Negro aggression by the cultural process. In *Person-
           ality in nature, society, and culture,* ed. C. Kluckhohn, H. A. Murray, and
           D. M. Schneider, pp. 597–608. New York: Alfred A. Knopf.
Puckett, N. N.
    1926   *Folk beliefs of the southern Negro.* Chapel Hill: University of North
           Carolina Press.
    1931   Religious folk beliefs of Whites and Negroes. *Journal of Negro History*
           16:9–35.
Redfield, R.
    1955   *The little community: viewpoints for the study of a human whole.* Chi-
           cago: University of Chicago Press.
    1956   *Peasant society and culture.* Chicago: University of Chicago Press.

Reid, I. DeA.
  1930 *Social conditions of the Negro in the Hill District of Pittsburgh.* Pittsburgh: General Committee on the Hill Survey.
  1939 *The Negro immigrant: his background, characteristics and social adjustment.* New York: Columbia University Press.
Riessman, F.
  1964 Low-income culture: the strengths of the poor. *Journal of Marriage and the Family* 26:417–21.
Rogler, L. H.
  1972 *Migrant in the city: the life of a Puerto Rican action group.* New York: Basic Books.
Ross, F. A.
  1934 *A bibliography of Negro migration.* New York: Columbia University Press.
Scott, E. J.
  1969 *Negro migration during the war.* New York: Arno Press.
Simmel, G.
  1908 Der streit. In *Soziologie untersuchungen über die formen der vergesellschaftung.* Leipzig: Duncker und Humbolt.
Slim, I.
  1967 *Pimp: the story of my life.* Los Angeles: Holloway House.
Smelser, N. J.
  1967 *Sociology: an introduction.* New York: John Wiley.
Smith, M. W.
  1959 Towards a classification of cult movements. *Man* 59:8–12.
Spain, R. B.
  1967 *At ease in Zion: social history of Southern Baptists, 1865–1900.* Nashville: Vanderbilt University Press.
Spier, L., et al.
  1959 Comment on Aberle's thesis of deprivation. *Southwestern Journal of Anthropology* 15:84–88.
Stein, M. B.
  1960 *The eclipse of community: an interpretation of American studies.* Princeton: Princeton University Press.
Stewart, W. A.
  1965 Urban Negro speech: sociolinguistic factors affecting English teaching. In *Social dialects and language learning,* ed. R. W. Shuy. Champaign, Ill.: National Council of Teachers of English.
  1966 Observations on the problems of defining Negro dialect. In *Conference on the language components in the training of teachers of English and reading: views and problems.* Washington, D.C.: Center for Applied Linguistics and the National Council of Teachers of English.
Suttles, G. D.
  1968 *The social order of the slum: ethnicity and territory in the inner city.* Chicago: The University of Chicago Press.
Thomas, W. I., and Znaniecki, F.
  1958 *The Polish peasant in Europe and America.* New York: Dover.

Thurman, H.
   1949   *Jesus and the disinherited.* New York: Abingdon-Cokesbury Press.
   1955   *Deep river: reflections on the religious insight of certain of the Negro spirituals.* New York: Harper and Row.
Time
   1972   Empty pockets on a trillion dollars a year. *Time,* March 13:66–74.
U. S. Bureau of the Census
   1935   *Negroes in the U.S.—1920–1932.* Washington, D.C.: U.S. Government Printing Office.
   1968   *Negro populations in the United States—1790–1915.* New York: Arno Press.
Valentine, C. A.
   1968   *Culture and poverty: critique and counter-proposals.* Chicago: University of Chicago Press.
   1969   Culture and poverty: critique and counter-proposals. *Current Anthropology* 10:181–201.
Vogt, V. O.
   1951   *Cult and culture: a study of religion in American culture.* New York: Macmillan.
Wallace, A. F. C.
   1956   Revitalization movements. *American Anthropologist* 58:264–81.
   1959   Towards a classification of cult movements. *Man* 59:25–26.
Warner, W. L.
   1941   Social anthropology and the modern community. *American Journal of Sociology* 46:785–96.
   1953   *American life: dream and reality.* Chicago: University of Chicago Press.
Washington, J. R., Jr.
   1970   *Black religion: the Negro and Christianity in the United States.* Boston: Beacon Press.
Weatherford, W. D.
   1957   *American churches and the Negro: an historical study from early slave days to the present.* Boston: Christopher Publishing House.
Whitten, N. E.
   1962   Contemporary patterns of malign occultism among Negroes in North Carolina. *Journal of American Folklore* 75:311–25.
Whyte, W. F.
   1961   *Street corner society.* Chicago: University of Chicago Press.
Willems, E.
   1970   Peasantry and city: cultural persistence and change in historical perspective, a European case. *American Anthropologist* 72:528–44.
Williams, M. D.
   1973a The Black community: a social prognosis: a brief note on the Black quest for community in Pittsburgh. Special Hillman Issue. *Pastoral Institute Newsletter* 1, no. 2:12–13.
   1973b Food and animals: behavioral metaphors in a Black Pentacostal church in Pittsburgh. *Urban Anthropology* 2:74–79.
Wilson, T. B.
   1965   *The Black codes of the South.* Tuscaloosa: University of Alabama Press.

Wood, W. W.
    1965   *Culture and personality aspects of the Pentecostal Holiness religion.* The
           Hague: Mouton.
Woodson, C. G.
    1921   *The history of the Negro church.* Washington, D.C.: Associated Pub-
           lishers.
Worsley, P.
    1957   *The trumpet shall sound.* London: Macgibbon and Kee.
Yinger, J. M.
    1970   *The scientific study of religion.* New York: Macmillan.

INDEX